WAS THE
REFORMATION
A MISTAKE?

WAS THE REFORMATION A MISTAKE?

WHY CATHOLIC DOCTRINE IS NOT UNBIBLICAL

MATTHEW LEVERING

With a Response by
KEVIN J. VANHOOZER

ZONDERVAN

Was the Reformation a Mistake?
Copyright © 2017 by Matthew Levering and Kevin J. Vanhoozer

This title is also available as a Zondervan ebook.

Requests for information should be addressed to:
Zondervan, *3900 Sparks Dr. SE, Grand Rapids, Michigan 49546*

ISBN 978-0-310-53071-8

Cover design: Darren Welch Design
Cover image: shutterstock.com
Interior design: Kait Lamphere

Printed in the United States of America

17 18 19 20 21 22 23 24 25 /DCI/ 15 14 13 12 11 10 9 8 7 6 5 4 3 2

To J. Todd Billings

CONTENTS

ACKNOWLEDGMENTS

I am grateful to Katya Covrett of Zondervan for the invitation to write this book. In commemoration of the Reformation, she and her colleagues came up with the topic and title, persuaded my eminent friend Kevin Vanhoozer to write an evangelical response within the book, and made it possible for me to undertake the task. Let me thank Kevin, my neighbor in Libertyville, Illinois, for bringing his characteristically brilliant intelligence, wit, and grace to his portion of the book. Writing a short book (the requested length of my portion was sixty thousand words) on a wide range of dense and complex five-hundred-year-old intractable Christian controversies poses personal and professional risks. I agreed to write such a book, however, because I wanted to attend to the five-hundredth anniversary of the Reformation in a way that would show appreciation for the love of the Word of God that has been manifested to me by numerous Protestant friends and colleagues.

The generosity and collegiality shown to me by evangelical theologians in the Chicago area since I moved here in 2013 has been a tremendous consolation and gift. Without being able to be in any way comprehensive, let me mention here the support and encouragement given me by Jack Bates, Chris Smith, Craig Hefner, Ty Kieser, Daniel Hill, Jon Laansma, Nicholas Perrin, Marc Cortez, Jeff Barbeau, Beth

Jones, Dan Treier, Keith Johnson, Greg Lee, Matthew Milliner, and George Kalantzis (all of Wheaton College), and also by Tom McCall, John Woodbridge, David Luy, Alex Pierce, David Moser, Lisa Sung, Doug Sweeney, Kevin Vanhoozer, and Geoffrey Fulkerson (all of Trinity Evangelical Divinity School, with the exception of David Moser who is now a doctoral candidate at Southern Methodist University). My Libertyville neighbor Scot McKnight reached out to me early on, and I am grateful for our lunches together and for his inspiring love of the gospel. Joel Willitts of North Park University graciously invited me to give a presentation on theological interpretation of Scripture to his class. Among the many evangelical theologians outside the Chicago area to whom I owe a significant debt—far too many to name here—let me mention just a few: Timothy George, Hans Boersma, Peter Leithart, Chad Raith, Dave Nelson, Michael Allen, Ryan Peterson, and Adam Johnson. None of the above, of course, bears responsibility for my positions in this book.

At Mundelein Seminary, my estimable dean, Fr. Thomas Baima, has long been at the center of Chicago-area and international ecumenical dialogues; he has my gratitude for all that he does for the seminary and for the church. I could not have undertaken this work without his support and that of Mundelein Seminary's rector, Fr. John Kartje, or without the generosity of James and Mary Perry, who, among their numerous works of love, endowed the Chair of Theology that I hold. To my extraordinary wife, Joy Levering, thank you for the blessings that you bear to all with whom you interact, and for all your gifts to me and to our treasured children. Joy, "you have ravished my heart" (Song 4:9); may God care for you and bless you everlastingly. I also wish to thank my beloved mother and father, who are committed Quakers, and my beloved brother Brooks and sister-in-law Heather, who are evangelical Christians.

During his tenure at Mundelein Seminary as the 2015–2016 Paluch Chair, Reinhard Hütter helped me to think about how to structure this book and gave excellent counsel. R. J. Matava read parts of an early version and offered trenchant criticism. David Luy assisted me tremendously in filling lacunae in the Luther sections and in helping me clarify the strictly limited purpose of these sections. David raised valuable questions about ways in which these sections might be misread, and I have worked to guard against such misunderstandings. Alex Pierce read the whole manuscript twice and saved me from a wide array of theological and textual infelicities. Jared Ortiz organized a reading group that read the introduction and four chapters of the manuscript, and that challenged me on numerous points and improved the final form of the manuscript greatly. The members of this reading group included Jared's Hope College colleagues Jonathan Hagood and Jack Mulder, as well as Len Baremen, Linda Baremen, Benjamin Currie, and Michael Page. Tremendous thanks to all of these generous souls. My son Andrew will be a freshman at Hope College this fall.

Let me dedicate this book to a Christian scholar and friend who has a heart for the gospel and a marvelous patience, generosity, gentleness, and brilliance: Todd Billings. We have shared many enriching times together at conferences, wonderful car rides (especially in Dallas-area ice storms!), and many a good meal. In his writings and in his person, Todd embodies the psalmist's teaching, "The fear of the LORD is the beginning of wisdom" (Ps 111:10).

INTRODUCTION

When I think of the Reformation, I think first of Protestant relatives, friends, and scholars who have contributed so much to my life and theological work. Insofar as we remain ecclesially and doctrinally divided, this is tragic and not in accord with Jesus's will for his disciples "that they may all be one" (John 17:21). Nonetheless, I cannot think of the Reformation merely in terms of tragic division because of all the wonderful insights and inspiring models of life that I have gained from Protestant Christians and from great Protestant thinkers of the past and present.

Since I hold to Catholic doctrinal positions, I consider that the Reformers made some doctrinal mistakes; this will become clear in the book's nine chapters. I do not call the Reformation "a mistake," however. The faith and lived example of my Protestant friends can hardly be reduced to "a mistake," nor are their profound scriptural and theological insights the fruit of a mere "mistake." God is doing something positive, something more than "drawing good from evil" (although God does that too), which will contribute to the richness of the unity of Christ's church—even if this divine work comes to fruition only in the final eschatological consummation of all things rather than, as I hope and pray, in the bringing together of separated Christians into the one church even in our day. I am deeply grateful for the Reformation's emphasis on love of Scripture, the authority of God's Word, salvation by God's grace, gospel preaching, Bible study, and personal faith and relationship with Christ.[1] These things too often have been taken for granted or neglected by Catholics both five-hundred years ago and today, and the Reformation continues to bring these central elements of Christianity to the attention of all Christians.

What I wish to do in this book is twofold. First, because the book was commissioned by Zondervan for the five-hundredth anniversary of Martin Luther's Ninety-Five Theses, I focus on nine issues raised by Luther at the outset of the Reformation that continue to divide Catholics and Protestants. These nine issues are the following: Scripture, Mary, the Eucharist, the existence of seven sacraments, monasticism, justification and merit, purgatory, the saints, and the papacy. I do not claim that these issues are the only ones that divide Catholics and Protestants, but they are significant ones. Thus, Luther is being deployed here to raise the main concerns that Protestants have about Catholic doctrine. The book does not intend to be a dialogue between *Luther* and Catholic theology.[2] I have organized this book into nine chapters, each of which begins by offering a thumbnail sketch of Luther's concerns about a specific issue. In each chapter I try to summarize in Luther's own words why he rejected the Catholic positions on these nine issues. As will become clear, the central reason was that he found these specific positions of the Catholic Church to be discordant with the scriptural Word of God.[3] Although Luther's rhetoric can be

1. As Louis Bouyer, C.O., points out with high praise, "Protestant worship, we may say, is basically a hearing of the Word of God in an atmosphere of faith and adoration, and this hearing is meant to arouse the response of obedience in faith, expressed in prayer that seeks to embrace the whole of life. . . . Direct, familiar, heart-to-heart intercourse with God, created, upheld, ceaselessly renewed by individual reading of the Bible, with prayer to God, which is felt, above all, as a response to his own Word—this, taken as its source, seen at its living heart, is Protestant spirituality" (Bouyer, *The Word, Church, and Sacraments in Protestantism and Catholicism* [San Francisco: Ignatius, 2004], 14–15).

2. Such a dialogue would need to fully examine Luther in his context and also engage the areas in which both Lutherans and Catholics no longer hold some views (such as virulent anti-Judaism) that were widespread five-hundred years ago.

3. For an appreciative portrait of the nature and influence of Luther's understanding of the scriptural Word of God, see Robert Kolb, *Martin Luther and the Enduring Word of God: The Wittenberg School and Its Scripture-Centered Proclamation* (Grand Rapids, MI: Baker Academic, 2016).

polemical (as was standard practice in his time),[4] he nicely articulates doctrinal concerns that Protestants today share.

Second, in each chapter I offer a biblical reflection, addressing the specific area of concern identified in the first section of the chapter. My biblical reflections seek to address the doctrinal concerns of the Reformation not by means of further historical retrieval (for example of the Council of Trent) but by offering my own contemporary reflection on Scripture aimed at conveying some biblical grounds for why Catholics hold the doctrinal positions that we do. To appropriate for my own purposes some words of N. T. Wright: "This is very important for those who, like me, believe that it's vital to ground one's beliefs in scripture itself."[5] Such biblical grounding, I would add, should not be conceived in a manner that would exclude, even theoretically, the need for the church's voice (as most Protestants would agree).[6] Scripture itself makes clear this need, as in Acts 15's description of the council of the apostles and elders in Jerusalem that debated the truth of the preaching of Paul and Barnabas. Proper biblical grounding should therefore not be restricted to biblical proof texts, although biblical

---

4. See for example the highly polemical language of Thomas More, *Responsio ad Lutherum*, ed. John M. Headley, trans. Sister Scholastica Mandeville, in *The Complete Works of St. Thomas More*, vol. 5, pt. 1 (New Haven, CT: Yale University Press, 1969).

5. N. T. Wright, *Surprised by Hope: Rethinking Heaven, the Resurrection, and the Mission of the Church* (New York: HarperCollins, 2008), 173. Wright is arguing against the Catholic doctrine of the intercession of the saints in the intermediate state between death and the general resurrection, and the implication is that Catholics do not ground their beliefs sufficiently in Scripture. I agree very much, however, with a point that Wright makes elsewhere: "the shorthand phrase 'the authority of scripture,' when unpacked, offers a picture of God's sovereign and saving plan for the entire cosmos, dramatically inaugurated by Jesus himself, and now to be implemented through the Spirit-led life of the church *precisely as the scripture-reading community*" (Wright, *The Last Word: Beyond the Bible Wars to a New Understanding of the Authority of Scripture* [New York: HarperCollins, 2005], 114).

6. Joseph Ratzinger argues that there is a tension in Luther's own thought, one that is also present in the other streams of the Reformation. "Despite the radicalism of his reversion to the principle of 'Scripture alone', Luther did not contest the validity of the ancient Christian creeds and thereby left behind an inner tension that became the fundamental problem in the history of the Reformation. . . . Scripture is Scripture only when it lives within the living subject that is the Church" (Ratzinger, *The Spirit of the Liturgy*, trans. John Saward [San Francisco: Ignatius, 2000], 167). For a nuanced account of *sola scriptura*, aware of the ecclesiological tension Ratzinger raises but arguing that the Reformation itself has the resources for resolving this tension, see Kevin J. Vanhoozer, *Biblical Authority after Babel: Retrieving the Solas in the Spirit of Mere Protestant Christianity* (Grand Rapids, MI: Brazos, 2016).

texts are central and necessary. Instead, as in Acts 15, proper biblical grounding is inseparable from the church's doctrinal reflection on the realities presented in the relevant biblical texts since Christ speaks to us through Scripture both as individuals and as his body the church.[7] What I do in my rudimentary biblical reflections, therefore, is attempt to exemplify, all too briefly, some basic elements of Catholic biblical reasoning about the disputed doctrines that have divided Christians in the West for the past five-hundred years. In doing so I show my agreement with Louis Bouyer that "the affirmations of Protestant theology on the unique transcendence of the Word of God as expressed in Holy Scripture" convey "the soundest Catholic tradition. . . . Saint Thomas Aquinas roundly affirms that the only possible basis for any doctrinal assertion is the Word of God, and, moreover, the Word of God as formulated by Scripture alone under direct divine inspiration."[8]

Both Protestant and Catholic readers may be somewhat frustrated by my approach. Why do I spend so much time in each chapter outlining Luther's concerns and then not respond to him directly? Why do I focus on Luther rather than also including Calvin, and why do I treat Luther's more polemical early works rather than, for example, his doctrinal catechisms? Why do my biblical reflections often unfold in an indirect style and often (though not always) lack argumentative edge, let alone systematic doctrinal rigor? Why do I not explain at the

---

7. Here I agree with the following remark of Keith L. Johnson's, even while I would augment it so as to underscore more clearly the communal/ecclesial way in which God wills to speak to each of us through Scripture: "Even though the Bible was written in a very different time and place than ours, God speaks to us through it to bring us to salvation in Christ. . . . God speaks to us personally through Scripture, not only to inform us about the true nature of reality but also to call us to live in this reality and make it our home" (Johnson, *Theology as Discipleship* [Downers Grove, IL: InterVarsity, 2015], 157).

8. Bouyer, *The Word, Church, and Sacraments in Protestantism and Catholicism*, 23–24. See also Chris R. Armstrong, *Medieval Wisdom for Modern Christians: Finding Authentic Faith in a Forgotten Age with C. S. Lewis* (Grand Rapids, MI: Brazos, 2016). This position, however, does not exclude "tradition" properly understood, since Scripture cannot be separated from the living apostolic community (the church) in which it was written, liturgically proclaimed, and canonically formed, and in which "the entire heritage of the apostles" was handed on (Yves Congar, O.P., *The Meaning of Tradition*, trans. A. N. Woodrow [San Francisco: Ignatius, 2004], 22). As Congar shows from the Fathers of the Church, no one should imagine "oral apostolic tradition as the transmission of secret doctrines whispered from mouth to mouth from one generation to the next" (Congar, 37).

outset of each chapter what the Catholic position on the disputed issue is today, or set forth important ecumenical advances such as the *Joint Declaration on the Doctrine of Justification*? Furthermore, do I imagine that my biblical reflections are going to change anyone's mind? Do I not realize that Protestants simply do not accept the exegetical inferences Catholics draw in formulating the disputed doctrines?

I have taken this twofold approach for the following reasons. First, in a book that had to be quite short, I wished to describe certain fundamental Protestant concerns—articulated paradigmatically by Luther at the very outset of the Reformation—about Catholic views on Scripture, Mary, the Eucharist, the papacy, and so forth. By means of Luther's powerful prose, I wanted to make it clear why these concerns are of such importance as to continue to divide Christians today, despite the significant ecumenical advances of the past century. Second, because insistence upon fidelity to the scriptural Word governs Luther's concerns, I wanted to clarify my concurrence with him on the matter of fidelity to the scriptural Word. Therefore, I did not want to set forth the Catholic position dogmatically; rather, it seemed better to offer biblical reasoning (with much of which Luther would agree) that provides grounds—not by itself, but as contextualized within the living liturgical and interpretative community over the course of the centuries—for the Catholic positions on the nine disputed issues.

I am aware that some of the modes of biblical reasoning that I employ are not accepted by many exegetes today, and I know that sometimes my arguments hinge upon interpretations of particular biblical passages that most exegetes today interpret differently. I also recognize that many Protestant readers and some Catholic readers will, in general, not be persuaded by my biblical reflections. Indeed, these brief biblical reflections, while striving to show that Catholic positions are not unbiblical, do not aim to persuade Protestants that the Catholic positions are in fact correct; much more work would need to be done to mount arguments with such a lofty goal in view. If I thought that a short book of mine would unite Protestants and Catholics on these nine disputed issues after five-hundred years of division, I would have to be completely crazy.

In my view, the underlying ecumenical issue is what counts as biblical evidence for a doctrinal judgment of truth. Ecumenically, then, the crucial thing is to perceive how a Catholic doctrinal judgment arises from Scripture on the basis of biblically warranted modes of biblical reasoning.[9] Catholic doctrine arises from Scripture, but it does so through a liturgically inflected and communal process of "thinking with" Scripture in ways that cannot be reduced to an appeal to biblical texts for irrefutable evidence of the particular reality expressed by the doctrinal judgment.[10] Thus, none of my biblical reflections constitutes a proof that aims to persuade the reader on historical or logical grounds. Even if my highly condensed biblical reflections were not filled with lacunae (as in fact they are), there would still be the need to read the biblical texts within the broader context of the living church's doctrinal development, the living liturgical community that ponders biblical realities over the course of time.

Since this broader context cannot be displayed in my chapters, I wish to make as clear as possible that in offering these biblical reflections, I am not trying to prove Catholic doctrine to Protestants. What I am trying to do is to offer some grounds for challenging the view that the Catholic positions on the topics treated in my nine chapters are "unbiblical," in the sense of being derived from modes of reasoning not warranted by Scripture and/or being not rooted in Scripture. Most Protestants today hold that certain Catholic positions on Scripture and its interpretation, Mary, the Eucharist, the seven sacraments,

---

9. I am not suggesting, of course, that either Protestants or Roman Catholics are homogenous when it comes to which sorts of biblical reasoning are viewed as "warranted."

10. By "liturgy," I mean the ritual worship of God's covenant people. For diverse but often complementary Protestant, Catholic, and Orthodox perspectives, see James K. A. Smith, *Desiring the Kingdom: Worship, Worldview, and Cultural Formation* (Grand Rapids, MI: Baker Academic, 2009); Geoffrey Wainwright, *Doxology: The Praise of God in Worship, Doctrine and Life; A Systematic Theology* (Oxford: Oxford University Press, 1984); Joseph Ratzinger, *The Spirit of the Liturgy*; Alexander Schmemann, *Introduction to Liturgical Theology*, trans. Asheleigh E. Moorehouse (Crestwood, NY: St. Vladimir's Seminary Press, 2003).

monasticism, justification and merit, purgatory, saints, and the papacy are not biblical and therefore are justifiably church-dividing. In order to deem a position "unbiblical," of course, one must have in view a set of modes of biblical reasoning warranted by Scripture, since it is by means of biblical reasoning that one deems a position "biblical."

Since my chapters must be short, I do not have space to summarize the Catholic doctrines under discussion. For readers not well acquainted with Catholic doctrine, therefore, I direct attention at the outset of each chapter to the specific paragraphs of the 1997 *Catechism of the Catholic Church* that treat the topic of the chapter, and I also often indicate other relevant documents of the Catholic Church, especially the documents of the Second Vatican Council.

BIBLICALLY WARRANTED MODES OF BIBLICAL REASONING: A BRIEF SKETCH

By arguing in favor of the validity of a variety of biblically warranted modes of reasoning about biblically revealed realities, I seek to be in accord with the procedure of Jesus himself in revealing the mysteries of salvation to us. Rather than writing a list of the contents of the gospel, Jesus called twelve disciples whom he prepared to share in his mission. Rather than presenting his twelve disciples with a list of doctrinal truths, the Lord Jesus made clear that his disciples would need to learn the truth about him in a communal and liturgical way, by living with him over a period of time and by being intimately related to him. As Paul emphasizes, the church continues likewise even after Jesus's ascension.

As the Gospels make clear, Jesus did things that only God can do, by forgiving sins (Mark 2:10) and by performing miracles. He identified himself as the Spirit-filled Messiah to the people gathered at the synagogue of Nazareth, by reading Isaiah 61:1–2 to the congregation and announcing its fulfillment in his person (Luke 4:16–30). But, as the Gospel of Mark makes especially clear, he did not explicitly explain his identity as the incarnate Son and Messiah, even to his disciples. Until after his resurrection, even his disciples did not understand why he had to suffer and die. Jesus repeatedly spoke to the crowds in parables, whose meanings he often explained only to his disciples. In addition, Jesus often taught about himself in liturgical settings, such as the synagogue service in Nazareth, the temple in Jerusalem where at the Feast of the Dedication he proclaimed that "I and the Father are one" (John 10:30), and the Feast of Booths where he proclaimed that "if any one thirst, let him come to me and drink. He who believes in me, as the scripture has said, 'Out of his heart shall flow rivers of living water'" (John 7:37–38). Jesus taught most profoundly, of course, on the Feast of Passover, when he proclaimed to his disciples that "I have earnestly desired to eat this passover with you before I suffer; for I tell you I shall not eat it until it is fulfilled in the kingdom of God" (Luke 22:15–16). When he disputed with Pharisees and Sadducees, he often did not turn to the biblical texts that strike us as clearest. For example, in order to show the superiority of the Messiah, he quoted Psalm 110:1. At other times, however, he did turn to clear texts, such as Malachi 3:1 regarding the office of John the Baptist (Luke 7:27) and Hosea 6:6 regarding God's desire that we be truly merciful (Matt 9:13).

After Jesus's resurrection, his way of teaching the central truths of faith required the disciples to come to a clearer and deeper understanding of these truths in communal and liturgical contexts. Knowing that this would be so, Jesus promised the disciples that he himself would teach them through the Holy Spirit in the years to come: "I have yet many things to say to you, but you cannot bear them now. When the Spirit of truth comes, he will guide you into all the truth. . . . He will glorify me, for he will take what is mine and declare it to you" (John 16:12–14). Through his Spirit of truth, Jesus ensured that his apostles and those to whom the apostles handed on the leadership of the church (such as Timothy) faithfully wrote and then drew together the books of Christian Scripture. Again through his Spirit of truth, Jesus ensures that Scripture would be interpreted faithfully by the church in handing down the gospel over the centuries. This enables Jesus in each generation to speak with truth and power to his body the church through Scripture. As Paul observes to Timothy, "All scripture is inspired by God and profitable for teaching, for reproof, for correction, and for training in righteousness" (2 Tim 3:16). This truth about Scripture is not in competition with the status of "the church of the living God" as "the pillar and bulwark of the truth" (1 Tim 3:15).

Since Jesus intended for us to learn the realities of faith together as God's people, he intended for us to receive his word from others. We receive his word, which strengthens and judges us, from the church that he governs through "the apostles and the elders" (Acts 15:6). The Holy Spirit has continued to "take what is mine [Jesus's] and declare it to you [the church]" (John 16:14, 15) over the centuries. Although the church remains under the judgment of Christ, the church's "standard of teaching" (Rom 6:17) continues today faithfully to instruct believers in the content of the gospel. When the Holy Spirit speaks Jesus's word to the church, the Spirit does so as the one who unites us to Christ as his friends (see John 15:15). What friends could not have borne to know about each other at the beginning of the friendship, they gradually appreciate as their friendship matures. The knowledge that friends have of each other continually develops in richness.[11] How much more must this be the case when the friend is the incarnate Lord, whom we

11. For another way of saying what I am trying to say here, see Joseph Ratzinger (Pope Benedict XVI), "Foreword," in his *Jesus of Nazareth: From the Baptism in the Jordan to the Transfiguration*, trans. Adrian J. Walker (New York: Doubleday, 2007), xi–xxiv. At xix–xx: "Modern exegesis has brought to light the process of constant rereading that forged the words transmitted in the Bible into Scripture: Older texts are reappropriated, reinterpreted, and read with new eyes in new contexts. . . . This is a process in which the word gradually unfolds its inner potentialities, already somehow present like seeds, but needing the challenge of new situations, new experiences and new sufferings, in order to open up. . . . [I]t is necessary to keep in mind that any human utterance of a certain weight contains more than the author may have been immediately aware of at the time. When a word transcends the moment in which it is spoken, it carries within itself a 'deeper value.' This 'deeper value' pertains most of all to words that have matured in the course of faith-history. For in this case the author is not simply speaking for himself on his own authority. He is speaking from the perspective of the common history that sustains him and that already implicitly contains the possibilities of its future, of the further stages of its journey." See also Maurice Blondel, *History and Dogma*, trans. Alexander Dru, in *The Letter on Apologetics & History and Dogma* (Grand Rapids, MI: Eerdmans, 1994), 221–87.

know preeminently in the communal worship that he commanded us to observe.

The reasoning prescribed by the Bible for interpreting biblical texts is hierarchically and liturgically contextualized, in the sense that the Spirit communicates the word of Christ to the people of God who are gathered for worship by "the apostles and the elders," and by those like Timothy whom the apostles (whose testimony to the gospel of Christ remains uniquely authoritative) appointed as their successors. Already in ancient Israel, in order to teach the Word of God, the divinely chosen leaders of God's people often read aloud the whole book of the law in the context of liturgically renewing the covenant through the offering of sacrifice. The teaching ministry of Ezra the scribe is representative. Ezra, active at the end of the Babylonian exile, "was a scribe skilled in the law of Moses which the LORD the God of Israel had given. . . . For Ezra had set his heart to study the law of the LORD, and to do it, and to teach his statutes and ordinances in Israel" (Ezra 7:6, 10). From the Persian king Artaxerxes, Ezra obtains the command to "appoint magistrates and judges who may judge all the people in the province Beyond the River [Israel], all such as know the laws of your God; and those who do not know them, you shall teach" (Ezra 7:25).

When Nehemiah has rebuilt the walls of Jerusalem, God's people assemble to learn the Word of God. Standing on a wooden pulpit, Ezra reads the entire book of the law to God's people, who stand during the reading and who, led by Ezra, ritually bow to the ground and worship God. Although "the ears of all the people were attentive to the book of the law" (Neh 8:3), some of them cannot understand; the book is not clear to them. Therefore, Ezra provides a number of assistants who help "the people to understand the law"; when Ezra reads a portion of God's Word, his assistants give "the sense, so that the people understood the reading" (Neh 8:7–8). The reading and interpretation of the Word of God here takes place within the context of the Feast of Booths, in which the people liturgically reenact the exodus experience. In this representative instance, liturgy and accurately hearing and interpreting

God's Word are inseparable: "They stood up in their place and read from the book of the law of the LORD their God for a fourth of the day; for another fourth of it they made confession and worshiped the LORD their God" (Neh 9:3). Ezra delivers a sermon in which he interprets the Word of God in the context of the whole of Israel's life of journeying with God, beginning with the creation and the choosing of Abraham. The meaning of the book of the law becomes clear within the context of the people of God, led by divinely appointed leaders. It is this people of God that are the bearers and living "subjects" of God's Word in history.[12]

A similar liturgically situated mode of reasoning about the realities described in the Bible is found in Jesus's conversation with two disciples on the road to Emmaus after his resurrection. Not recognizing him, the two disciples give him a basic synopsis of what has happened "concerning Jesus of Nazareth, who was a prophet mighty in deed and word before God and all the people, and how our chief priests and rulers delivered him up to be condemned to death, and crucified him. But we had hoped that he was the one to redeem Israel" (Luke 24:19–21). They go on to say that "some women of our company" went to his tomb and returned to proclaim that the tomb was empty and that they had received a message from angels telling them that Jesus was alive (Luke 24:22–23). Jesus responds by interpreting the whole of Scripture for them, showing that it is precisely these events to which the whole of God's Word has pointed. Jesus tells them, "'O foolish men, and slow of heart to believe all that the prophets have spoken! Was it not necessary that the Christ should suffer these things and

---

12. See Ratzinger/Benedict XVI, "Foreword," xx–xxi: "The Scripture emerged from within the heart of a living subject—the pilgrim People of God—and lives within this same subject. One could say that the books of Scripture involve three interacting subjects. First of all, there is the individual author or group of authors to whom we owe a particular scriptural text. But these authors are not autonomous writers in the modern sense; they form part of a collective subject, the 'People of God,' from within whose heart and to whom they speak. Hence, this subject is actually the deeper 'author' of the Scriptures. And yet likewise, this people does not exist alone; rather, it knows that it is led, and spoken to, by God himself, who—through men and their humanity—is at the deepest level the one speaking."

enter into his glory?' And beginning with Moses and the prophets, he interpreted to them in all the scriptures the things concerning himself" (Luke 24:25–27). Even then, however, the two disciples do not understand; they do not recognize him. But shortly afterwards, when at the table Jesus "took the bread and blessed, and broke it, and gave it to them"—echoing the events of the Last Supper—"their eyes were opened and they recognized him" (Luke 24:30–31). The truth of God's Word, both of the risen Lord present before them and of the Word of his Scripture, becomes manifest to the two disciples in and through Christ's liturgical action of blessing. Joel Green, who (mistakenly in my view) rejects any "eucharistic" overtones here, nonetheless grants that "the revelatory significance afforded the moment of sharing the table cannot be overlooked."[13] When God has gathered us in worship and praise, God reveals the meaning of his Word to us.

Another biblically warranted mode of biblical reasoning that involves communal discernment is found in Paul's letters. In Romans 4, Paul argues that Genesis 15:6 is about the contrast between salvation by faith and salvation by works. This is not a reading that modern biblical scholars (at least those not guided by a prior Christian commitment) would be likely to find within Genesis 15 itself. In 1 Corinthians 10, Paul argues that

> our fathers were all under the cloud, and all passed through the sea, and all were baptized into Moses in the cloud and in the sea, and all ate the same supernatural food and all drank the same supernatural drink. For they drank from the supernatural Rock which followed them, and the Rock was Christ. (1 Cor 10:1–4)

Again, modern biblical scholars could not easily agree with Paul's reasoning here. Certainly, in the actual text of the Torah (see Exod 17 and Num 20), the rock seems to be quite stable and rock-like. From the

---

13. Joel B. Green, *The Gospel of Luke* (Grand Rapids, MI: Eerdmans, 1997), 843.

perspective of modern biblical scholars, the human author(s) of Exodus and Numbers would not have identified this rock with the coming Messiah of Israel. Furthermore, although Paul associates the manna and the miraculous spring of water with the Eucharist and baptism, the earlier biblical description of Israel's exodus journey, including the crossing of the Red Sea, does not present it in baptismal terms. The book of Exodus presents the manna simply as bodily food, even if God-given.

My point is not that Paul is offering ungrounded speculation about God's Word, nor am I saying that Paul's biblical reasoning about the realities of salvation is wrong (by no means!). Likewise, in highlighting the communal and liturgical character of biblical reasoning according to Ezra and Jesus, I am not suggesting that the gospel is intrinsically obscure to the individual mind or that we can only understand what the Bible teaches when we are gathered in worship. Nor, let me emphasize, am I making some kind of negative blanket statement about modern biblical interpretation or Reformation-era biblical interpretation. I am simply suggesting that the actual biblical ways in which God brings about his people's understanding of his Word deserve attention when the question is what modes of biblical reasoning have a proper role in grounding Christian doctrinal judgments of truth. Even if (uninspired) interpreters cannot replicate the work of the (inspired) apostolic authors, the Holy Spirit may guide the church in Spirit-guided modes of biblical reasoning that, while rooted in more than the plain sense of the text, should not be called unbiblical.

Thus, as many contemporary Protestant and Catholic scholars recognize, the doctrinal development of earlier centuries cannot be judged on the basis of whether they follow the path of clear biblical proof, although true doctrinal development must be grounded in a coherent set of biblical texts and must employ biblically warranted modes of biblical reasoning.[14] Although Paul's approach to biblical

---

14. For recent Protestant scholarship that recognizes this point, see for example Karlfried Froehlich, with Mark S. Burrows, *Sensing the Scriptures: Aminadab's Chariot and the Predicament of Biblical Interpretation* (Grand Rapids, MI: Eerdmans, 2014); Richard B. Hays, *Reading Backwards:*

interpretation is not normative for post-biblical interpreters in any strong or determinative sense, it does provide biblical warrant for similar modes of biblical reasoning practiced by the church under the guidance of the Spirit in later centuries. Jesus's decision to teach in parables, to teach in liturgical contexts, and to teach through chosen emissaries appointed to lead his church (the apostles) also needs to be given due weight in contemporary reasoning about biblical realities. When asked to show what convinces us that Scripture supports the doctrinal positions by which we articulate the content of our faith, we must point to specific biblical texts, but we must also keep in mind that the modes of biblical reasoning that we find in Scripture are not normally aimed at providing logical or historical proofs, but instead emphasize participation in the living liturgical community that receives and ponders the Word of God. As the New Testament scholar Richard B. Hays concludes on the basis of his exhaustive analysis of the Gospels' interpretation of (Old Testament) Scripture, "the Evangelists received Scripture as a complex body of texts given to the community by God, who had scripted the whole biblical drama in such a way that it had multiple senses. Some of these senses are hidden, so that they come into focus only *retrospectively*."[15]

Figural Christology and the Fourfold Gospel Witness (Waco, TX: Baylor University Press, 2014); Hans Boersma, *Heavenly Participation: The Weaving of a Sacramental Tapestry* (Grand Rapids, MI: Eerdmans, 2011), especially chapters 8–10; Ephraim Radner, *Time and the Word: Figural Reading of the Christian Scriptures* (Grand Rapids, MI: Eerdmans, 2016). See also the theo-dramatic and performative-communicative mode of biblical reasoning that characterizes the work of Kevin J. Vanhoozer: Vanhoozer, *Remythologizing Theology: Divine Action, Passion, and Authorship* (Cambridge: Cambridge University Press, 2010); Vanhoozer, *The Drama of Doctrine: A Canonical-Linguistic Approach to Christian Theology* (Louisville: Westminster John Knox, 2005). For concrete analysis of doctrinal development, cautioning against seeking biblical proofs as we understand them today, see Khaled Anatolios, *Retrieving Nicaea: The Development and Meaning of Trinitarian Doctrine* (Grand Rapids, MI: Baker Academic, 2011); Lewis Ayres, *Nicaea and Its Legacy: An Approach to Fourth-Century Trinitarian Theology* (Oxford: Oxford University Press, 2004).

15. Richard B. Hays, *Echoes of the Scripture in the Gospels* (Waco, TX: Baylor University Press, 2016), 358. Hays goes on to say: "Let us be clear about the implication of the Evangelists' example at this point. If we insist—as much modern criticism has done—that the legitimate interpretation of Israel's Scripture must be strictly constrained by the (historically reconstructed) intention of the ancient Hebrew authors, or by the meaning that could have been understood by readers in the original historical settings of the Old Testament texts, we are declaring a priori that the Gospel writers were wrong and misguided and that their claims to revelatory

The intended audience of my book is Bible-believing Christians who continue to resonate with the concerns that have divided Protestant and Catholic Christians for five hundred years. My biblical reflections aim to show that even if one disagrees with judgments made in the course of Catholic doctrinal development, the Catholic positions on the nine disputed doctrines should not be rejected as unbiblical or as lacking in biblical grounding—at least given the Catholic view (shared by many Protestants as well) of biblically warranted modes of biblical reasoning. I do not have space in my biblical reflections to address all the points that historical-critical exegetes would raise today. In offering brief biblical sketches as a preliminary and incomplete response to common concerns about the biblical foundations of Catholic doctrines, I hope to suggest that these Catholic doctrines are biblical and do not justify ecclesial division, while also making clear that biblically warranted communal and liturgical modes of biblical reasoning are necessary for appreciating Catholic doctrinal judgments. I recognize, of course, that Protestants too value communal and liturgical modes of biblical reasoning, and I recognize that I am not offering new biblical arguments that Protestants have not encountered elsewhere during the past five centuries.

WEEDS AND WHEAT:
THE REFORMATION IN CONTEXT

Before proceeding, let me make some additional observations about whether the Reformation was a "mistake," as my book's title asks in light of the five-hundredth anniversary. In the Gospel of Matthew, Jesus's

---

retrospective reading are false. . . . The canonical Evangelists, through their artful narration, offer us a different way to understand the New Testament's transformational reception of the Old as a paradigm-shattering but truthful disclosure of things 'hidden from the foundation of the world' (Matt 13:35; freely quoting Ps 78:2). This hermeneutical sensibility locates the deep logic of the intertextual linkage between Israel's Scripture and the Gospels not in human intentionality but in the mysterious providence of God, who is ultimately the author of the correspondences woven into these texts and events, correspondences that could be perceived only in retrospect. In short, *figural interpretation discerns a divinely crafted pattern of coherence within the events and characters of the biblical narratives*" (ibid., 359). Along quite similar lines, see my *Participatory Biblical Exegesis: A Theology of Biblical Interpretation* (Notre Dame, IN: University of Notre Dame Press, 2008).

preaching of the kingdom of heaven includes his sobering parable of the wheat and the weeds. In the parable, the servants ask the householder whether they should uproot the weeds, which have been sown by Jesus's enemy. The householder replies, "No; lest in gathering the weeds you root up the wheat along with them. Let both grow together until the harvest; and at harvest time I will tell the reapers, Gather the weeds first and bind them in bundles to be burned, but gather the wheat into my barn" (Matt 13:29–30). Thus, Jesus expected that there would be both wheat and weeds in his inaugurated kingdom (the church of the Holy Spirit), until the final consummation of that kingdom.

Let me be clear that I am not identifying the Reformation with the "weeds." Quite the opposite, a great profusion of weeds seems to have plagued the Catholic Church in the fourteenth and fifteenth centuries. Not that the tenth century was much better for the church, and indeed weeds have abounded at all times, including our own, and we must all pray for Christ's mercy insofar as our hearts are divided and we are far from pure "wheat." Nonetheless, the particularly disastrous popes of the fourteenth and fifteenth centuries revealed an extraordinarily urgent need for reform of the church. On a local level, no doubt, many areas of Europe had solidly functioning churches, no small achievement given the grim prevalence of plagues and wars. Caricatures of the fourteenth and fifteenth centuries as monolithic periods of desolate drought in the spiritual life of laypeople or clergy are demonstrably erroneous, even though there were clearly some devotional abuses.[16] But despite the need to reject easy caricatures, there was in fact a massive institutional problem characterized by a lack of holiness and an abuse of power, especially papal abuse but certainly not limited to it.

During these two centuries, furthermore, the intellectual elite were moving away from the Catholic Church, as can be seen in the writings

---

16. See Eamon Duffy, *The Stripping of the Altars: Traditional Religion in England, 1400–1580*, 2nd ed. (New Haven, CT: Yale University Press, 2005); Augustine Thompson, O.P., *Cities of God: The Religion of the Italian Communes, 1125–1325*, 2nd ed. (University Park, PA: Penn State University Press, 2006).

of a number of the great Renaissance humanists. They were discovering new historical and political methods, and they were paying greater attention to the pre-Christian past and to the history of the church. Although the development of doctrine had always been recognized, the real extent of post-biblical doctrinal development had not been previously appreciated. Furthermore, since the popes of this time were often engaged in fornication, greed, and warmongering, the question had to be raised as to whether Jesus Christ could have intended such an institution as the Catholic Church. To many who were trained in Renaissance historiography, the evidence in favor of anything like the current form of the Catholic Church came to appear rather shaky. Instead, it seemed plausible that the bishops of Rome had gradually seized power and led the Catholic Church into its present ruin of Mary- and saint-focused piety, of selling indulgences on a grand scale, of lavish ecclesiastical lifestyles, of poorly educated clergy and scripturally ignorant laity, of neo-Pelagian theology, and so forth.

To call the Reformation a "mistake" in such a context would be absurd. I hold that the Reformers made mistakes, but that they chose to be reformers was not a mistake. There had to be a Reformation, and it is good that the Reformation shook up a status quo in Rome and elsewhere that was unacceptable and untenable. In this sense, the Protestant Reformation cannot be dismissed as a mere "mistake," even if in my view it mistakenly deemed some Catholic doctrines to be unbiblical and church-dividing. In addition, for Catholics the Reformation also includes the Catholic response; rather than speaking of a "Counter-Reformation," we should speak of the ongoing reformation of the church led by those who did not break with the papacy, often benefiting from correctives put forward by the Reformers. Although I differ from the Reformers with respect to the biblical grounding of the Catholic doctrines they disputed, they were right in seeking reform, in perceiving the large extent of post-biblical doctrinal development, and in insisting upon grace, faith, and Scripture at the very heart of Christianity.

WHAT THE PRESENT BOOK IS AND IS NOT

The present book aims to stimulate positive ecumenical conversation, in the context of the five-hundredth anniversary of the Reformation. I have intended to write an irenic book that focuses on two tasks, namely ensuring that Protestant doctrinal concerns (brilliantly articulated by Luther) are heard and understood by Catholics today, and attempting to meet these doctrinal concerns in a brotherly way on the shared ground of authoritative Scripture. Let me reiterate that my biblical reflections are not meant to stand as demonstrative evidence for the Catholic position. They aim simply to identify certain significant biblical texts upon which—if there were agreement about the biblically warranted modes of interpreting Scripture and of making doctrinal judgments (such as the status of church councils and of typological reasoning)—Catholics and Protestants might build together. I hold that in these nine disputed doctrinal areas, Catholic biblical reasoning should at least not be rejected as unbiblical.

With its strict limitations of space, this book does not pretend to be a full-fledged theological work along scholarly lines. Each topic that I treat here ought to be treated in a book or in several books, and indeed a very large pile of such books have been written over the past five hundred years (elsewhere, I have myself contributed to this pile). In this book, I generally quote only Luther and Scripture. Although my focus necessarily involves areas in which Luther challenges established Catholic doctrines, my purpose is not to drive a sharp wedge between Luther and his Catholic context.[17] Nor is my purpose to explore the developments in Luther's thought over the course of his career or to distinguish him from later Reformers. Rather, I am employing his thought solely to set forth nine doctrinal concerns shared by most

---

17. Luther's broader relationship to Catholicism is beyond my purview. For contrasting positions, see for example David S. Yeago, "The Catholic Luther," in *The Catholicity of the Reformation*, ed. Carl E. Braaten and Robert W. Jenson (Grand Rapids, MI: Eerdmans, 1996), 13–34; Daphne Hampson, *Christian Contradictions: The Structures of Lutheran and Catholic Thought* (Cambridge: Cambridge University Press, 2001); Heiko A. Oberman, *The Two Reformations: The Journey from the Last Days to the New World*, ed. Donald Weinstein (New Haven, CT: Yale University Press, 2003).

Protestants today. For those seeking a scholarly and thorough presentation of Luther's theology, I recommend Bernhard Lohse's *Martin Luther's Theology: Its Historical and Systematic Development.*[18]

In each of the nine chapters that follow, I offer a brief introduction and then move directly into Luther's concerns, which are followed by my brief biblical reflection. Readers might wish that, prior to presenting Luther's position or prior to presenting my biblical reflection, I had offered in each chapter a more fleshed-out framework for my exposition. Such a framework might provide a sense of to what extent I think Luther was arguing properly against the evident corruptions of the church of his time, an explanation of the Catholic doctrine which Luther criticizes and for which I am providing biblical support, or a fully developed argumentative stance. But I have decided not to give the chapters this kind of framework. By framing each chapter in a standard way, I would be suggesting that each chapter should be read as a full-fledged argument for the doctrine at issue, whereas (due to space limitations) none of my chapters makes a fully developed argument. Obviously, I do make arguments in the biblical reflections, and in each chapter I arrive at a conclusion favorable to the Catholic position. But this book is nowhere near a fully developed argument in which Protestant views confront my own Catholic biblical exposition, and one or the other must win. It cannot be such a book, not least because my biblical reflections (with much of the content of which I think Protestants will agree) are meant to be a preliminary sketch of biblical reasoning rather than to prove the clear presence of Catholic doctrines in Scripture.

One final note. I recognize that in the chapters that follow, there is a structural asymmetry between the sections on Luther and my biblical reflections. The sections on Luther present the criticisms Luther levied at the Catholic Church five hundred years ago, but these sections do not set forth the broader outlook within which Luther registers his objections to Catholic doctrine in the nine disputed areas. Whereas Luther's positions are propounded from the perspective of his polemical edge, my biblical

---

18. Bernhard Lohse, *Martin Luther's Theology: Its Historical and Systematic Development*, trans. Roy A. Harrisville (Minneapolis: Fortress, 1999).

reflections develop biblical themes or affirmations in a generally nonpolemical manner, and many of these affirmations are ones to which Luther would have no objection. The result is a twofold problem: it may seem that Luther and Catholics today have much less doctrinal agreement than they actually do, and a productive ecumenical conversation can hardly be generated when the two sets of discourses are asymmetrically related.

In response, let me underscore once more that I recognize that Luther and Catholics (then and now) are largely playing on the same side. We agree about the triune God, the incarnation of the Son of God, the saving death of Christ, his glorious resurrection and ascension, the priority of the grace of the Holy Spirit, the authority of Scripture, the centrality of faith, and many other such things. In writing this book, I focused on the nine church-dividing issues precisely because there is already so much important agreement. Again, I employ Luther's early polemical writings simply as a convenient way of presenting the nine areas of difference in the context of the five-hundredth anniversary of the Reformation. Even when other Protestants do not agree with Luther's particular solutions (or when Luther later upholds positions quite close to the Catholic ones he criticized), general agreement remains among Protestants about the need to jettison the nine Catholic doctrines on biblical grounds. The purpose of my biblical reflections, then, is not to generate ecumenical conversation between Catholics and Luther's writings—an ecumenical conversation that in fact has been ongoing for more than half a century and that has already borne much fruit[19]—but rather to return to Scripture and seek to work toward an increasingly shared biblical framework for the nine issues that Luther identified as problematic and that continue today to divide Catholics and Protestants.

---

19. See most recently the 2015 joint statement of the Evangelical Lutheran Church in America and the United States Conference of Catholic Bishops, "Declaration on the Way: Church, Ministry and Eucharist," available at the USCCB website. See also such volumes as, among others, *The Eucharist as Sacrifice: Lutherans and Catholics in Dialogue III* (New York: National Committee for The Lutheran World Federation; Washington, DC: Bishops' Committee for Ecumenical and Interreligious Affairs, 1967); Bilateral Working Group of the German National Bishops' Conference and the Church Leadership of the United Evangelical Lutheran Church of Germany, *Communio Sanctorum: The Church as the Communion of Saints*, trans. Mark W. Jeske, Michael Root, and Daniel R. Smith (Collegeville, MN: Liturgical, 2004).

CHAPTER 1

SCRIPTURE

The subject of this chapter is Scripture and its interpretation. For the Catholic Church's position today on this subject, the reader should consult paragraphs 51–141 of the *Catechism of the Catholic Church*, as well as the Second Vatican Council's *Dei Verbum* and Benedict XVI's recent apostolic exhortation *Verbum Domini*.[1] Protestants and Catholics agree that Scripture is God's authoritative Word. The disputed question then is how God's scriptural Word is handed on and interpreted. Having discovered to their dismay that (in their view) several of the Catholic Church's doctrinal teachings were not in fact scripturally grounded, Luther and the other Reformers sought to renew the church on better doctrinal foundations. My proposal in my biblical reflection is that Scripture teaches that the church is the faithful interpreter of Scripture under the guidance of the Holy Spirit. If this is so, then it follows that if the church failed to be able to faithfully determine matters of doctrinal truth for the whole people of God in each generation and across generations, Scripture itself would fail in its truth.

LUTHER'S CONCERN

In Martin Luther's 1520 "An Appeal to the Ruling Class of German Nationality as to the Amelioration of the State of Christendom," he

---

1. See the *Catechism of the Catholic Church*, 2nd ed. (Vatican City: Libreria Editrice Vaticana, 1997).

inquires into why the pope's interpretation of Scripture must be accepted while contrary interpretations, even when set forth by intelligent and reputable scholars, must be rejected. He begins by noting with rhetorical force that "the Romanists profess to be the only interpreters of Scripture, even though they never learn anything contained in it their lives long."[2] These "Romanists" claim that even if a pope is morally decadent and intellectually inept, his formal teaching about matters of faith cannot be in error. This claim, however, does not itself have a scriptural basis, and therefore is an invention of the Romanists.

Indeed, this Romanist claim makes Scripture itself useless. Why should Scripture be consulted when (allegedly) the truth is found instead in the tradition as understood by the pope? Scripture here takes a decided backseat to the pope, who is supposed to be a servant of Scripture. According to the Romanists, the church under the pope is guaranteed by the Holy Spirit to arrive at the right interpretation in matters of faith. The Holy Spirit here allegedly guides even a morally corrupt and faithless pope (or a morally corrupt and faithless church), despite the fact that such a pope (or church) could not have the indwelling of the Spirit promised by Christ. Furthermore, once all authority rests in the decision of the pope and in the established teaching of the Catholic Church, appealing to the actual text of Scripture no longer has real authority, since the church under the pope will not admit to a single error in matters of faith. Indeed, all copies of Scripture could be burned, and the church could simply go on as before, making its own decisions and directed by its supposedly Spirit-inspired (but obviously corrupt) leaders.

Luther suggests that the church under the pope would do well to recall St. Paul's observation that people who are attempting to speak God's Word should listen to each other (see 1 Cor 14:30), as well as to Jesus's confirmation of the prophecy that "they shall all be taught by God" (John 6:45). From such biblical testimonies, it would seem

---

2. Martin Luther, "An Appeal to the Ruling Class of German Nationality as to the Amelioration of the State of Christendom," in *Martin Luther: Selections from His Writings*, ed. John Dillenberger (New York: Anchor, 1962), 412.

that neither the pope nor whatever happens to be traditional in the church should not have the last word, when confronted with a better interpretation of Scripture. After all, Luther emphasizes, Scripture never says that the most powerful person in the church must be believed, and Scripture never says that morally corrupt and ignorant shepherds will be infallible leaders of Christ's flock. Luther also points out that the pope's claim to be able to make a definitive interpretation cannot be tested. If the pope erred, how could this be demonstrated if no appeal to Scripture and no independent interpreters were allowed? It is a vicious circle: believe my interpretation of Scripture because Scripture, according to my interpretation, grants me infallible interpretative authority.

Fortunately, humble persons can still read Scripture and, in faith, receive the Holy Spirit. Such persons will be able to perceive, as Luther does, that Scripture itself gives no warrant to the papal domination of biblical interpretation. Here two biblical texts seem to stand in Luther's way: Matthew 16:19 and Luke 22:32. With regard to the former, Luther answers that the "keys of the kingdom of heaven" (Matt 16:19) are given not only to Peter but "to the whole Christian community," and, besides, the keys "have no reference to doctrine or policy, but only to refusing or being willing to forgive sin."[3] So the keys cannot be appealed to exegetically as a basis for the unlikely papal claim never to have made a doctrinal error. With regard to Luke 22:32, where Jesus tells Peter "I have prayed for you that your faith may not fail," Luther points out that the faith of many popes, as shown by their deeply immoral behavior, has already failed. Thus, Jesus was praying for Peter and "for all apostles and Christians"—for all who have real faith—but certainly not for all popes.[4]

Luther hammers home the sheer incongruity of the notion that popes can interpret Scripture better than others. He urges, "Think it over for yourself. You must acknowledge that there are good Christians among us who have the true faith, spirit, understanding, word, and mind of

---

3. Ibid., 413.
4. Ibid.

Christ."[5] Once this is acknowledged, then surely the "mind of Christ" (cf. 1 Cor 2:16) is possessed better by those who have faith than by those who do not; and a quick tour through fifteenth-century popes (my example, not Luther's, although he would agree with me) suggests that faith was not their strongest attribute. Those who have the "mind of Christ" are by definition able to interpret the Word of God. Luther draws the evident conclusion: "Why ever should one reject their opinion and judgment, and accept those of the pope, who has neither that faith nor that spirit?"[6] Luther also points out that the Nicaean confession of one, holy church is not a confession of one, holy pope; we should instead believe in the church, which cannot be concentrated "entirely in one man."[7] The point is that the pope should not have determinative authority regarding the interpretation of Scripture in the church.

Luther seeks to liberate Scripture from captivity to the pope, so that the Word of God can freely speak to believers without the distortive weight of the false interpretations and inventions added by the church under the papacy over the course of centuries. The freedom and capacity of Christians truly to hear God's Word is attested by St. Paul: "The spiritual man judges all things, but is himself to be judged by no one" (1 Cor 2:15). For Luther, there are such spiritual men alive today, and it is unlikely that the pope is among them. No matter what the grounds may be, Luther argues, it can never be right "to allow the spirit of liberty—to use St. Paul's term—to be frightened away by pronouncements confabricated by the popes."[8] Instead, God's Word has been given to believers so that believers might interpret it. When believers do so, they find that the church under the pope has invented numerous things not found in Scripture and has distorted the gospel of grace. The only possible thing that believers can do, therefore, is to follow the Word of God, come what may. In proclaiming their Christian

---

5. Ibid.
6. Ibid., 414.
7. Ibid.
8. Ibid.

liberty to obey the Word of God, believers should invite the pope, and the entire church under the domination of the pope, to follow the true scriptural path. Luther exhorts, "We ought to march boldly forward, and test everything the Romanists do or leave undone. We ought to apply that understanding of the Scriptures which we possess as believers, and constrain the Romanists to follow, not their own interpretation, but that which is in fact the better."[9] For Luther, there is no reason why believers cannot reform the church and overcome the Romanists.

What if, however, the Romanists cite all sorts of learned and powerful authorities? Should we not listen to the biblical reasoning of those to whom we are subject, and who excel us in authority and perhaps also in learning? Luther replies that God's pattern is to speak his Word through the weak rather than through the powerful. As examples, he offers Abraham's being taught by Sarah (Gen 21:12) and Balaam being taught by his ass (Num 22:28). He asks rhetorically, "Since God once spoke through an ass, why should He not come in our day and speak through a man of faith and even contradict the pope?"[10] Lest someone think that contradicting the pope is always wrong, he reminds them of Paul's stern correction of Peter (Gal 2:11). When dealing with the Word of God, therefore, Christians have the responsibility to hear and speak the Word, even at great personal cost and even in the face of powerful authorities. Luther states that "it is the duty of every Christian to accept the implications of the faith, understand and defend it, and denounce everything false."[11] Put more bluntly, "Even if the pope acts contrary to Scripture, we ourselves are bound to abide by Scripture."[12] Nothing that the pope (or the church under the pope) teaches that does not "abide by Scripture"—that invents things that distort the gospel of grace and faith or that impinge upon Christian freedom—can be accepted by Christian believers.

---

9. Ibid.
10. Ibid.
11. Ibid., 414–15.
12. Ibid., 415.

Once the unbiblical authority of the pope has been removed, every doctrine taught by the pope must be vetted for its accordance to the Word of God. Every doctrine or practice that does not have clear biblical warrant must be rejected. Throughout his post-1517 career, Luther labored tirelessly at this task of reform. In his 1525 "The Bondage of the Will," disputing against Desiderius Erasmus, Luther responds to the charge that the church's authority is needed because Scripture is not always clear. He rhetorically asks Erasmus, "Is it not enough to have submitted your judgment to Scripture? Do you submit it to the Church [under the pope] as well?—why, what can the Church settle that Scripture did not settle first?"[13] Luther goes on to say that either Scripture will be the judge and measure, or else the church will be; both cannot have the determinative role. The key question, then, is whether one objects "to there being a judge [namely, Scripture] of the Church's decisions."[14] In Luther's view, Erasmus would prefer peace to truth, and that is why Erasmus wishes to accept the church even when it goes against or beyond Scripture.

Erasmus, of course, goes further and argues that Scripture is often not fully clear, given the depths of the mysteries involved. Therefore, Scripture cannot be easily interpreted and thus cannot itself easily be the determinative measure of doctrinal questions, since one theologian-exegete will say this and another that. Although Luther grants that the mysterious depths of God cannot be plumbed and are not plumbed by Scripture, he denies that Scripture fails to be clear. Indeed, he considers that "the notion that in Scripture some things are recondite and all is not plain was spread by the godless Sophists . . . who have never yet cited a single item to prove their crazy view; nor can they."[15] Once one posits that Scripture itself is unclear, believers who lack learning give up on reading Scripture, since they imagine that God does not teach them clearly through it. Luther suggests that Satan uses the notion of

---

13. Martin Luther, "The Bondage of the Will," in *Martin Luther: Selections*, 167–203, at 170.
14. Ibid.
15. Ibid., 172.

Scripture's obscurity "to scare off men reading the sacred text, and to destroy all sense of its value."[16]

Does this mean, then, that Luther is actually denying that Scripture can be difficult? On the contrary, Luther knows full well that "many *passages* in the Scriptures are obscure and hard to elucidate."[17] But the reason for their difficulty is not due "to the exalted nature of their subject, but to our own linguistic and grammatical ignorance"; and, besides, such difficulty "does not in any way prevent our knowing all the *contents* of Scripture."[18] These contents fundamentally are Jesus Christ, the incarnate Son; the triune God; Christ's suffering on the cross for our sins; and Christ's resurrection, ascension, and everlasting reign. If one reads Scripture correctly, one finds Jesus Christ. He is not obscure or hidden, but rather makes all things clear. Luther concludes, "You see, then, that the entire content of the Scriptures has now been brought to light, even though some passages which contain unknown words remain obscure."[19] The Light has come and illuminated not only the whole of Scripture but also the mysteries of salvation and the Trinity. Thus, those who claim that mere believers cannot be trusted to understand Scripture, with the result that the church under the pope must interpret it for them, are being disingenuous.

In emphasizing that "the contents of Scripture are as clear as can be," Luther also points out that the words (or passages) that are obscure are made clear by other passages in Scripture. He observes, "What God has so plainly declared to the world is in some parts of Scripture stated in plain words, while in other parts it still lies hidden under obscure words."[20] Even if some passages are rather obscure, the whole is bathed in light. God has revealed himself clearly, just as a fountain remains bathed in light whether or not someone in a dark alley can see the fountain clearly. Luther lays down a challenge to Erasmus and any

---

16. Ibid.
17. Ibid.
18. Ibid.
19. Ibid.
20. Ibid., 173.

others who appeal to the obscurity of Scripture: "Come forward then, you, and all the Sophists with you, and cite a single mystery which is still obscure in the Scripture."[21]

Even if there were difficulties in the Scriptures, Luther adds that God has illumined the minds of believers so that they can understand God's Word. But this illumination is not only for an elite; rather, it is available to anyone who does not insist upon remaining blind. Thus, Luther is willing to grant that "to many people a great deal remains obscure; but that is due, not to any lack of clarity in Scripture, but to their own blindness and dullness, in that they make no effort to see truth which, in itself, could not be plainer."[22] For scriptural descriptions of such blindness, he cites 2 Corinthians 3:15, "a veil lies over their minds," and 2 Corinthians 4:3–4, "even if our gospel is veiled, it is veiled only to those who are perishing. . . . The god of this world has blinded the minds of the unbelievers, to keep them from seeing the light of the gospel of the glory of Christ, who is the likeness of God." Luther concedes that there are people for whom Scripture's clear revelation of the light of Christ remains dark, but such people have in fact transferred "the darkness of their own hearts on to the plain Scriptures of God."[23] If one has rejected the Holy Spirit and possesses a heart darkened against Christ, one surely will not be able to understand God's Word which speaks clearly of Christ. This point regarding the necessity of the Spirit explains the incomprehension of atheists and applies as readily to erudite Scripture scholars and theologians (and of course also to bishops and the pope). As Luther remarks, "Nobody who has not the Spirit of God sees a jot of what is in the Scriptures. . . . Even when they can discuss and quote all that is in Scripture, they do not understand or really know any of it."[24]

In "The Bondage of the Will," Luther's central argument is that

---

21. Ibid.
22. Ibid.
23. Ibid.
24. Ibid., 174.

Scripture itself denies that we are free in matters of salvation: God moves our will by his grace, and we are entirely passive under this movement. As something of an aside within this argument, Luther's defense of the clarity of Scripture comes in response to examples of scriptural obscurity given by Erasmus, including "the distinction of persons in the Godhead, the union of the Divine and human natures of Christ, and the unpardonable sin."[25] Luther responds that Erasmus has failed to understand what Scripture aims to communicate and what Scripture does indeed clearly communicate. In Luther's view, "Scripture makes the straightforward affirmation that the Trinity, the Incarnation and the unpardonable sin are facts. There is nothing obscure or ambiguous about that. You imagine that Scripture tells us *how* they are what they are; but it does not, nor need we know."[26] Scripture tells us what we need to believe for salvation—indeed it gives "the plainest proofs of the Trinity in the Godhead and of the humanity of Christ"—but it does not satisfy our curiosity on all matters.[27] Although we can be blinded to what Scripture reveals if we reject the Spirit, nonetheless Scripture itself is perfectly clear and perspicuous, so that in fact "nothing whatsoever is left obscure or ambiguous, but all that is in the Scripture is through the Word brought forth into the clearest light and proclaimed to the whole world."[28]

This understanding of Scripture stands behind Luther's insistence to Pope Leo, in Luther's 1520 "The Freedom of a Christian," that "in all other matters I will yield to any man whatsoever; but I have neither the power nor the will to deny the Word of God."[29] Neither the church under the pope, nor the pope himself can claim special authority to interpret Scripture, because Scripture (as God's Word) is clear to those who possess the Spirit and because Scripture judges and interprets the church rather than vice-versa. Thus, in theological disputation

---

25. Ibid.
26. Ibid.
27. Ibid.
28. Ibid., 175.
29. Luther, "The Freedom of a Christian," in *Martin Luther: Selections*, 45.

Luther is willing to debate anyone so long as Scripture remains the free judge and measure of all Christian claims: "I acknowledge no fixed rules for the interpretation of the Word of God, since the Word of God, which teaches freedom in all other matters, must not be bound [cf. 2 Tim 2:9]."[30]

BIBLICAL REFLECTION

Upon hearing the Word of God, the people of God must obey it with faith, even if this can be easier said than done. For example, at the time of King Josiah, the high priest found the "book of the law" in the temple and the leaders of Israel came to the painful realization that "our fathers have not obeyed the words of this book" (2 Kgs 22:13). Josiah organized a solemn covenant renewal, in which he read the book of the law to the whole people and then made "a covenant before the LORD, to walk after the LORD and to keep his commandments and his testimonies and his statutes, with all his heart and his soul, to perform the words of this covenant that were written in this book; and all the people joined in the covenant" (2 Kgs 23:3). Much earlier, in the days of Joshua, the imperative of obedience to God's Word is summed up in the people's promise to Joshua: "The LORD our God we will serve, and his voice we will obey" (Josh 24:24). Joshua adds their promise, and some further statutes, to the "book of the law": "So Joshua made a covenant with the people that day, and made statutes and ordinances for them at Shechem. And Joshua wrote these words in the book of the law of God; and he took a great stone, and set it up there under the oak in the sanctuary of the LORD" (Josh 24:25–26). In this act of solemn covenant renewal, Joshua warns the people that they have promised to

---

30. Ibid., 50. It is worth noting, however, that Luther himself wrote (and commissioned) catechisms and confessions of faith, which were enforced (along with the ecumenical symbols) as normative standards of doctrine in Lutheran congregations, and so I do not wish to suggest or imply that Luther rejected ecclesiastical authority *tout court*. The texts I cite above are (mostly) intended to refute the unassailability of papal authority. I present these texts to convey what I take to be a fundamental dimension of Protestant understanding of the relationship between Scripture and its human interpreters.

obey God's Word. Joshua tells the people, "Behold, this stone shall be a witness against us; for it has heard all the words of the LORD which he spoke to us; therefore it shall be a witness against you, lest you deal falsely with your God" (Josh 24:27).

The paradigmatic case of the people's failure of obedience is Israel's crafting of a golden calf to worship. In Exodus 32, when Moses descends Mount Sinai and hears the singing of the people in celebration of their idol,

> Moses' anger burned hot, and he threw the tables [containing the Decalogue] out of his hands and broke them at the foot of the mountain. And he took the calf which they had made, and burnt it with fire, and ground it to powder, and scattered it upon the water, and made the people of Israel drink it. (Exod 32:19–20)

For most of the exodus out of Egypt, the people complain bitterly against God and against Moses and Aaron. Even at the very time that God is leading them to conquer the Promised Land, the people cannot stop complaining. Becoming fearful that the inhabitants of the land would be too strong for them,

> The congregation raised a loud cry; and the people wept that night. And all the people of Israel murmured against Moses and Aaron; the whole congregation said to them, "Would that we had died in the land of Egypt! Or would that we had died in this wilderness! Why does the LORD bring us into this land, to fall by the sword?" (Num 14:1–3)

The people of God make clear that they would prefer to be back in Egypt. Although they repent soon afterward, God decrees that the punishment for their continual disobedience and lack of trust is that "none of the men who have seen my glory and my signs which I wrought in Egypt and in the wilderness, and yet have put me to the proof these ten times and have not hearkened to my voice, shall see the land which I swore to give to their fathers" (Num 14:22–23).

Disobedience to the Word of God marks the New Testament as well. On the one hand, such disobedience is the sign of the world's sinfulness. The evangelist John states that "the true light that enlightens every man was coming into the world. He was in the world, and the world was made through him, yet the world knew him not. He came to his own home, and his own people received him not" (John 1:9–11). But on the other hand, disobedience to the Word of God—refusal to hear it—marks the earliest Christian community as well. Writing to the church in Corinth, Paul describes an instance of such disobedience with shame, since it consists in the tolerance of sexual immorality forbidden by God. Paul tells the Corinthians, "It is actually reported that there is immorality among you, and of a kind that is not found even among pagans; for a man is living with his father's wife. And you are arrogant! Ought you not rather to mourn?" (1 Cor 5:1–2).

This is a clear case of disobedience to the Word of God; however, there are also cases among the Corinthians in which it is not clear who authoritatively speaks the Word of God. Paul criticizes this factionalism, arguing that Christ ought to be enough. He remarks,

> It has been reported to me by Chloe's people that there is quarreling among you, my brethren. What I mean is that each one of you says, "I belong to Paul," or "I belong to Apollos," or "I belong to Cephas," or "I belong to Christ." Is Christ divided? Was Paul crucified for you? Or were you baptized in the name of Paul? (1 Cor 1:11–13)

Christ is not divided, but divisions are present nonetheless. Paul explains that "there must be factions among you in order that those who are genuine among you may be recognized" (1 Cor 11:19). Despite this unintentional contribution made by factions, Paul not surprisingly warns in the starkest terms against them. Decrying false messengers of the Word of God, he observes that "we are not, like so many, peddlers of God's word; but as men of sincerity, as commissioned by God, in the sight of God we speak in Christ" (2 Cor 2:17). He suggests that other messengers of God's Word have been altering it deviously, and he contrasts this with his own openness: "We have renounced disgraceful, underhanded ways; we refuse to practice cunning or to tamper with God's word, but by the open statement of the truth we would commend ourselves to every man's conscience in the sight of God" (2 Cor 4:2).

One can imagine the confusion of the members of the Corinthian church. How were they to know who was proclaiming to them the truth of God's Word? Paul suggests that they will find that the false messengers who "tamper with God's word" can be known by their sneakiness, but to many members of the Corinthian church it must have seemed difficult to be assured of who was proclaiming the true Word of God and thereby to be assured of what Word should be obeyed.

Indeed, Paul himself does not rely on the Corinthian congregation's ability to differentiate between the sneakiness of those who pervert the Word of God and the sincerity of Paul who rightly proclaims it. Rather, Paul appeals to his apostolic authority over the community. It is because of Paul's authority—given by Christ—that the community can know that he proclaims the true Word of God that commands obedience. With reference to his own interpretative authority, he warns the Corinthians that he "cannot do anything against the truth, but only for the truth," and he adds, "I write this while I am away from you, in order that when I come I may not have to be severe in my use of the authority which the Lord has given me for building up and not for tearing down" (2 Cor 13:8, 10). He proclaims the true Word of God, and he knows that he proclaims the true Word of God because the Lord has given him authority.[31]

Paul tells the Galatians that his apostolic authority comes "not from men nor through man, but through Jesus Christ and God the Father" (Gal 1:1). Confident that he is proclaiming the true Word of God and

31. See Hans Urs von Balthasar, *Paul Struggles with His Congregation: The Pastoral Message of the Letters to the Corinthians*, trans. Brigitte L. Bojarska (San Francisco: Ignatius, 1992).

that those who disagree with him about central points are falsifying the Word of God, he complains sharply about the behavior of the Galatians, some of whom have been persuaded that Paul himself is falsifying the Word of God. Paul remarks, "I am astonished that you are so quickly deserting him who called you in the grace of Christ and turning to a different gospel—not that there is another gospel, but there are some who trouble you and want to pervert the gospel of Christ" (Gal 1:6–7). He defends his authority and the authority of his gospel as rooted in a divine revelation personally given to him by the risen Christ. He also defends his authority to truly proclaim the Word of God on the grounds that his interpretation has been confirmed by Cephas (Peter), with whom Paul spent "fifteen days" (Gal 1:18) a few years after his conversion. Paul adds that "because of false brethren secretly brought in" (Gal 2:4), he had to defend to the apostles in Jerusalem the truth of his interpretation of the Word of God. Although he never had any doubt that his interpretation was true, he is pleased to say that "when they [the apostles in Jerusalem] perceived the grace that was given to me, James and Cephas and John, who were reputed to be pillars, gave to me and Barnabas the right hand of fellowship" (Gal 2:9).

This episode is reported in more detail in the book of Acts. According to Acts 15:1, "Some men came down from Judea [to Antioch] and were teaching the brethren, 'Unless you are circumcised according to the custom of Moses, you cannot be saved.'" Paul rejected this as a false interpretation of God's Word. However, in the end it proved impossible for the matter of interpretation to be settled at Antioch. Instead, representatives of the church in Antioch, including Paul, were appointed to go to Jerusalem and obtain the definitive judgment of the apostles in Jerusalem, led by Peter and James. Acts records that "after there had been much debate" (Acts 15:7), the first authoritative speech was delivered by Peter. In this speech, Peter tells of his own ministry to the Gentiles, and sums up the gospel as follows: "We believe that we shall be saved through the grace of the Lord Jesus, just as they [Gentile Christians] will" (Acts 15:11). Then, after Paul and his colleague

Barnabas have spoken, James stands up to say that the Gentiles need not keep the Torah in full, although they should abstain from idols, from unchastity, and from eating strangled animals and blood. In the letter that the church in Jerusalem sends to Antioch announcing this decision, the leaders of the church in Jerusalem state that their decision "has seemed good to the Holy Spirit and to us" (Acts 15:28). The Holy Spirit stands behind their authoritative interpretation of God's Word. The mandate to obey the authoritative interpretations of the leaders of the church fits also with the injunction of Hebrews 13:17: "Obey your leaders and submit to them; for they are keeping watch over your souls."

Unfortunately, the church is not immune from bad leaders. Paul shows himself to be all too aware of this fact when he takes leave of the church in Ephesus, a city that he prophetically knows that he will never visit again. He warns the elders of the church in Ephesus,

> Take heed to yourselves and to all the flock, in which the Holy Spirit has made you guardians, to feed the church of the Lord which he obtained with his own blood. I know that after my departure fierce wolves will come in among you, not sparing the flock; and from among your own selves will arise men speaking perverse things, to draw away the disciples after them. (Acts 20:28–30)

The most alarming element here is that these "fierce wolves" will come precisely from the elders or leaders of the church. They will speak "perverse things," that is, false interpretations of the Word of God, and they will do so in a manner that will make it difficult for ordinary believers to recognize that their interpretations are false. In light of this coming situation, Paul urges the elders to rely upon God and upon "the word of his grace" (Acts 20:32), and to remember Paul's own teachings, since as he recalls "for three years I did not cease night or day to admonish every one with tears" (Acts 20:31).

Not surprisingly, however, the meaning of the Word of God according to Paul's own teachings can be disputed. Here 2 Peter 3 is instructive.

That epistle recalls first that "our beloved brother Paul wrote to you according to the wisdom given him, speaking of this [the coming day of the Lord] as he does in all his letters" (2 Pet 3:15–16). But then 2 Peter sounds a note of sharp warning. With reference to Paul's letters, 2 Peter avers, "There are some things in them hard to understand, which the ignorant and unstable twist to their own destruction, as they do the other scriptures. You therefore, beloved, knowing this beforehand, beware lest you be carried away with the error of lawless men and lose your own stability" (2 Pet 3:16–17). If it were easy to avoid losing one's stability by listening to false interpreters of God's Word, then 2 Peter would not caution believers so sharply against such a plight. After all, as 2 Peter openly admits, there are passages in Paul's letters that are quite "hard to understand." Some interpreters will understand Paul to mean one thing, while other interpreters will understand him to mean the opposite. If both interpreters exhibit learning and piety, and if both interpreters possess at least some claim to authority, who is to decide between them?

In the second letter of John, we find the admonishment that whoever "does not abide in the doctrine of Christ does not have God; he who abides in the doctrine has both the Father and the Son" (2 John 9). The second letter of John assumes that we know what the doctrine is, since it continues, "If any one comes to you and does not bring this doctrine, do not receive him into the house or give him any greeting" (2 John 10). The problem arises when we are unsure of the exact content of the doctrine. In cases of dispute, how do we assure ourselves about the precise content of the "doctrine of Christ"?

Dissensions among Christians continued after the death of the apostles, involving core elements of what obeying God's Word requires. Attributing these dissensions to "later times," 1 Timothy 4:1 remarks that "the Spirit expressly says that in later times some will depart from the faith by giving heed to deceitful spirits and doctrines of demons." According to 1 Timothy, the "minister of Christ Jesus" must resist such deceitful doctrines and must instead lift up "the words of the faith" and "the good doctrine" as distinct from "godless and silly myths" (1 Tim 4:6–7). Again, the problem is that if "godless and silly myths" were obviously godless and silly, and if the "good doctrine" could always easily be known, then there would be no real need to worry about dissensions in "later times." Since Paul is sometimes difficult to understand and since other biblical teachings can be difficult as well, one cannot claim that those who are well versed in Scripture will easily be able to demonstrate for the whole church what the right interpretation of God's Word is on any particular disputed issue. Some recourse to authoritative leaders of the whole church will always be necessary, just as we find in Acts 15 and elsewhere. This befits the fact that "the church of the living God" is "the pillar and bulwark of the truth" (1 Tim 3:15), thanks to the Spirit who guides the church "into all the truth" (John 16:13).

In 2 Timothy 3:16–17, we learn the power of Scripture as God's Word: "All scripture is inspired by God and profitable for teaching, for reproof, for correction, and for training in righteousness, that the man of God may be complete, equipped for every good work." At the same time, it is clear that God does not intend for Scripture to function without the ability of the church's leaders to determine authoritatively what Scripture means on a disputed point. Although some of the leaders of the church may fall into error, the Holy Spirit ensures that the church's leadership serves all members of the church by enabling us to know true doctrine and to obey the Word of God. Paul's second letter to Timothy describes just such a role for the church's leaders, who are to "preach the word, be urgent in season and out of season, convince, rebuke, and exhort, be unfailing in patience and in teaching" (2 Tim 4:2). Indeed, 2 Timothy warns of a coming time when each member of the church will want to determine for himself or herself what Scripture means: "For the time is coming when people will not endure sound teaching, but having itching ears they will accumulate for themselves teachers to suit their own likings, and will turn away from listening to the truth and wander into myths" (2 Tim 4:3–4).

When people simply follow "their own likings," the necessary stance of self-effacing obedience to God's Word goes missing. Such a situation does not measure up to the scriptural depiction of authoritative leaders such as Peter, Paul, and Timothy (as well as Moses, Joshua, and Josiah), who are commissioned by God to serve God's people.

The church has authoritative leaders appointed by Christ, and their interpretations are binding for the whole people of God under the guidance of the Holy Spirit. This does not mean that the church's authoritative leaders make no errors, since they obviously do so. It means solely that they are preserved, in their solemn determinations of binding doctrine, from an error that would negate the church's mediation of the true gospel to each generation and that would negate the church's standing as "the pillar and bulwark of the truth." Under the Spirit's guidance, the church as led by the apostles and by those whom they appointed as successors (down to the present day) feeds the flock of Jesus Christ with the true doctrine of the Word of God rather than with "godless and silly myths" or the "doctrines of demons." Certainly, the successors of the apostles do not have the unique status of the apostles, since the latter received the Word of God directly from Christ. Furthermore, as Paul says, it is quite evident that there will be bad leaders, poorly disposed to Christ, even among the successors of the apostles.

Everyone can agree that the church needs leaders and that these leaders will exercise teaching authority. The question is whether and when the teaching of these leaders is normative, that is to say, is sustained in truth by the Holy Spirit in order to enable believers over the centuries to receive "sound teaching" about the Word of God. The Catholic Church holds that due to the working of the Holy Spirit rather than to human power, the successors of the apostles are able truthfully to do what the apostles and elders meeting at Jerusalem did, with the result that the church over the centuries does not fail in the truthfulness of its mediation of the gospel.

CHAPTER 2

MARY

A central task of the Reformation involved reorienting devotion to the Virgin Mary and affirming solely those aspects of her life to which Scripture bears clear witness. Readers who do not know what the Catholic Church teaches about Mary should see paragraphs 484–511 of the *Catechism of the Catholic Church*, as well as paragraphs 52–69 of Vatican II's *Lumen Gentium* and John Paul II's encyclical *Redemptoris Mater*.[1] In my biblical reflection, I set forth some biblical grounds for praising and pondering Mary in the ways that Catholics do, without claiming that these biblical grounds are demonstrative on their own, outside of the fuller context of biblically warranted modes of biblical reasoning. I identify biblical passages and connections that have informed and guided Catholic biblical reasoning about Mary over the centuries. Mary has a unique relation to Christ in both his incarnation and his crucifixion, a relation that enables Christ to call her both "mother" and "woman," and that flows from and explains the marvelous divine favor that she has received.

LUTHER'S CONCERN

Martin Luther discusses the Virgin Mary mainly in sermons and at appropriate (but brief) places in his biblical commentaries, rather than

---

1. See *Lumen Gentium*, in *Vatican Council II*, vol. 1, *The Conciliar and Post Conciliar Documents*, rev. ed., ed. Austin Flannery, O.P. (Northport, NY: Costello, 1996), 350–426. For papal documents such as *Redemptoris Mater*, see www.vatican.va.

in his more famous treatises. In 1521 during the period of his most influential writings, he published a commentary on Mary's Magnificat (see Luke 1:46-55). He emphasizes that Mary's song of praise flows from her direct enlightenment by the Holy Spirit, since "no one can correctly understand God or His Word unless he has received such understanding immediately from the Holy Spirit."[2] In Luther's commentary, he focuses on the way in which God lifts up and enables to triumph those who, in the eyes of the world, are powerless and wretched. Mary appears as an exemplar of Luther's theology of grace. He remarks that God "looks into the depths and helps only the poor, despised, afflicted, miserable, forsaken, and those who are nothing."[3] Mary has no works—Luther imagines that "Annas' or Caiaphas' daughter would not have deigned to have [Mary] for her humblest lady's maid"—but by unconditional grace and by her faith in the angel's message, Mary "finds herself the Mother of God, exalted above all mortals."[4] Luther urges that we reflect deeply on the greatness of her motherhood, which he observes is a "pure grace and not a [merited] reward."[5] He states appreciatively that "men have crowded all her glory into a single word, calling her the Mother of God. No one can say anything greater of her or to her, though he had as many tongues as there are leaves on the trees, or grass in the fields, or stars in the sky, or sand by the sea. It needs to be pondered in the heart what it means to be Mother of God."[6]

In her Magnificat, Mary praises God alone, giving no credit or attention to any works of her own and refusing to become "puffed up" by her status.[7] Luther points out that "having such overwhelming honors heaped upon her head, she does not let them tempt her, but acts as though she did not see it" and "clings only to God's goodness,"

2. Martin Luther, "The Magnificat," trans. A. T. W. Steinhaeuser, in *Luther's Works*, vol. 21, ed. Jaroslav Pelikan and Helmut T. Lehmann, American edition (Philadelphia: Fortress, 1956), 297–358, at 299.
3. Ibid., 300.
4. Ibid., 302, 308.
5. Ibid., 327.
6. Ibid., 326.
7. Ibid., 308.

which is "known by her in faith alone."[8] Her focus is entirely upon God, and so she gives no credence to those false teachers who too often persuade the human spirit to "fall upon the external works and rules and imagine it can attain to godliness by means of them."[9] Mary will be called blessed by all generations, according to Luther, because of God's gracious regard for her. In this way, all generations will praise not so much Mary as God's grace: "Not *she* is praised thereby, but God's *grace* toward her."[10] Unlike those who "magnify themselves" rather than God, Mary "does not desire herself to be esteemed; she magnifies God alone and gives all glory to Him. She leaves herself out and ascribes everything to God alone, from whom she received it."[11] Along these lines, Luther argues that those humans who suppose themselves to be lifted up by their own works are criticized by Mary's Magnificat, while Mary praises those who are "hungry" and thus depend solely on grace rather than upon works. Crediting Mary for her exemplary faith, Luther observes that "where there is no faith, there must necessarily be many works; and where these are, peace and unity depart, and God cannot remain."[12]

Luther affirms that Mary was sinless throughout her life, due to God's grace. In commenting on the Magnificat, he states that Mary "freely ascribes all to God's grace, not to her merit. For though she was without sin, yet that grace was far too great for her to deserve it in any way."[13] Elsewhere in his writings, he affirms that she was conceived by sinful parents but was not herself marked by sin, although he does not take an explicit position on the doctrine of the immaculate conception.[14]

Regarding the doctrine of Mary's assumption, August 15, 1522 marks the last time Luther preached explicitly on the "Feast of the Assumption." In his sermon, he makes clear that he cannot accept Mary's assumption,

---

8. Ibid., 309.
9. Ibid., 304.
10. Ibid., 321.
11. Ibid., 308.
12. Ibid., 305.
13. Ibid., 327.
14. See Luther, *Luther's Works*, 53:640, a text dating from 1543, shortly before his death.

because the doctrine lacks biblical foundation. He states that the gospel text "tells us nothing about Mary being in heaven," and so although no one doubts that she is in heaven, we do not know whether she is present in body and soul.[15] We know only that she is alive with God, as Jesus teaches in Matthew 22 that Abraham, Isaac, and Jacob are. As an exegetical principle for judging true doctrine, Luther holds that "those things that are necessary to believe which you must always preserve, which Scripture clearly reveals, are to be markedly distinguished from everything else. For faith must not build itself upon what Scripture does not clearly prove."[16] The doctrine of Mary's assumption goes beyond what Scripture "clearly reveals," and so Luther rejects it as not resting "squarely on Scriptures" and therefore as not properly belonging to Christian doctrine: "Our faith always must rest upon what is known. We do not make articles of faith out of what doesn't rest squarely on Scriptures, else we would daily make up new articles of faith."[17]

Although the observance of the Feast of Mary's Assumption persisted for a time in some Lutheran areas, its content was profoundly revised so as to solely emphasize that Mary is now alive with God. Insofar as he could, Luther did away with the observance of this feast as unbiblical, and on the same grounds he also ended the liturgical feast of Mary's conception as well as the feast celebrating her birth. As Miri Rubin remarks, Luther retained only the explicitly biblical Marian "feasts of the Annunciation, the Visitation and the Purification."[18] On biblical grounds, he accepted that she was and is perpetually virginal.

In his commentary on the Magnificat, Luther cautions that we should "not make too much of calling her [Mary] 'Queen of Heaven,' which is a true-enough name and yet does not make her a goddess who could grant gifts or render aid, as some suppose when they pray and flee to

---

15. Martin Luther, "Feast of the Assumption (August 15, 1522)," in *Festival Sermons of Martin Luther*, trans. Joel R. Baseley (Dearborn, MI: Mark V Publications, 2005), 145.

16. Ibid., 146.

17. Ibid.

18. Miri Rubin, *Mother of God: A History of the Virgin Mary* (New Haven, CT: Yale University Press, 2009), 369.

her rather than to God."[19] Luther makes clear that praying to Mary in a manner that sets her up as an object of worship or as more merciful or more powerful than her Son is a terrible error. In his commentary on the Magnificat, however, he allows Christians to request Mary's intercession. He notes that although "she does nothing" and "God does all," nonetheless "we ought to call upon her, that for her sake God may grant and do what we request. Thus also all other saints are to be invoked, so that the work may be every way God's alone."[20] Luther emphasizes that Mary is a passive instrument of God's work. For Luther, Mary's Magnificat testifies that "I [Mary] am but the workshop in which He performs His work; I had nothing to do with the work itself. No one should praise me or give me the glory for becoming the Mother of God, but God alone and His work are to be honored and praised in me."[21] There is no hint here of a participation or cooperation in her Son's work.

In his commentary on the Sermon on the Mount (1532), Luther notes that it is the devil who has instigated and fostered "the rascality and devilish sorcery [the monks] have been practicing under the holy name of Christ, Mary, the holy cross, or St. Cyprian," and he warns against such things as "the worship of all the saints."[22] He adds that we must "not let ourselves be diverted by their [false prophets'] claims of the signs and wonders that Mary and other saints have done, nor by the skillful way they throw dust into our eyes to lead us away from the Word."[23] He goes on to complain specifically about "rosaries, pilgrimages, the worship of saints, Masses, monkery, and other special and self-chosen works," since "there is nothing here about Christ, or about faith, Baptism, and the Sacrament, or about obedience and the good works which Christ teaches me to practice within my station, in my relations with my neighbor. Instead, there is the exact opposite."[24]

19. Luther, "The Magnificat," in *Luther's Works*, 327–28.
20. Ibid., 328–29.
21. Ibid., 329.
22. Martin Luther, "The Sermon on the Mount," trans. Jaroslav Pelikan, in *Luther's Works*, 21:3–294, at 272.
23. Ibid., 273.
24. Ibid., 274.

BIBLICAL REFLECTION

The Old Testament knows the joy of bearing a child. Consider Eve's happy remark,"I have gotten a man with the help of the LORD" (Gen 4:1) and the joy of Sarah when she bore Isaac and proclaimed (with a play on words upon her son's name), "God has made laughter for me; every one who hears will laugh over me" (Gen 21:6). In God's covenant with Israel, the covenant was passed down through generations, since the covenantal people were God's family, God's own people. If Sarah had not been able to bear a child, the covenant could not have been handed on; the same is true in each generation of Israelite women, since the continuance of the covenant requires the bearing of children. Thus, the reality of the covenant augments the natural significance of motherhood.

Within the context of the covenant and of their desire for motherhood, various women of Israel display the faithfulness of God and their own God-given faithfulness. Initially, Sarah cannot have a child, and after Abraham complains to God that "I continue childless, and the heir of my house is Elie'zer of Damascus" (Gen 15:2) and that "a slave born in my house will be my heir" (Gen 15:3)—words that must have cut Sarah to the heart—she has her Egyptian maid bear a child for her by Abraham. Not surprisingly, this strategy does not work out well, although the Lord does not abandon the child, Ishmael. God continues to promise Abraham that "I will make you exceedingly fruitful; and I will make nations of you, and kings shall come forth from you" (Gen 17:6). Abraham laughs at God's promises and assumes that God must be talking about Ishmael: "Shall Sarah, who is ninety years old, bear a child?" (Gen 17:17). God makes his promise known to Sarah, who tries to hide her own laughter from God. During this time, Sarah is nearly taken from Abraham by a local king in whose territory they are living; God has to intervene to remove Sarah from Abimelech. The upshot is that "the LORD visited Sarah as he had said, and the LORD did to Sarah as he had promised. And Sarah conceived, and bore Abraham a son in his old age" (Gen 21:1–2). Sarah, aware that she had given birth to the son of God's covenantal promise, rejoiced: "God has made laughter for me" (Gen 21:6). There is great joy—even if God soon tests Abraham by commanding him to sacrifice Isaac (a test to ensure that, for the continuation of the covenant and for the promised multitude of descendants, Abraham depends not on himself but on God).

Abraham's grandson Jacob receives a new name from God after a night of striving with God out of a desire for divine blessing: "Your name shall no more be called Jacob, but Israel, for you have striven with God and with men, and have prevailed" (Gen 32:28). But Israel's career is unthinkable without his mother Rebekah, who enables him to gain his father's blessing and to be the one who carries forward God's covenantal promises. Rebekah favors her younger son, and it is Rebekah who develops the plan in which Jacob takes the blessing of the first-born away from his brother Esau. As we learn, "Isaac loved Esau, because he ate of his game; but Rebekah loved Jacob" (Gen 25:28). Rebekah wins, and her love for Israel stands at the very origin of the people of Israel.

Consider too the family of Judah, from whom King David and Jesus Christ descended. Judah's wife bore him two sons, both of whom died as adults before having children. Tamar, the wife of Judah's deceased first-born son, decides to insist upon her right to have a child, a right that Judah is thwarting. She pretends to be a harlot and Judah "went in to her, and she conceived by him" (Gen 38:18). Judah later acknowledges the child and says of Tamar, "She is more righteous than I," since she has ensured the fulfillment of what was due to her and to Judah's descendants (Gen 38:26).

Consider also Hannah, who weeps and prays because she cannot have a child, despite the protests of her husband Elkanah, who asks: "Why do you not eat? And why is your heart sad? Am I not more to you than ten sons?" (1 Sam 1:8). When God blesses her with a child and she makes good on her vow to consecrate the child to the covenantal service of the Lord, she rejoices in the Lord's life-giving power. She proclaims,

> He raises up the poor from the dust;
>> he lifts the needy from the ash heap,
> to make them sit with princes
>> and inherit a seat of honor.
> For the pillars of the earth are the LORD's
>> and on them he has set the world.
> He will guard the feet of his faithful ones. (1 Sam 2:8–9)

In the era of Davidic kingship, the "queen mother" had an exalted position in the court. Just as there were bad kings, so also there were bad queen mothers. The devout King Asa has to remove Maacah, a devotee of the goddess Asherah, "from being queen mother" (2 Chr 15:16). When Israel goes into exile in Babylon, it is specified that "the king's mother" (2 Kgs 24:15) is taken into exile. The privilege of being the king's mother meant that she is listed right after the king in the list of exiles. When Bathsheba, mother of King Solomon, goes to ask a favor of the king, she is given her due place of honor: Solomon "sat on his throne, and had a seat brought for the king's mother; and she sat on his right" (1 Kgs 2:19). This does not mean that he must grant her request, and in this case he does not grant it, since her request is not right. But it does show that the Israelite respect for the mothers of those in the line of God's covenant (in this case, the Davidic covenant) extends to the era of the kingship. We tend to assume that the mother of the king is a forgettable and insignificant person, but the opposite was the case in Israel. As the Lord says through the prophet Jeremiah in his prophecy of humiliation and exile, "Say to the king and the queen mother: 'Take a lowly seat, for your beautiful crown has come down from your head'" (Jer 13:18).

In all these ways, motherhood is shown to be central for the covenantal people of God. Through the prophet Isaiah, God foretells that salvation will come to Israel through a child, a son in the royal line of David, even though the Davidic kingship came to an end in 586 BC. The prophecy states,

There shall come forth a shoot from the stump of Jesse,
    and a branch shall grow out of his roots.
And the Spirit of the LORD shall rest upon him,
    the spirit of wisdom and understanding,
    the spirit of counsel and might,
    the spirit of knowledge and the fear of the LORD.
And his delight shall be in the fear of the LORD. (Isa 11:1–3)

This "shoot from the stump of Jesse" will not only be a son of David (and of Jesse) but also will have a mother. Thus, when King Ahaz of Judah is in despair about the future of his kingdom, Isaiah tells him at the Lord's command: "Hear, then, O house of David! Is it too little for you to weary men, that you weary my God also? Therefore the Lord himself will give you a sign. Behold, a young woman [or virgin] shall conceive and bear a son, and shall call his name Immanuel" (Isa 7:13–14), a name that means "God is with us." Isaiah urges the people to wait for the fulfillment of this sign. Even though it now seems that the Lord is "hiding his face from the house of Jacob" (Isa 8:17), in the future God will bring it about in Galilee that

    the people who walked in darkness
        have seen a great light . . .
    For to us a child is born,
        to us a son is given;
    and the government will be upon his shoulder,
        and his name will be called
    "Wonderful Counselor, Mighty God,
        Everlasting Father, Prince of Peace." (Isa 9:2, 6)

This child of the "young woman" or "virgin" will reign always, thanks to the power of the Lord.

In the prophecy of Isaiah, Israel is repeatedly called "daughter of Zion." Isaiah's prophecy begins with Israel in a state of deep desolation.

> Your country lies desolate,
>   your cities are burned with fire;
> in your very presence
>   aliens devour your land. . . .
> And the daughter of Zion is left . . .
>   like a besieged city. (Isa 1:7–8; cf. Lam 1:6)

As Lamentations 2:13 puts it,

> What can I liken to you, that I may comfort you,
>   O virgin daughter of Zion?
> For vast as the sea is your ruin;
>   who can restore you?

In this context, marked by exile and desolation, the Lord promises redemption and restoration:

> Loose the bonds from your neck,
>   O captive daughter of Zion.
>
> For thus says the Lord: "You were sold for nothing, and you shall
> be redeemed without money." (Isa 52:2–3)

Tellingly, the Lord proclaims,

> Say to the daughter of Zion,
>   "Behold, your salvation comes;
> behold, his reward is with him,
>   and his recompense before him." (Isa 62:11)

Mary is the "daughter of Zion"—the embodiment of the holy people of Israel—who first greets the redemption of Israel, and she is also the virgin (or "young woman") who rejoices with Sarah and Hannah in God's faithfulness in sending a Son. In her womb the prophecy of Zechariah, which is a prophecy for all God's people, is first fulfilled: "Sing and rejoice, O daughter of Zion; for lo, I come and I will dwell in the midst of you, says the LORD" (Zech 2:10). In all this, Mary stands as the "handmaid of the Lord" (Luke 1:38) who humbly accomplishes Israel's mission of obedient love of the Lord. In the fullness of time, when Elizabeth meets Mary in the Gospel of Luke, Elizabeth cries out, "Blessed are you among women, and blessed is the fruit of your womb!" (Luke 1:42).[25] Elizabeth goes further in paying her respects to Mary: "Why is this granted me, that the mother of my Lord should come to me?" (Luke 1:43). She perceives how blessed Mary is since Mary is the mother of the Lord. In her womb Mary carries the child who is "the Son of God" (Luke 1:35). Elizabeth proclaims that Mary is more blessed than any other mere human because Mary is the mother of the Son of God.

We know from the Gospel of John that the one whom Mary bears is "the Word" who in the beginning "was with God, and . . . was God" (John 1:1). In the womb of Mary, the divine "Word became flesh and dwelt among us, full of grace and truth; we have beheld his glory, glory as of the only Son from the Father" (John 1:14). Can anything earthly compare with the privilege that Mary enjoyed of bearing the divine Word as her child? Certainly, God bestowed wonderful gifts upon many others, such as Abraham, David, and the twelve disciples. But the intimacy of being the mother of the Son of God, of bearing the incarnate Son in one's womb (not merely a physical episode but also a spiritual one, as mothers can attest), surely is a gift beyond all others. No role in salvation history, other than that of Jesus, is more exalted or decisive.

As the one "blessed among women," Mary knows that it is no work of hers, but rather it is God's gift. Her response to Elizabeth shows

---

25. For a historical-critical analysis of some of the biblical texts about Mary, arguing that Mary and Joseph conceived Jesus through sexual intercourse, see Andrew T. Lincoln, *Born of a Virgin? Reconceiving Jesus in the Bible, Tradition, and Theology* (Grand Rapids, MI: Eerdmans, 2013).

who she is, in her supreme humility and her rejoicing on behalf of all Israel. She knows that "henceforth all generations will call me blessed" (Luke 1:48). She is the one whom God has chosen in sending his Son to become flesh for the salvation of the world. She is called blessed because of the gift she has received, and in praising her blessedness we praise the greatness of what God has done for his people. That God has rendered her truly fit to receive this gift is shown by the perfect humility in which she responds with pure praise of God.

> My soul magnifies the Lord,
> and my spirit rejoices in God my Savior . . .
> for he who is mighty has done great things for me,
> and holy is his name. (Luke 1:46–47, 49)

How is it that she responds without pride? How is it that she can say yes to God on behalf of all Israel and the whole human race? The answer appears in the angel Gabriel's greeting to her: "Hail, full of grace, the Lord is with you!" (Luke 1:28). The Lord has prepared her to be the mother of the Lord. Her motherhood does not merely consist in serving as a mere physical conduit, which would be less than a fully human motherhood. Rather, she has been prepared spiritually through God's gracious power within her for her vocation as mother to her Son, so that she will be able to raise him from infancy in humble love. She is the first disciple of Christ.

Mary does not presume upon her strength; she does not receive the angel's greeting as though such an extraordinary visit and greeting were her due. She is "greatly troubled at the saying" (Luke 1:29) because she knows that the God of Israel, whom we cannot approach without holy fear, is present. But she asks for no further purification. She does not say, as Simon Peter does when Jesus calls him to discipleship, "Depart from me, for I am a sinful man, O Lord" (Luke 5:8). She does not say, as the prophet Isaiah does when he is called to be a prophet, "Woe is me! For I am lost; for I am a man of unclean lips" (Isa 6:5). She simply wonders with holy and human fear what this greeting could mean. Then the angel explains to her precisely what the work is: "Do not be afraid, Mary, for you have found favor with God. And behold, you will conceive in your womb and bear a son, and you shall call his name Jesus" (Luke 1:30–31).

How is it that she has "found favor with God"? It is because God has prepared her; she is "full of grace." In other words, the Lord has dwelt within her so that she lacks pride and is filled with faith and love. To enjoy "favor with God" is not to receive a greater status in the terms of this world. It is spiritual favor, true grace that frees the human person for "righteousness to eternal life" (Rom 5:21). Mary is free to respond fully and simply to God, because God's "favor"—God's grace—means that she does not need to respond as Isaiah and Peter do. No uncleanness of spirit weighs down her response. She freely takes on the vocation of bearing Israel's Lord and Messiah: "Behold, I am the handmaid of the Lord; let it be to me according to your word" (Luke 1:38). As her Son later says to his Father, "Not my will, but thine, be done" (Luke 22:42), or as he says to the crowd, "'Who is my mother, and who are my brethren?' And stretching out his hand toward his disciples, he said, 'Here are my mother and my brethren! For whoever does the will of my Father in heaven is my brother, and sister, and mother'" (Matt 12:48–50). Unlike the twelve disciples who are often found arguing about "which of them was the greatest" (Luke 9:46), Mary faithfully mirrors the humility of her Son, whose identity she pondered "in her heart" (Luke 2:19). God's gracious presence within her enables her to freely give herself completely to the Father's will: "Let it be to me according to your word."

How should Jesus's followers think about his mother? Certainly, they, like "all generations," should call her blessed. They should raise their minds to the fullness of the incarnation of the Son of God by praising the holy and humble "Yes" that she gave, a "Yes" that models what our response must be. On the cross, Jesus commands his mother to take his beloved disciple for her own son, and he commands his beloved disciple to love his (Jesus's) mother as his own mother: "When Jesus saw his mother, and the disciple whom he loved standing near, he said to his mother, 'Woman, behold, your son!' Then he said to the disciple, 'Behold, your mother!' And from that hour the disciple took her to his own home" (John 19:26–27). All disciples who are loved by Jesus and who love the crucified Lord should imitate the beloved disciple by recognizing Mary as their mother who is "blessed among women" because she is the mother of her Son.

When we are "one body in Christ" (Rom 12:5), we share his mother. This is important because she shows us what discipleship involves, and it is also important because she embodies holy Israel (daughter Zion in whose midst God dwells) and calls us to be aware that we, in whom her Son dwells spiritually, are "the Israel of God" (Gal 6:16) and "God's temple" (1 Cor 3:17). Finally, it is important because Mary loves us in her love for her Son. Christ came to inaugurate the kingdom of God, a communion of persons who share in his love, who are members of his body, and who pray for each other and ask for each other's prayers. As the first disciple, Mary prays for us in Christ, and we are in communion with her and are helped by her prayers, since Christ wishes for his church to be an interpersonal communion of love.

Mary remained at the cross because she loved her Son and because her love was powerful enough to suffer with Jesus. From the outset, God's grace fits her to take up her cross and follow her Son, just as Jesus commands all his disciples to do (see Matt 16:24). Mary literally follows Jesus to the cross (see John 19:25). Her presence at the foot of the cross is like that of the beloved disciple (and of Mary Magdalene and Mary the wife of Clopas), but it is rooted in the unique vocation she alone received in being the mother of the Son. The Gospel of Luke connects her motherhood with suffering, when it reports Simeon's prophecy upon seeing the infant Jesus:

Simeon blessed them and said to Mary his mother,

> "Behold, this child is set for the fall and rising of many in Israel,
> and for a sign that is spoken against
> (and a sword will pierce through your own soul also),
> that thoughts out of many hearts may be revealed."
>   (Luke 2:34–35)

Mary might have expected a different kind of greatness. After all, when the angel Gabriel promised that "you will conceive in your womb and bear a son," Gabriel also told her,

> He will be great, and will be called the Son of the Most High;
> and the Lord God will give to him the throne of his father David,
> and he will reign over the house of Jacob for ever;
> and of his kingdom there will be no end. (Luke 1:31–33)

That must have sounded great, but in fact her mission was first to share in her Son's humble suffering. He was mocked when he returned to Nazareth and proclaimed that he himself was the eschatological servant prophesied by Isaiah. In Nazareth, where he and his mother had lived for years, the members of the synagogue, including his own friends, became incensed at his words (which they misunderstood as either crazy or arrogant) and "led him to the brow of the hill on which their city was built, that they might throw him down headlong" (Luke 4:29; cf. Mark 3:21).

No doubt Mary suffered then, and she also suffered when, as Jesus went "through cities and villages, preaching and bringing the good news of the kingdom of God" (Luke 8:1), "his mother and his brethren came to him" (Luke 8:19) and tried to reach him but could not because the crowd gathered around him was too great. Jesus's messianic mission was to establish a family united by faith in him rather than by literal kinship ties. Thus, Mary is exalted by grace, not merely by a blood-relationship. She is certainly "blessed among women" as his mother, but that exaltation comes to her in the form of grace.

Mary suffered originally because her betrothed husband, Joseph, "resolved to send her away quietly" because "before they came together she was found to be with child" (Matt 1:18–19). Although Joseph did not send her away, because an angel warned him in a dream that the child "conceived in her is of the Holy Spirit" (Matt 1:20), the original misunderstanding of her pregnancy was a humiliation for her, even though Joseph treated her with kindness. At the end of her pregnancy, furthermore, she had to travel with Joseph to take part in a census at Bethlehem, where "there was no place for them in the inn" (Luke 2:7) and so she gave birth in a stable, away from family, friends, and midwife. Soon after, she had to flee with Joseph and her baby to Egypt because of Herod's persecutions (Matt 2:13–15). In all this she was being configured from the outset to her Son, who says of himself, "Foxes have holes, and birds of the air have nests; but the Son of man has nowhere to lay his head" (Matt 8:20).

In pondering the glory of her Son, revealed to her by the angel, she began to perceive the mystery of her own suffering in relation to the unique mission of her Son. When Jesus goes missing during a family trip to Jerusalem, she confronts him after he is found in the temple: "Son, why have you treated us so? Behold, your father and I have been looking for you anxiously" (Luke 2:48). Although only a boy of twelve, he has been teaching the elders in the temple. He responds to Mary: "How is it that you sought me? Did you not know that I must be in my Father's house?" (Luke 2:49). His path leads toward the cross and toward the Father. Configured to him by grace, having emptied herself and acted as "the handmaid of the Lord," his mother is to join him there at the cross, where all disciples who love him must also be. As Jesus says, "A disciple is not above his teacher, but every one when he is fully taught will be like his teacher" (Luke 6:40), and "whoever does not bear his own cross and come after me, cannot be my disciple" (Luke 14:27). Repeatedly, Mary contemplates her Son intensely, as part of her full interior configuration to her Son and Redeemer: "Mary kept all these things, pondering them in her heart" (Luke 2:19).

Was Mary's attention to her Son diverted by having other children? We do not have clear biblical evidence on this point, but it is noteworthy that although Jesus obviously has "brethren" (Acts 1:14), among them "James the Lord's brother" (Gal 1:19), they are never identified as children of Mary. We are not told that "James the Lord's brother" is the son of Jesus's mother, rather than the son of close relative, such as "Mary the mother of James" (Luke 24:10), or a half-sibling from a previous marriage of Joseph. We are told, however, that Joseph quickly learns that Mary's Son is "of the Holy Spirit" (Matt 1:20) and is "Christ the Lord" (Luke 2:11). Joseph knows from the outset that Mary's womb is uniquely God's temple and that Mary's Son is her (and Joseph's) Lord, to whose nourishment and life they must devote all their energies. If Mary had other sons and daughters, they would have been responsible for caring for her after Jesus's death, whereas in fact the beloved disciple takes Mary into his home.

It can seem quite surprising, even disturbing, that in the Gospel of John, Jesus often calls his mother "woman," which seems impolite or disrespectful. At the wedding at Cana—a scene filled with symbolic imagery regarding God's covenantal marriage with Israel—Jesus's mother tells him that the wine has run out. Jesus responds, "O woman, what have you to do with me? My hour is not yet come" (John 2:4). At the cross, he again impersonally addresses his mother as "woman": "Woman, behold, your son!" (John 19:26).

Note that in both cases, Jesus is speaking in the context of his mission to accomplish the purification of God's people. In Cana he changes water into wine using jars whose normal purpose was to hold water "for the Jewish rites of purification" (John 2:6), and on the cross he dies for the sins of the people. This aspect of purification from sin—the reversal of Adam and Eve's fall—sheds light on Jesus's use of the term "woman" in addressing his mother in John 2 and 19.

To appreciate how this is so, we must first recall the account of Adam and Eve's fall. In Genesis 3, Eve has not yet received her name;

she is called simply "the woman" (Gen 3:2). Tempted by the "serpent," she eats from the divinely forbidden fruit of the Tree of the Knowledge of Good and Evil, and prompts her husband to eat. This act of rebellion is discovered by God, who curses the serpent and promises,

> I will put enmity between you and the woman,
>   and between your seed and her seed;
> he shall bruise your head,
>   and you shall bruise his heel. (Gen 3:15)

Of course, this imagery derives from the human aversion to snakes and from the common experience of being bitten by snakes, which are sometimes poisonous. But there is also a much deeper symbolic meaning in play, as we should expect given the rich concentration of symbolism in Genesis 1–3. Specifically, the symbolism of Genesis 3:15 foreshadows the overcoming of the original sin through a future struggle between the "woman" (and her "seed") and the "serpent." In this struggle, seemingly both the woman's seed and the serpent will be harmed; the serpent's head will be crushed, and the woman's seed (or descendant) will be fatally wounded.

Given this background, we gain insight into Jesus's addressing his mother as "woman" at Cana (John 2:4) and at the cross (John 19:26). Although his use of the term "woman" may seem to be rudely impersonal, he has a very good reason for it. Note once more the significance of Cana and the cross: both involve the reversal of sin and the consummation of the covenantal marriage between God and his people that God has intended from the very beginning. All humans are children of "the woman" Eve; now, in Christ, all humans are called to be adopted children of Mary in her Son. The point is that Mary is the "woman" of the new covenant; she is the new Eve who participates intimately in the work of redemption that her Son, the new Adam, accomplishes by his cross in fulfilment of the promise of Genesis 3:15.

This helps to explain why in another Johannine text, the book of Revelation, Mary is again identified as "woman." In Revelation 12:1, we find "a great portent . . . in heaven," namely the appearance of "a woman clothed with the sun, and the moon under her feet, and on her head a crown of twelve stars." The reference to twelve stars indicates Israel (with its twelve tribes) and/or the church (with the twelve disciples). Importantly, "she was with child and she cried out in her pangs of birth, in anguish for delivery" (Rev 12:2). She is opposed by "a great red dragon," a serpent, who "stood before the woman who was about to bear a child, that he might devour her child when she brought it forth" (Rev 12:3–4). She then bears the child, "one who is to rule all the nations with a rod of iron," and the child is "caught up to God and to his throne" (Rev 12:5). This child is Jesus Christ. In the war that follows, the "woman" flees and is pursued by the dragon, who is infuriated by the divine aid she receives and who goes "off to make war on the rest of her offspring" (Rev 12:17). The "woman" here is a symbol of the church. The typology of the book of Revelation connects Mary as "woman" with the church as "woman." The church, too, bears children—namely, all those united to Christ through faith and baptism. But the "woman" against whom the serpent fights in Revelation 12 cannot be separated from Mary as the new Eve, whose seed conquers the serpent, since the "woman" bears a son "who is to rule all the nations with a rod of iron."

Here we again see the unique participation of Mary in the life of her Son. As Simeon prophesied, the "woman," Mary, suffered a sword in her own heart at the cross. Her suffering was certainly not salvific—since her Son is her Savior—but her suffering at the foot of the cross was uniquely united with her Son's suffering, just as through motherhood (and by grace) she was uniquely united with her Son's incarnation.

This raises a further question. In uniquely suffering with her Son, did Mary receive a unique share in his exaltation? Note that Romans 6:5 states that "if we have been united with him in a death like his, we shall certainly be united with him in a resurrection like his," and Romans 8:17 observes that we will be "fellow heirs with Christ, provided we suffer with him in order that we may also be glorified with him." Has this bodily glorification happened to Mary, due to her unique sharing in Christ's sufferings?

The New Testament does not give us a direct answer, but neither is it silent. In Revelation 12:1, the sign that appears "in heaven" is the "woman clothed with the sun, with the moon under her feet," and this woman is linked typologically to both Mary and the church. The "woman" appears "in heaven." Does this mean that Mary, with her Son, is "in heaven" (and not simply as a disembodied soul), called to sit at the right hand of the King as the queen mother? In considering this question, we should examine Revelation 11:19, the verse that directly precedes 12:1. In Revelation 11:19, another significant typological image occurs. There we read, "Then God's temple in heaven was opened, and the ark of his covenant was seen within his temple; and there were flashes of lightning, loud noises, peals of thunder, an earthquake, and heavy hail." The "ark of his covenant" is within "God's temple in heaven." The question then is how the "ark" within his temple (11:19) relates to the "woman" in heaven (12:1).

Recall that in Israel's ark of the covenant, the Word of God was contained. It was contained both in the two tablets of stone on which God wrote the Ten Commandments (see Deut 10:5) and in the "book of the law" that Moses wrote down (Deut 31:26). Some manna and the rod of Aaron were also in the ark. By comparison with the ark, Mary contained in her womb the Word of God and "the bread of life" (John 6:48), her Son. When David was bringing the ark up to Jerusalem, "David danced before the LORD with all his might," and he was "leaping and dancing before the LORD" (2 Sam 6:14, 16). Similarly, when Mary, bearing Jesus in her womb, comes near to Elizabeth (who is pregnant with John the Baptist), "the babe leaped in her [Elizabeth's] womb"; and Elizabeth joyfully recognizes "the mother of my Lord" and proclaims that "when the voice of your greeting came to my ears, the babe in my womb leaped for joy" (Luke 1:41, 43–44). From his place in Elizabeth's womb, John the Baptist responds to the pregnant

Mary in the same way that David responds to the ark of the covenant, namely by leaping with joy.

Thus, when "God's temple in heaven was opened" and when "a great portent appeared in heaven" (Rev 11:19–12:1), what appears in heaven is linked with Mary—"the ark of his covenant" and a "woman clothed with the sun." Since Mary uniquely shares in the mission of Christ (though Christ alone is the Redeemer), this twofold typological vision of what seems to be Mary in heaven fits with the exaltation that Christ receives after his suffering and also fits with the promise that if we suffer with Christ we will be raised with him. Her unique bond with Christ gives a reason for why she would be fully present in heaven, with her risen and ascended Son, prior to the general resurrection. As "queen mother," she takes an exalted "seat" (see Jer 13.18) at the right hand of her Son the King at the restoration of Israel.

The typological connections that are present in these New Testament references to Mary accord with the typological reasoning that the New Testament often employs to convey truth about the central figures of the history of salvation. For example, the New Testament depicts Jesus as the new Adam, the new Moses, the new Joshua, and the new Solomon. The biblical images that are connected with Mary have been interpreted by the Catholic Church to signify that Mary, due to her unique participation in the mysteries of her Son, is indeed the "ark of the covenant" and the "woman" whom the eyes of faith can perceive to be fully in heaven (body and soul) with her Son. Likewise, the Catholic Church has interpreted the biblical references to Mary's grace, to her humility, and to her configuration to her Son to mean that as the new Eve she was fully free in her "Yes" to God, thanks to God preparing her by freeing her from sin at her conception due to the merits of her Son's passion. Her obedient "Yes" on behalf of the whole human race flowed from God's grace and favor, because "God so loved the world that he gave his only Son" (John 3:16).[26]

---

26. See David Braine, "The Virgin Mary in the Christian Faith: The Development of the Church's Teaching on the Virgin Mary in Modern Perspective," *Nova et Vetera* 7 (2009): 877–940.

CHAPTER 3

∽∾

THE EUCHARIST

The Reformers all agreed that the Catholic Church has made significant errors about the Lord's Supper, not only regarding the nature of Jesus's presence in the Eucharist but also and especially regarding the Catholic doctrine that the Mass is a "sacrifice" insofar as it sacramentally re-presents Christ's sacrifice (and thereby intimately unites believers to Christ's once-and-for-all saving action). For readers who are not acquainted with the Catholic understanding of the Eucharist, I recommend paragraphs 1322–1419 of the *Catechism of the Catholic Church*, as well as paragraphs 1–14 of Vatican II's *Sacrosanctum Concilium* and John Paul II's encyclical *Ecclesia de Eucharistia.*[1] My biblical reflection sets forth the covenantal and sacrificial dimensions of God's relationship with Israel, and suggests that the celebration of the Eucharist by the church should ultimately be understood in light of the Passover lamb of the exodus. As in previous chapters, my biblical reflection attempts to lay foundations for doctrinal reflection rather than spelling out the doctrinal development that has proceeded, over the centuries, via biblically warranted modes of biblical reasoning.

---

1. *Sacrosanctum Concilium*, in *Vatican Council II*, 1–36.

LUTHER'S CONCERN

In his 1520 treatise *The Babylonian Captivity of the Church*, Martin Luther lodges three main criticisms against the doctrine of the Eucharist as understood by the Catholic Church prior to the Reformation. These criticisms concern the refusal to allow the laity to partake of the eucharistic cup (due to the danger of dropping the precious blood, as well as no doubt to the danger of spreading disease), the doctrine of transubstantiation, and the neglect of the Eucharist's meaning as a promise or oath to which the proper response is faith (a neglect caused by the doctrine of the eucharistic sacrifice which in Luther's view turns the Eucharist into a work by which the church saves itself). Let me set forth these three criticisms in more detail.

First, Luther points out that there is no scriptural justification for the withholding of the cup from the laity. According to Luther, the scriptural passages that teach about the Eucharist are solely "the gospel passages on the Lord's Supper, and St. Paul in I Corinthians 11."[2] In his view John 6 is about faith, not about the Eucharist at all. When one turns to the Gospels, one finds that Jesus does not withhold the cup from any of his disciples. Indeed, Jesus commands that all drink of the cup. Nonetheless, the "Romanists" hold that "it was entrusted to the free judgment of the church to administer which kind she preferred" to the laity.[3] But Luther notes that the Romanists here are able to bring forth no scriptural support for this claim, and can only say, "The church has so ordained."[4] In fact, it is the pope and bishops who have so ordained, in their rebellion against Jesus's own words and in their tyrannizing over believers. Thus, Luther observes that "it is not the church which ordained these things, but those who tyrannize over the church without the consent of the church, which is the people of God."[5]

---

2. Martin Luther, "The Babylonian Captivity of the Church," in *Martin Luther: Selections*, 257.
3. Ibid., 258.
4. Ibid., 260.
5. Ibid.

Even so, a certain theologian—representing "fair-speaking toadies of the pope"—argues that 1 Corinthians 11, with its critique of factions at Corinth, bears favorably upon the church's ability to withhold the cup from the laity.[6] Luther demolishes this argument by making clear that Paul certainly did not have in mind anything to do with withholding the cup. The conclusion follows on firm scriptural grounds: "To deny both kinds to the laity is impious and oppressive; and it is not in the power of any angel, nor of any pope or council [i.e. the Council of Constance, which ruled on this matter] whatever to deny them."[7] Neither the "Roman dictatorship"[8] nor a council of bishops can rightly teach anything against the express word of Scripture, although popes and councils (such as that of Constance) have repeatedly done so, to the detriment of the people of God. Must then all believers receive under both kinds? Luther states that there is no explicit scriptural teaching on this point, and so Jesus evidently "left the matter to each man's choice."[9] The sin consists only in forbidding the laity to receive the cup.

Second, Luther argues for the view that in the Eucharist the body and blood of Jesus are present in, with, and under the bread and wine, and he argues against the view that in the Eucharist the substance of the bread and wine are changed by God into the substance of Christ's body and blood (i.e., transubstantiation). Here Luther recalls his student years, in which he read Pierre d'Ailly's argument that had the church not condemned consubstantiation (according to which the bread and wine continue to be substantially present in the Eucharist), it would be much more reasonable to hold than is transubstantiation. Arguing that the church has no authority to impose a belief on this matter, as the church in fact did at the Council of Lyons, Luther holds that each person must be free to believe in transubstantiation or consubstantiation, and for his part he insists simply that Christ's body and blood are *really* present,

6. Ibid., 261.
7. Ibid., 263.
8. Ibid.
9. Ibid., 264.

albeit in a noncircumscriptive manner. Scripture does not say that the bread and wine are changed in "substance"; after all, Paul and Acts call the Eucharist the breaking of bread. All the confusion about the accidents of bread and wine remaining and the accident of quantity serving in place of the substance derives from Aristotelian philosophy rather than from Scripture. In the Gospels and in 1 Corinthians 11, Jesus and Paul speak of the bread without going on to say that the bread is no longer there once Jesus's body is present. Just as two natures can be present in one Jesus, so also two natures can be present in the eucharistic bread/body of Christ and wine/blood of Christ. Although this is his position, Luther grants that transubstantiation remains possible and not heretical. What he rejects is that the church has any authority to doctrinally compel believers to hold transubstantiation.

Third, Luther criticizes the doctrine of eucharistic sacrifice as "the most wicked abuse of all," both because of its falsehood and because of its prevalence: "There is no belief more widely accepted in the church to-day, or one of greater force, than that the mass is a good work and a sacrifice."[10] Once one holds that the Eucharist is a sacrifice, then it becomes possible to offer the Mass for particular persons for the remission, in some way, of some of the punishments due to their sins. Participating in the celebration of a Mass, too, is seen to be a meritorious (sacrificial) work on the part of the persons who participate. The result is that "the special feasts, the confraternities, intercessions, merits, anniversaries, and memorial days" enable priests to make money by saying Mass, since "things of this kind are bought and sold in the church, dealt in and bargained for; the whole income of priests and monks depending on it."[11]

Does the doctrine of eucharistic sacrifice have a foundation in Scripture? Luther urges his readers to clear their minds of all later accretions, and to begin by focusing on the words of institution uttered by Jesus. If we do so, Luther thinks that we will no longer "be carried

---

10. Ibid., 271.
11. Ibid.

about by every wind of doctrine, as we have been carried about till now by irreverent doctrine, man-made, and contrary to the truth."[12] Against the man-made doctrine of eucharistic sacrifice, Jesus's words of institution show clearly that the Eucharist, quite simply, is a testament. According to numerous passages in the New Testament, a testament is a will that one makes in view of one's death, a binding promise regarding the inheritance that one wills to give to one's heirs. Jesus has his death in view, and he appoints as his heirs those who have faith in him and in his promise. In his words of institution, what does Jesus promise to give his heirs? He promises to give them the remission of sins. The truth of Jesus's testament is confirmed by his death (a death foreshadowed by the earlier testaments or covenants found in the Old Testament).

In the Mass, then, we simply are called to believe in Jesus's testament. Thus, in terms of preparation for participating in the Mass, we must realize that "we cannot prepare ourselves for it by any works, by the use of force, or by any merits; but only by faith."[13] God's Word demands the response of faith. Once faith alone has brought us into communion with God, "then love succeeds faith, and gives rise to every good work," none of which pertain to the salvation brought about by faith.[14] In the Mass, therefore, Jesus reminds us that he has confirmed his promise or testament irrevocably by his death, which his body and blood signify. With faith in his testament, we partake in his body and blood. As Luther says, "Who would not weep inward tears and in very joy surrender himself entirely to Christ, if he believed firmly and without doubt that this inestimable promise of Christ's belonged to him?"[15] Thus the Mass is solely about Jesus's promise of forgiveness of sins and eternal salvation for those who believe, and our attitude at Mass should be nothing other than joyful faith.

Unfortunately, only the priests know the words of institution; the

---

12. Ibid., 272.
13. Ibid., 273–74.
14. Ibid., 274.
15. Ibid., 275–76.

common people do not even hear them. The result has been dire sacrilege: "Satan has taken advantage of this lamentable condition of ours to remove every trace of the real mass from the church."[16] At the Eucharist, instead of worshiping God with faith, believers attempt to offer God a good work that we think will be of benefit to us, and we prepare for Mass by means of all sorts of things (for example, confession or prayer) other than faith in the divine promise. Believers come to Mass prepared to do a work rather than prepared to embrace in faith an unmerited promise. Yet, do not Jesus's body and blood serve to symbolize a sacrifice? Luther answers that just as God symbolized his promise to Noah by means of a rainbow, God gives his own body and blood simply to confirm his greatest promise.

It follows that "in the mass, the word of Christ is the testament, the bread and wine are the sacrament."[17] Of these two, it is obviously Christ's word that is most important, because the sacrament is simply a sign of Christ's word. Faith in Christ's word is what everything hinges upon, and so, as Luther remarks, "I am able daily, indeed hourly, to have the mass; for, as often as I wish, I can set the words of Christ before me, and nourish and strengthen my faith by them."[18] Sadly, the scholastic theologians ("perfidious teachers") in their disputations about the Eucharist almost always ignore the centrality of testament and faith, and instead talk endlessly about transubstantiation and "*opera operata*, participations, and the fruits of the mass."[19] This focus on our own works destroys the Mass, which in fact is about the wondrous bequest that Jesus wills for us to inherit by faith and without any merit of our own, no matter how holy or well-prepared we imagine ourselves to be.

In a nutshell, those who innocently trusted in the church led by the pope have become exiles from their true inheritance. The Mass "has been transformed, by the teaching of godless men, into a good

---

16. Ibid., 276.
17. Ibid., 279.
18. Ibid.
19. Ibid., 279, 281.

work."[20] It has been transformed into a sacrificial work that accomplishes, whenever it is done, some benefit. It is as though we imagined we could earn what Jesus promises us, or as though we wished to do Jesus a good turn. Luther laments, "This ignorance of the testament, and this servitude of the sacrament, are things that go beyond tears. . . . With unheard-of perversity, we mock at the mercy of the Giver; for we give as a work what we should be accepting as a gift."[21] The Eucharist is intended only to prompt the response of personal faith, and yet people pay money to have Masses said for the souls of dead loved ones, whose opportunity to have faith has come and gone. Each person must respond on his own with his own faith, and so the Eucharist as a sacrifice could not do any good to anyone even if it were not the sacrilege that it is.

Are not the prayers of the Mass good works? Luther grants that they are, but he emphasizes that "the prayers are not the mass, but the works of the mass."[22] The Mass itself is the testament and the sacrament, and both aim solely at the response of faith. We can pray for others, but we cannot celebrate the Mass for others, since the latter requires an act of personal faith. The words of the canon of the Mass, therefore, deeply mislead believers and turn them away from the words of Jesus. In the canon of the Mass, the Eucharist is clearly presented as a sacrifice, a good work. By contrast, Jesus at the Last Supper shows us what the reality of the Eucharist is. At the Last Supper, he simply said the words of the testament over bread and wine; he certainly did not immolate himself. Once we return to Jesus's own words and example, we can see that the church has turned "something we receive" into "something we offer."[23]

There is, however, something that we do offer, which explains where the words of the canon of the Mass originally came from. Namely, the early church collected food and drink to distribute to the poor, and this offering, which originated through God's bounty, was lifted up to God

---

20. Ibid., 282.
21. Ibid.
22. Ibid., 285.
23. Ibid., 287.

by the priest (who took a portion of it to consecrate as the Eucharist). While saying the words of institution in the vernacular, the priest would lift up the consecrated bread and cup so that all could see and be stimulated anew to respond to Christ's testament with faith. Originally, then, the use of "sacrifice" (a sacrifice of praise) and "offering" served a good purpose, but "in these corrupt and most perilous times" the use of these terms impedes the gospel, which is necessarily "superior to all the canons and collects."[24] Luther adds that since the Mass is not a sacrifice, but rather is the lifting up of Christ's testament and sacrament regarding his gift of unmerited mercy, priests and laity are on completely equal footing in the Mass.

BIBLICAL REFLECTION

Let me begin by reflecting upon the Passover. After Joseph dies, the people of Israel fall into a state of slavery and oppression in Egypt. The Lord hears his people's groaning and sends Moses to lead the people out of Egypt and into the promised land. God appears to Moses and says,

> I have heard the groaning of the people of Israel whom the Egyptians hold in bondage and I have remembered my covenant. Say therefore to the people of Israel, "I am the LORD, and I will bring you out from under the burdens of the Egyptians, and I will deliver you from their bondage, and I will redeem you with an outstretched arm and with great acts of judgment." (Exod 6:5–6)

The goal of this redemption from Egyptian bondage is giving the people a deeper relationship with their God.

Since the people's will to escape their oppression has been crushed by the weight of slavery, God must act on their behalf. He does so by sending ten plagues with the purpose of demonstrating his saving power

---

24. Ibid., 289.

and compelling Pharaoh to let the people of Israel go. Prior to sending each plague, God sends Moses to Pharaoh with the request, "Let my people go, so they may serve me" (Exod 8:20). The service that God wants from his people is sacrificial worship. Moses tells Pharaoh, "We must go three days' journey into the wilderness and sacrifice to the LORD our God as he will command us" (Exod 8:27). Freedom from slavery and the journey to the promised land are linked to serving God through sacrificial worship, suggesting thereby that false worship is itself a form of slavery and exile from home.

In Exodus 11, after the first nine plagues had failed to change Pharaoh's mind, God promises to deliver one final and decisive plague—namely, God will exact the punishment of death upon the firstborn of Egypt. God tells Moses, "About midnight I will go forth in the midst of Egypt; and all the first-born in the land of Egypt shall die, from the first-born of Pharaoh who sits upon his throne, even to the first-born of the maidservant who is behind the mill" (Exod 11:4–5). God will not inflict this punishment upon the Israelites. But in order to avoid receiving the punishment of the death of their first-born, the people of Israel cannot simply remain passive; rather, they must enact a sacrificial ritual. Each household must select an unblemished lamb; and on the fourteenth day of the month of Abib, "the whole assembly of the congregation of Israel shall kill their lambs in the evening" (Exod 12:6; cf. Exod 13:4). This sacrificial slaughtering of the unblemished lambs is what God uses to spare the people of Israel from the slaughtering of their first-born. God commands each household to "kill the passover lamb. Take a bunch of hyssop and dip it in the blood which is in the basin, and touch the lintel and the two doorposts with the blood which is in the basin" (Exod 12:21–22). When God sees the blood of the unblemished lamb marking the door of the household, God will spare the household the punishment that the Egyptians receive.

At Passover, then, God spares the Israelites from the punishment of death through the blood of an unblemished lamb. Recall that the promised punishment of disobedience to God is death (Gen 2:17).

Due to the Passover sacrifice of the unblemished lamb, by which God spares the people from the punishment of death (just as God spared Abraham's son Isaac by providing "the lamb for the burnt offering" [Gen 22:8]), the people begin the exodus from Egyptian slavery to dwell with God in the promised land. The Passover sacrifice therefore indicates the mode by which God's people will come to dwell with him in an intimate way.

During the exodus, Moses renews the covenant between God and Israel by means of the "blood of the covenant which the LORD has made with you" in accordance with "the book of the covenant" (Exod 24:7–8). Moses sprinkles the sacrificial blood first upon the altar and then upon the people. With Aaron, Nadab, Abihu, and seventy elders of Israel, Moses ascends the mountain (Sinai) where "they saw the God of Israel" and "they beheld God, and ate and drank" (Exod 24:10–11).

Much later, when the prophet Daniel confesses the sins of Israel, the angel Gabriel comes to Daniel and tells him that, in fact, the time of sinful exile is coming to an end and the restoration of Israel is at hand. Gabriel instructs Daniel to expect a messianic figure who will undergo a sacrificial death as part of the restoration of Israel. Gabriel states, "Seventy weeks of years are decreed concerning your people and your holy city, to finish the transgression, to put an end to sin, and to atone for iniquity, to bring in everlasting righteousness, to seal both vision and prophet, and to anoint a most holy place" (Dan 9:24). Gabriel tells Daniel to expect the restoration of Jerusalem by "an anointed one, a prince," but to expect first a tribulation at the end of which "an anointed one shall be cut off, and shall have nothing" (Dan 9:25–26).

A similar restoration of Israel is depicted in the book of Zechariah. The Lord promises,

> I will signal for them and gather them in,
>   for I have redeemed them,
>   and they shall be as many as of old.
> Though I scattered them among the nations,

yet in far countries they shall remember me,
and with their children they shall live and return.
(Zech 10:8–9)

In case the theme of new exodus is still not clear, the Lord adds, "They shall pass through the sea of Egypt, and the waves of the sea shall be smitten" (Zech 10:11; cf. Exod 14:21–22). As the prophecy continues, we find that the Lord himself promises to become "the shepherd of the flock doomed to be slain for those who trafficked in the sheep" (Zech 11:7).

The Lord goes on to proclaim that in his coming day, he "will pour out on the house of David and the inhabitants of Jerusalem a spirit of compassion and supplication, so that, when they look on him whom they have pierced, they shall mourn for him, as one mourns for an only child, and weep bitterly over him, as one weeps over a first-born" (Zech 12:10). He states that in his coming day, which will bring about the new exodus, he will set up "a fountain" that will cleanse all Israel from sin. That day will involve a profound tribulation.

> Strike the shepherd, that the sheep may be scattered; . . .
> In the whole land, says the LORD,
>   two thirds shall be cut off and perish,
>   and one third shall be left alive.
> And I will put this third into the fire
>   and refine them as one refines silver,
>   and test them as gold is tested. (Zech 13:7–9)

The result of this tribulation will be the intimate dwelling of the people with God: "They will call on my name, and I will answer them. I will say, 'They are my people'; and they will say, 'The LORD is my God'" (Zech 13:9).

Isaiah 53 describes God's suffering servant who will endure "the chastisement that made us whole" and who will bear "the iniquity of us all" (Isa 53:5–6).

> By oppression and judgment he was taken away;
>   and as for his generation, who considered
> that he was cut off out of the land of the living,
>   stricken for the transgression of my people? (Isa 53:8)

After enduring this tribulation unto death in order to "make many to be accounted righteous" (Isa 53:11), the servant will receive a glorious reward from God. The result will be the long-promised fulfillment of the covenantal marriage between God and his people, Israel.

> For your Maker is your husband,
>   the LORD of hosts is his name;
> and the Holy One of Israel is your Redeemer,
>   the God of the whole earth he is called. (Isa 54:5)

These prophecies indicate why Jewish expectation of the restoration of Israel was widespread in Jesus's time. This background helps us to appreciate what Jesus intends to accomplish when he tells his disciples,

> Behold, we are going up to Jerusalem; and the Son of man will be delivered to the chief priests and the scribes, and they will condemn him to death, and deliver him to the Gentiles; and they will mock him, and spit upon him, and scourge him, and kill him; and after three days he will rise. (Mark 10:33–34)

Put simply, Jesus plans to endure the prophesied tribulation on behalf of God's people, and "to give his life as a ransom for many" (Mark 10:45).[25] Fulfilling the messianic prophecy of Zechariah 9:9, Jesus rides into Jerusalem to the acclaim of the people. He cleanses the temple as an

---

25. See Brant Pitre, *Jesus and the Last Supper* (Grand Rapids, MI: Eerdmans, 2015). For further background, see Pitre, *Jesus, the Tribulation, and the End of the Exile: Restoration Eschatology and the Origin of the Atonement* (Grand Rapids, MI: Baker Academic, 2005). For a much different exegetical perspective, see Ben Witherington III, *Making a Meal of It: Rethinking the Theology of the Lord's Supper* (Waco, TX: Baylor University Press, 2007).

eschatological sign (see Zech 14:21; Mark 11:15), and he prophesies the destruction of the temple (Mark 13:2). He is the new temple, as is made especially clear in John 2:19–21 but as the other gospels show as well.[26] He is also the new Passover Lamb, the "Lamb of God, who takes away the sins of the world" (John 1:29), the one of whom it is truly said that "not a bone of him shall be broken" (John 19:36; cf. Exod 12:46; 1 Pet 1:19).

How does the Last Supper relate to the new Passover? Jesus's Last Supper has the elements of a Passover meal. In Mark 14:12, we read that "on the first day of Unleavened Bread, when they sacrificed the passover lamb, his disciples said to him, 'Where will you have us go and prepare for you to eat the Passover?'" Jesus tells them that they will find a room in Jerusalem already prepared; and they go there to make ready for "the passover" (Mark 14:16). Could it be that Jesus envisions himself as the sacrificial lamb of a "new Passover," by whose blood the people of Israel will be restored and the nations gathered to Israel?[27] Certainly, Jesus makes clear that by his death he will establish the promised new covenant. Thus, at his Last Supper, he "took bread, and blessed, and broke it, and gave it to them, and said, 'Take; this is my body.' And he took a cup, and when he had given thanks he gave it to them, and they all drank of it. And he said to them, 'This is my blood of the covenant, which is poured out for many'" (Mark 14:22–24). Jesus calls upon the new covenant community—the inaugurated kingdom of God and the restored Israel—to liturgically participate in his paschal sacrifice in the period between his death and the consummation of the kingdom. He commands his disciples: "Do this in remembrance of me" (Luke 22:19).

To understand what kind of "remembrance" this is, we need once more to recall the exodus narrative. After commanding the ritual of

---

26. See Nicholas Perrin, *Jesus the Temple* (Grand Rapids, MI: Baker Academic, 2010).

27. See Pitre, *Jesus and the Last Supper*. Pitre argues that at the Last Supper, Jesus shows that he is the new Passover sacrifice by whose blood, in the eschatological tribulation, the people of Israel will be restored and the nations gathered to Israel in the new exodus, whose ultimate destination is the new creation and the resurrection of the dead (of which Jesus is the firstfruits).

the sacrifice of the unblemished lamb and the seven days of eating unleavened bread, God instructs the Israelites:

> In this manner you shall eat it: your loins girded, your sandals on your feet, and your staff in your hand; and you shall eat it in haste. It is the LORD's passover. . . . This day shall be for you a memorial day, and you shall keep it as a feast to the LORD; throughout your generations you shall observe it as an ordinance for ever. (Exod 12:11, 14)

The ritual is a way of entering into the past salvific event and making it present. Thus, after detailing the Passover ritual that each generation must perform, Moses tells the people, "You shall tell your son on that day [the annual feast of Passover], 'It is because of what the LORD did *for me* when *I* came out of Egypt'" (Exod 13:8; emphasis added). Similarly, in his farewell discourse, Moses speaks as though each generation of Israelites belongs to the "you" who fled Egyptian slavery: "You shall eat no leavened bread with it [the Passover lamb]; seven days you shall eat it with unleavened bread, the bread of affliction—for you came out of the land of Egypt in hurried flight—that all the days of your life you may remember the day when you came out of the land of Egypt" (Deut 16:3). The liturgy of the Passover is a remembrance that takes each generation back to the first Passover.

It is also worth recalling here that on the exodus journey, God fed his people with manna as their daily bread: "The people of Israel ate the manna forty years, till they came to a habitable land; they ate the manna, till they came to the border of the land of Canaan" (Exod 16:35). Likewise, Jesus feeds those who follow him in faith in his new exodus, but this time with himself as the "bread of life" (John 6:48). In the Gospel of John, after observing that eternal life requires faith in him, Jesus states, "I am the bread of life. Your fathers ate the manna in the wilderness, and they died. This is the bread which comes down from heaven, that a man may eat of it and not die. I am the living bread which came down from heaven" (John 6:48–51). Here Jesus presents himself as the new manna, the food that will strengthen us to attain the goal of the new exodus, namely "eternal life" or dwelling with God. Jesus goes on to explain that "the bread which I shall give for the life of the world is my flesh" (John 6:51). He adds that "he who eats my flesh and drinks my blood has eternal life, and I will raise him up at the last day. For my flesh is food indeed, and my blood is drink indeed. He who eats my flesh and drinks my blood abides in me, and I in him" (John 6:54–56).

This startling claim fits with the view that at the Last Supper, Jesus is instituting a new Passover in which his disciples (and later believers) are to participate by consuming him sacramentally as the new paschal lamb for the new exodus. In faith, we participate in his paschal sacrifice by means of an act of liturgical remembrance, in which what we eat and drink sacramentally is the paschal flesh and blood of Jesus. Jesus thereby unites us in his body and strengthens us on the new exodus journey to the fullness of the kingdom of God. The unitive power of our eucharistic participation in Christ's sacrifice is expressed by Paul: "The cup of blessing which we bless, is it not a participation in the blood of Christ? The bread which we break, is it not a participation in the body of Christ? Because there is one bread, we who are many are one body, for we all partake of the one bread" (1 Cor 10:16–17).

Paul also reminds the Corinthians what their liturgical remembrance involves. He repeats the command that Jesus gave his disciples at the Last Supper.

> I received from the Lord what I also delivered to you, that the Lord Jesus on the night when he was betrayed took bread, and when he had given thanks, he broke it, and said, "This is my body which is for you. Do this in remembrance of me." In the same way also the cup, after supper, saying, "This cup is the new covenant in my blood. Do this, as often as you drink it, in remembrance of me." (1 Cor 11:23–25)

He then explains what this liturgical remembrance accomplishes: "For as often as you eat this bread and drink the cup, you proclaim the Lord's death until he comes" (1 Cor 11:26). In the new covenant established by Jesus's cross, we "proclaim the Lord's death" through liturgical "remembrance" and by our lives of self-giving love. Our liturgical remembrance of him is false if we do not imitate his self-giving love but instead "eat of the bread and drink of the cup" in "an unworthy manner" marked by selfishness (1 Cor 11:27–28). Paul exhorts the Corinthians to live in accord with the fact that "Christ, our paschal lamb, has been sacrificed" (1 Cor 5:7).

In remembering Jesus's paschal sacrifice liturgically, the church shares in his one sacrifice and his self-offering to the Father in the Holy Spirit. Our liturgical "remembrance" is a participation in his Passover and in his body as the "living bread" or true manna, since what we offer is "the bread which comes down from heaven," Jesus's flesh, which is given "for the life of the world" (John 6:50–51). In making this offering, the church does not offer a new sacrifice, but rather shares through solemn liturgical remembrance, as Jesus's body, in the single Passover offering of the Lamb. As a participation in the paschal action of Jesus by which he offers his body and blood for the restoration of his people, the Eucharist saves us from the punishment of death and unites us to him in the new exodus journey to perfect dwelling with God. In the faith-filled action of liturgical remembrance by which we offer and consume the body and blood of "our paschal lamb" (1 Cor 5:7), we share in his one saving sacrifice so intimately that it becomes *our own*, as the offering of the whole "body of Christ" (1 Cor 12:27) to the Father in the Spirit. The eucharistic sacrifice is our (the church's) offering of Jesus's saving sacrifice, in such a manner that we are perfectly joined to it through a perfect sacramental communion in his body and blood which we offer.

CHAPTER 4

THE SEVEN SACRAMENTS

When the Reformers scoured the Bible for evidence about the sacraments instituted by Jesus, they did not find the seven that the Catholic Church holds to exist. The Catholic Church's enumeration and practice of the sacraments developed over the centuries, and the Reformers expressed significant concerns about the result. Readers unfamiliar with the Catholic Church's teachings about the seven sacraments should turn especially to paragraphs 1113–1134 and 1210–1666 of the *Catechism of the Catholic Church*. My biblical reflection explores biblical support for the four sacraments whose sacramental status Martin Luther rejected immediately: confirmation, marriage, ordination, and extreme unction (now called the sacrament of the anointing of the sick). After offering an account of what a Christian "sacrament" is, I set forth some of the biblical foundations of each of these four sacraments in turn. Without being able here to track all the biblically warranted modes of biblical reasoning at work in the development of sacramental doctrine, I hope to show something of the biblical basis behind the disputed sacraments.

LUTHER'S CONCERN

In *The Babylonian Captivity of the Church*, Martin Luther teaches that there are three sacraments: baptism, the Eucharist, and confession of sins. He notes that "without doubt, confession of sins is necessary, and in accordance with the divine commandments," and as evidence he cites Matthew 3:6, Matthew 18:15–19, and 1 John 1:9.[1] While affirming the validity of private confession, he states, "What I reject is solely that this kind of confession should be transformed into a means of oppression and extortion on the part of the pontiffs," by whom he means mainly the pope and bishops, although he also urges that the church should "give free permission for any brother or sister [i.e. any layperson] to hear confessions of secret sins."[2] He especially excoriates Rome for the demand for satisfaction, construed otherwise than as the "renovation of life."[3] The resulting focus on works among believers, says Luther, is another of the "monstrous things we owe to thee, O thou whose seat is in Rome, together with thy soul-destroying laws and rituals."[4]

The so-called sacraments of the church led by the pope are, according to Luther, no sacraments at all. Finding no supporting scriptural evidence, Luther rejects the sacramental standing of confirmation, marriage, ordination, and extreme unction. Confirmation, Luther holds, is a particularly obvious case. He states, "It is difficult to understand what the Romanists had in mind when they made the sacrament of confirmation out of the laying on of hands."[5] Christ laid on hands

---

1. Luther, "The Pagan Servitude of the Church," in *Martin Luther: Selections*, 319. Dillenberger notes that this text is more commonly titled "The Babylonian Captivity of the Church," and I have retained this more common title in the body of my text.

2. Ibid., 319, 321. Although Luther defends confession of sins on biblical grounds, the sacramental status of "confession" is admittedly somewhat reduced by the end of this text. During his career, Luther continues to see confession as a quasi-sacrament, but subsumes it underneath baptism. Even so, in "The Babylonian Captivity of the Church," he accepts it along with baptism and the Eucharist on biblical grounds, and so I do not defend it in this chapter. See Ronald K. Rittgers, *The Reformation of the Keys: Confession, Conscience, and Authority in Sixteenth-Century Germany* (Cambridge, MA: Harvard University Press, 2004).

3. Luther, "The Pagan Servitude of the Church," in *Martin Luther: Selections*, 322.

4. Ibid., 323.

5. Ibid., 324.

to do all sorts of things; and the apostles, too, laid on hands for purposes (notably ordination) that can be shown to be unrelated to any alleged sacrament of confirmation. Likewise, many things are said to strengthen believers, including bread, and so if spiritual strengthening is the purpose of the sacrament of confirmation, then the eucharistic bread itself could be "confirmation."

Luther supposes that once the bishops had given all the real work (preaching, baptizing, and celebrating the Eucharist) to their priests, the bishops needed something to do and so they gave themselves—in a further insult to Christ's sole authority—responsibility for a new sacrament, "confirmation." Certainly, Jesus Christ did not institute confirmation as a sacrament. For Luther, a sacrament must contain the twin salvific elements of promise and faith. As Luther notes, Christ did not connect this combination of promise and faith to the laying on of hands. And although Christ did say "they will lay their hands on the sick, and they will recover" (Mark 16:18), this laying on of hands cannot be a sacrament because it does not happen regularly. At best, then, confirmation can be used by the church, like the consecration of water. Surely, it can only help to lay on hands and pray over a person, since prayer always helps. However, this action is not a sacrament, and because there is no salvific promise attached to it, it does not in itself promote salvation.

Luther spends more time discussing marriage, but he is equally persuaded from the outset that it cannot be a sacrament. Scripture attaches no divine promise to marriage, nor did Jesus institute marriage, which has existed since Adam and Eve. Luther states bluntly, "There is no Scriptural warrant whatsoever for regarding marriage as a sacrament."[6] Certainly, marriage can be a metaphor or allegory, as it is in Ephesians 5; but this does not mean that it is a sacrament. Luther focuses on the fact that marriage has always existed. What then is the difference between our marriages today and the pagan marriages of

---

6. Ibid., 326.

our forebears? Their marriages were real and binding, too. On what grounds would marriage, while remaining in outward form entirely the same, suddenly become a "sacrament" when it takes place in the church?

In the Latin text of Ephesians 5, marriage is presented as a *sacramentum*, and Luther knows that some consider that this passage clearly indicates Christian marriage's sacramental status. He replies that those who make this claim demonstrate their ignorance of Greek. The Greek term translated as *sacramentum* is *mysterion*, and this term means a "sacred, secret, and recondite thing itself."[7] In 1 Timothy 3:16, Paul calls Jesus himself a *mysterion* in this sense. Those who read Ephesians 5:31–32 as being about a "sacrament" of marriage, therefore, do not care about the actual meaning of scriptural words. Instead, "they [the Romanists] have brought verbal meanings, human customs and such like, into the sacred writings, transforming the proper meaning into what they themselves have fabricated, turning anything into anything else."[8] In the case of Ephesians 5:32, the *mysterion* under discussion is the union of Christ and the church; the *mysterion* (or *sacramentum*) is not the marriage of a man and a woman. And the *mysterion* is by no means a "sacrament" in the sense of a sign of a sacred thing, but rather means "something at once hidden and of great importance."[9] Luther grants that the marriage of man and woman is a "material allegory" or "figure" of the *mysterion* of Christ and the church, but marriage is not thereby a sacrament, since there is no divine institution or promise in the New Testament.[10] Again, Luther emphasizes that Paul clearly indicates where the *mysterion* or *sacramentum* lies, namely in the Christ-church relationship and not in human marriage. But even if it were otherwise, the word *mysterion* does not mean what the Romanists mean by "sacrament." In defending the correct interpretation of *mysterion*, Luther aims to defend, against the Romanists, "the certainty and purity

---

7. Ibid., 327.
8. Ibid.
9. Ibid., 328.
10. Ibid., 328–29.

of faith and the Scriptures."[11] Better to remain with God's Word in the Scripture than to hold stubbornly to what mere men, no matter how holy, have invented.

Luther goes on to criticize the church led by the pope for creating several impediments to valid marriage—impediments that can be sidestepped by those with the money for dispensations. The church likewise traffics in annulments. Luther claims that these matters should rather be left up to prudent Christians rather than canon lawyers: "Remember that Christian love has no need of any laws at all," so long as a true Christian is present to exercise prudence.[12] Following Matthew 5:32, Luther also insists that Christ allowed divorce in the case of fornication. Therefore, it is wrong that "the Romanists do not allow the re-marriage of a man separated from his wife by divorce."[13] At the same time, Luther states that he abhors divorce so greatly "that I prefer bigamy to divorce, yet I do not venture an opinion whether bigamy [practiced by the patriarchs in the Old Testament] should be allowed."[14] Regarding divorce, he makes clear that he does not intend to lay down any principles, but rather the key is that the matter must not be "settled by the mere fiat of the pope or of the bishops. Rather, if two learned and good men were to agree, in Christ's name and in Christ's spirit, and issue a pronouncement, I myself would prefer their verdict even to that of a council."[15]

Turning next to the sacrament of holy orders as practiced by the Catholic Church, Luther begins by stating his position clearly: "This was unknown as a sacrament to the church of Christ's time, the doctrine having been devised by the church of the popes."[16] Christ nowhere ordained any man or instituted such a sacrament by means of a promise of grace. In taking this position, Luther is not condemning the rite; he

---

11. Ibid., 329.
12. Ibid., 332.
13. Ibid., 339.
14. Ibid.
15. Ibid., 340.
16. Ibid.

is simply denying its status as a sacrament. The grounds upon which he does so are clear: "we ought to try . . . to have everything assured, unassailable, plainly confirmed by Scripture, before it is put forward as an article of the faith."[17] Once these scriptural requirements are in place, it becomes apparent there is in fact not "a single tittle of evidence" for the sacramental status of holy orders.[18]

Luther emphasizes here that the church itself possesses no power to institute divine sacraments on its own, since it cannot give divine promises of grace. He responds to the way in which "the Romanists pretentiously claim that anything instituted by the church has no less authority than what has been ordained by God, since the church is governed by the Holy Spirit."[19] Such a claim is false because "the word of promise" always precedes the church, which is built up solely by faith in Christ's word of promise. The church cannot give itself a divine promise. Rather, as Luther says, "she was instituted by God's promises, and not God's promise by her. For the word of God is beyond comparison superior to the church. She is a created thing, and, being such, has no power to institute, to ordain, or to make; but only to be instituted, to be ordained, and to be brought into being."[20]

Luther is well aware that the response to him, made by those who adhere to the church as led by the pope, is that "the church has the power of distinguishing the word of God from the word of man."[21] He gladly grants that the church does indeed have this power, and to confirm this point he cites Augustine's statement that "moved by the authority of the church, he believed in the gospel, because it [the church] proclaimed that this was the gospel."[22] In distinguishing the Word of God from the word of man, however, the church does not have the power to overthrow the Word of God. The church is never superior to

---

17. Ibid.
18. Ibid.
19. Ibid., 341.
20. Ibid.
21. Ibid.
22. Ibid.

the gospel that it proclaims. The truth seizes the church, rather than the church rationalistically seizing the truth. Luther states, "Similarly by the illumination of the Spirit, when doctrines come up for decision and approval, the church possesses a 'sense' whose presence is certain, though it cannot be proved."[23] This admission seems to confirm that when the church says that holy order is a sacrament, it is a sacrament. But Luther inquires into in whom the authoritative church consists. After all, he says, who was present when the church decided upon seven sacraments, and how can we be sure that the authoritative church was in fact truly present in the gathering that made the decision? As he puts it, "For when these decrees were passed, it was customary for only a few bishops and doctors, and no others, to be present; and who knows if they constituted a church possessing the Spirit? It was possible that they did not constitute a church, and that they all erred."[24]

Indeed, given that they overrode the gospel by claiming the power to institute a sacrament (a promise of grace) where God did not institute one, we can be sure that they were just a group of bishops and were not, in fact, the church. According to Luther, that is what happened at the numerous councils claimed to be authoritative by the Church of Rome. He observes, "Councils have often erred, especially that of Constance, which was the most wicked of them all."[25] Against the claim to authority made by the church led by the pope and the councils that it has approved, Luther appeals to the "church universal" and its authority: "There is reliable proof only of what has received the assent of the church universal, and not merely that of Rome."[26] The "church universal" here includes all churches and believers that oppose the claims made for and by the Church of Rome.

Moving from ecclesiology to history, Luther notes that, among the church fathers, the "seven sacraments" are only present in Dionysius the

---

23. Ibid.; I capitalized the word "Spirit" here.
24. Ibid., 342; I have capitalized "Spirit."
25. Ibid.
26. Ibid.

Areopagite, who is "more of a Platonist than a Christian" and whose theology is caught up in a web of allegories rather than first being solidly grounded "in the proper and simple sense of Scripture."[27] Even had Dionysius put forth better arguments, he knew nothing of a pope (let alone of cardinals and archbishops), and so in any case his arguments in favor of seven sacraments cannot truly serve the church of the pope.

The false teaching that holy orders is a sacrament is further under-lined for Luther by the teaching that the sacrament of holy orders imparts a "character" or permanent distinctive configuration to Christ. Luther challenges the provenance of this doctrine: "I would ask whence do such ideas arise, and on whose authority and for what reason have they become established?"[28] The point is that the church led by the pope has been inventing doctrines that have no foundation in God's Word or institution. Luther adds, "Not that we are unwilling for the Romanists to be free to invent, to say, or to assert, whatever they like; but we also insist on our own freedom. . . . It is sufficient that, for the sake of concord, we should accommodate ourselves to their ceremonies and idiosyncrasies; but we refuse to be compelled to accept them as necessary for salvation."[29] The false teachings of the church led by the pope can perhaps be tolerated, but they cannot be accepted in any way if the church led by the pope insists that such teachings are binding upon everyone for salvation.

Luther is well aware that the church dates the institution of the priesthood to Holy Thursday, when Christ commissioned his twelve disciples to celebrate the Eucharist and when he showed them other marks of favor. In response, Luther notes that Christ gave no promise and said no words of ordination; all that Christ did was to command: "Do this in remembrance of me" (Luke 22:19). Why is it that these words should be taken to convey sacramental ordination, and when was this connection to ordination made? In this regard Luther points

---

27. Ibid., 343.
28. Ibid., 344.
29. Ibid.

out, "Not one of the ancient Fathers asserts that priests were ordained when those words were used. What then is the origin of this new piece of intelligence?"[30] Answering his rhetorical question, Luther speculates that the origin may have been the desire on the part of the church led by Rome to separate clergy and laity as widely as possible, and to exalt the clergy over their fellow baptized Christians. By making ordination a sacrament, the church led by Rome gained a tool for the oppression and subjection of the laity and of the gospel. Insisting that the common priesthood of the baptized should be recognized as the only sacramental priesthood found in the church, Luther finds that "the sacrament of ordination is the prettiest of devices for giving a firm foundation to all the ominous things hitherto done in the church, or yet to be done. This is the point at which Christian fellowship perishes, where pastors become wolves, servants become tyrants, and men of the church become worse than men of the world."[31]

Luther goes on to emphasize that priests, whose main task is preaching, do not need an extra sacrament in order to be able to serve their fellow Christians. He notes that the whole body of Christians (the baptized priesthood) should be at the center, rather than encouraging priests to lord it over laity: "All of us who are Christians are also priests. Those whom we call priests are really ministers of the word and chosen by us; they fulfill their entire office in our name."[32] The distinction between "papal priests" and "Christian priests" is that the latter actually preach at the bequest of the Christian people and are "the husband of one wife" (1 Tim 3:2), whereas the former receive a mere "man-made ceremonial" that they mistakenly consider a sacrament and that requires them to be unmarried and celibate.[33] Luther forcefully cries out, "O! the disgrace which these monstrous priesthoods bring upon the Church of God! Where can you find priests who know the

---

30. Ibid., 345.
31. Ibid.
32. Ibid.
33. Ibid., 346–47.

gospel, not to mention preach it?"[34] Arguing that in ancient times the laity administered the sacraments, Luther insists once more that "every one who knows that he is a Christian should be fully assured that all of us alike are priests, and that we all have the same authority in regard to the word and the sacraments, although no one has the right to administer them without the consent of the members of his church, or by the call of the majority."[35] The supposed "sacrament" of holy orders is at most a rite confirming the congregational call to the ministry of preaching; anything else would be mere slavery to the pope. Thus, it can be hoped that by ridding the church of the sacrament of holy orders we might restore to Christians their "joyful liberty" and full equality as baptized believers.[36]

The last of the four false sacraments identified by Luther is extreme unction. Luther considers it to be a ceremony that "theologians of the present day" have made into a sacrament for those on the brink of death, as a man-made parallel to baptism.[37] Responding to James 5:14–15 and to defenders of the sacrament, Luther questions the apostolic character of the letter of James, and adds that "no apostle was licensed to institute a sacrament on his own authority, or, to give a divine promise with an accompanying sign."[38] Since Christ did not institute the sacrament in the Gospels, it is not a sacrament. Furthermore, the actual words of James 5:14–15 pertain to illnesses of all kinds, not solely to illnesses at the brink of death, and James 5:15 describes people recovering from their illness rather than dying. Thus, the Romanists rely upon a biblical text that they deliberately misread. If extreme unction were a sacrament and did in fact efficaciously accomplish what it signifies, then dying people would be healed by it, which experience shows is not the case. Additionally, James 5:14 speaks of the elders of the congregation making a visit of mercy in order to pray over the sick person, whereas

---

34. Ibid., 348.
35. Ibid., 348.
36. Ibid., 350.
37. Ibid.
38. Ibid., 351.

the church of the pope merely sends one priest—and usually a young priest at that. Luther suggests that in fact James 5:14–15 is connected with Mark 6:13 and Mark 16:18, both of which describe the disciples' ability to heal the sick. Defenders of the sacrament, of course, can make no claim that it heals the sick; rather, it does nothing more than help to prepare the sick for death. Luther concludes that extreme unction is a fine and spiritually beneficial custom, but it is not a sacrament.

As a final note, Luther responds to those who think that these four "sacraments" are true because they come from the authority of the papacy. He notes first that these "sacraments" actually had their origin among university professors. Secondly, he explains that the church led by the pope has been corrupted by the fact that, beginning around the year 500, the papacy became corrupted to the point of being "preeminent, indeed unrivalled, in violence, craftiness, and superstition."[39] The difference between the early church and their popes, on the one hand, and the church today and its popes, on the other, is so great that one must choose whether "the early popes were not true pontiffs of Rome, or else those of the present day are not true pontiffs."[40] In fact, whichever option one chooses leads directly to the conclusion that the popes of the present day are usurpers, who have no valid authority in the universal church. To this point Luther adds that, after all, confirmation and extreme unction are superfluous, since baptism suffices for our life, and the Eucharist prepares us for our death.[41]

BIBLICAL REFLECTION

Paul's teachings about the relationship of baptism to Christ's cross can help us to understand what a Christian sacrament is. Paul remarks, "Do you not know that all of us who have been baptized into Christ

---

39. Ibid., 356.
40. Ibid.
41. For an Anglican defense of the seven sacraments—including the argument that "Christ instructs us to observe all seven" (p. 69)—see Andrew Davison, *Why Sacraments?* (London: SPCK, 2013), ch. 6.

Jesus were baptized into his death? We were buried therefore with him by baptism into death" (Rom 6:3–4). To be united with Christ's death is necessary because "all have sinned" and all "are justified by his [God's] grace as a gift, through the redemption which is in Christ Jesus, whom God put forward as an expiation by his blood, to be received by faith" (Rom 3:23–25). Each of us needs to be united to the blood of Christ, by which Christ reconciles the whole world to God. As Paul comments, "God shows his love for us in that while we were yet sinners Christ died for us," and "we are now justified by his blood" (Rom 5:8–9). Baptism unites us with Christ's saving death. Paul equally emphasizes that union with Christ's cross leads to union with Christ's resurrection: "If we have died with Christ, we believe that we shall also live with him" (Rom 6:8). We thereby become, by God's grace, "a new creation" (Gal 6:15), ontologically changed by our union with Christ in the Spirit.[42] Paul also makes clear that Christ's saving cross is "to be received by faith" (Rom 3:25). Thus, Paul states that "in Christ Jesus you are all sons of God, through faith" (Gal 3:26). Baptism unites us with Christ's death, but in a way that involves not only the sacrament—water baptism—but also faith. Taking baptism as an example of what a Christian sacrament is, then, we can say that the sacraments of faith are visible signs instituted by Jesus Christ that unite us to the saving power of Christ's passion—and thus also to his resurrection.[43]

Let me begin with confirmation. The Gospel of John describes the risen Jesus breathing his Spirit upon the disciples: "Jesus said to them again, 'Peace be with you. As the Father has sent me, even so I send you.' And when he had said this, he breathed on them, and said to them, 'Receive the Holy Spirit'" (John 20:21–22). Is this sending of

---

42. See Daniel A. Keating, *Deification and Grace* (Naples, FL: Sapientia, 2007); as well as Fr. David Vincent Meconi, S. J., and Carl E. Olson, eds., *Called to Be the Children of God: The Catholic Theology of Human Deification* (San Francisco: Ignatius, 2016).

43. For twentieth-century development in Catholic sacramental theology, see Dominic M. Langevin, O. P., *From Passion to Paschal Mystery: A Recent Magisterial Development concerning the Christological Foundation of the Sacraments* (Fribourg, Switzerland: Academic Press Fribourg, 2015).

the Holy Spirit an event that only the apostles experience? The book of Acts makes clear that the answer is no. For example, when Peter goes to the household of the Gentile centurion Cornelius, Peter proclaims the gospel to Cornelius's household and "the Holy Spirit fell on all who heard the word" (Acts 10:44). The sending of the Holy Spirit upon them does not replace baptism, since Peter immediately "commanded them to be baptized in the name of Jesus Christ" (Acts 10:48). The sending of the Spirit by the risen and ascended Lord is part of Christian initiation, and cannot be reduced to or equated with baptism.

Does Jesus will for this sending of the Spirit, however, to take the form of a distinct *sacrament* of the church, namely a visible sign willed by Jesus that unites believers more deeply to the saving power of his cross? In considering this question, it may be worth noticing that the sending of the Holy Spirit is associated with a particular visible sign at Pentecost. That visible sign is fire: "And there appeared to them tongues as of fire, distributed and resting on each one of them" (Acts 2:3). This resting of the Spirit upon the disciples strengthens their public witness to faith in Christ, so that they are enabled to proclaim "the mighty works of God" (Acts 2:11).

Recall also the prophecy from Isaiah 61, which in the Nazareth synagogue Jesus applied to himself: "The Spirit of the Lord is upon me, because he has anointed me to preach good news to the poor" (Luke 4:18). Anointing was a common theme among God's people, Israel—for example, when God commanded Moses to anoint the tent of meeting and all its instruments with oil and to "anoint Aaron and his sons . . . as priests" by means of "holy anointing oil" (Exod 30:30–31). In the exodus from Egypt, God instructed Moses that this anointing oil "shall not be poured upon the bodies of ordinary men, and you shall make no other like it in composition; it is holy, and it shall be holy to you" (Exod 30:32).

The symbolism of the anointing oil also appears in the prophecy of Ezekiel. Describing his covenant with Israel, God recounts in Ezekiel 16:9, "I bathed you [Israel] with water and washed off your blood from you, and anointed you with oil." If water is here associated with the forgiveness of sins, the anointing with oil is associated with further initiation into God's people. Another place that we encounter the symbol of oil in association with strengthening is Psalm 89:20–21, which states,

> I [the Lord] have found David, my servant;
>> with my holy oil I have anointed him;
> so that my hand shall ever abide with him,
>> my arm also shall strengthen him.

This anointing with holy oil strengthens David for the conquering of his enemies.

Another messianic psalm states

> Your divine throne endures for ever and ever.
>> Your royal scepter is a scepter of equity;
>> you love righteousness and hate wickedness.
> Therefore God, your God, has anointed you
>> with the oil of gladness above your fellows. (Ps 45:6–7)

This royal anointing with the "oil of gladness" parallels Christ's being anointed with the Holy Spirit, since Christ is the one who "will reign over the house of Jacob for ever; and of his kingdom there will be no end" (Luke 1:33). If we read the Gospel of Luke's proclamation of Christ in light of this messianic psalm, the "oil of gladness" here can be said to represent the Holy Spirit.

It is the risen and ascended Jesus who anoints believers with the Holy Spirit. In the earliest church, Jesus sent the Holy Spirit upon believers either with the visible sign of tongues of fire or without need for a visible sign. Given that the Holy Spirit's anointing is a royal anointing into Christ's mission—establishing "a royal priesthood" (1 Pet 2:9)—we can see that it also connects symbolically with the "oil of gladness." Hebrews 6:2 speaks about "ablutions [βαπτισμῶν]" and the "laying on of hands." While the "ablutions" seem to differ from baptism itself, the "laying on of hands" seems to refer to a ritual connected with the outpouring or anointing of the Spirit upon the new believer.[44] Jesus's anointing of each believer with the Holy Spirit, in the ongoing Pentecost that sustains the inaugurated kingdom of God, occurs in the church through a sacramental "laying on of hands" that employs anointing oil as its sacramental sign.[45]

The next disputed sacrament is marriage. Marriage takes place when two persons, a man and a woman, bond themselves freely to each other for the purposes of mutual fellowship and the procreation and raising of children.[46] Genesis 2:24 explains that "a man leaves his father and his mother and cleaves to his wife, and they become one flesh." Ephesians 5 quotes Genesis 2:24 and immediately adds, "This is a great mystery, and I mean in reference to Christ and the church" (Eph 5:32). When entered into by two Christians, the natural bond of marriage between a man and a woman is a sign of the reality that "Christ loved the church and gave himself up for her, that he might sanctify her, having cleansed her by the washing of water with the word" (Eph 5:25–26). The self-giving of the Christian man and woman to each other in marriage is a sign of Christ's sacrificial self-giving for us.

Does Jesus, however, intend for marriage to take on a sacramental significance in his inaugurated kingdom? He was certainly aware of the significance of marriage in the prophetic texts of Israel. In promising the new covenant, God presents himself as Israel's true "husband" (Jer 31:32), despite Israel's infidelity. In the prophecy of Isaiah, immediately after the portrait of the Suffering Servant who "bore the sin of many, and made intercession for the transgressors" (Isa 53:12), God states,

---

44. See Harold W. Attridge, *The Epistle to the Hebrews: A Commentary on the Epistle to the Hebrews* (Minneapolis: Fortress, 1989), 164; Craig R. Koester, *Hebrews: A New Translation with Introduction and Commentary* (New Haven, CT: Yale University Press, 2001), 311.

45. From an evangelical perspective, the distinction between baptism and confirmation is challenged by Ronald P. Byars, *The Sacraments in Biblical Perspective* (Louisville: Westminster John Knox, 2011), 144–45.

46. For discussion see Perry J. Cahall, *The Mystery of Marriage: A Theology of the Body and the Sacrament* (Chicago: Hillenbrand, 2016).

> Fear not, for you will not be ashamed;
>> be not confounded for you will not be put to shame;
> for you will forget the shame of your youth,
>> and the reproach of your widowhood you will remember
>> no more.
> For your Maker is your husband,
>> the LORD of hosts is his name;
> and the Holy One of Israel is your Redeemer,
>> the God of the whole earth he is called. (Isa 54:4–5)

Israel has sinned against her "husband," but thanks to the coming work of the Lord as Redeemer, Israel will be united perfectly to her "husband" the Lord. Similar prophecies characterize the book of Hosea. For example, Hosea prophesies, "In that day, says the LORD, you will call me, 'My husband.' . . . I will betroth you to me for ever; I will betroth you to me in righteousness and in justice, in steadfast love, and in mercy" (Hos 2:16, 19).

Jesus justifies the fact that his disciples do not fast by proclaiming himself to be the "bridegroom" of Israel (Matt 9:15; Mark 2:19; Luke 5:34). In the Gospel of John, John the Baptist uses similar marital imagery in presenting himself as "the friend of the bridegroom" (John 3:29) who prepares the way for Christ, the bridegroom. When his disciples tell him about Jesus, John the Baptist joyfully proclaims, "He who has the bride is the bridegroom; the friend of the bridegroom, who stands and hears him, rejoices greatly at the bridegroom's voice; therefore this joy of mine is now full" (John 3:29). In the Gospel of John, Jesus's first miracle is at a wedding feast, and this miracle indicates that the divinely promised purification of the bride (Israel) has arrived through Jesus. In the book of Revelation, the church is depicted "as a bride adorned for her husband" (Rev 21:2) and as "the Bride, the wife of the Lamb" (Rev 21:9).

When Jesus identifies himself as the divine bridegroom, he ensures that marriage among Christians will be a sign that reminds believers of the bridegroom (Jesus) and his bride (Israel/church).[47] On the cross, Jesus knowingly perfects and forever secures the marriage of God and his people. Christian marriage therefore is a sign of the saving power of Christ's cross, as Ephesians 5 indicates. It follows that among Christians, marriage between a man and a woman operates as a sign that unites believers to Christ's cross, and so marriage is a sacrament of his inaugurated kingdom.

Ordination, or holy orders, is the third disputed sacrament. The question here is whether Jesus wanted his church to be hierarchically organized and to have a ministerial priesthood that is commissioned by means of a *sacrament* to teach, govern, and sanctify his people. Jesus certainly does not wish to renew or extend the Levitical priesthood. Instead, he chooses twelve disciples as a sign of the eschatological Israel. He tells them that in the world to come, "when the Son of man shall sit on his glorious throne, you who have followed me will also sit on twelve thrones, judging the twelve tribes of Israel" (Matt 19:28). Could it be, then, that either Jesus assumed there would be no lengthy interim period between his resurrection and his second coming, or he intended for the apostles to be the only ordained hierarchy in the church's history, with no need for a "sacrament" that visibly and distinctively unites the successors of the apostles to the power of Christ's passion and resurrection?

According to the Gospel of Luke, after praying all night Jesus chose the twelve from among a larger group of disciples. The evangelist reports, "In these days he went out into the hills to pray; and all night he continued in prayer to God. And when it was day, he called his disciples, and chose from them twelve, whom he named apostles" (Luke 6:12–13). These twelve, however, are not the only ones whom Jesus sent on mission in his name. When the time came for him to "set his face to go to Jerusalem" for his final Passover, Jesus "appointed seventy others, and sent them on ahead of him, two by two, into every town

---

47. See Brant Pitre, *Jesus the Bridegroom: The Greatest Love Story Ever Told* (New York: Random House, 2014).

and place where he himself was about to come" (Luke 9:51 and 10:1). He expects them not to rely on money or connections but to carry with them solely his peace. In sharing Christ's peace with those who receive it in faith, the seventy are expected to do the works of Christ by sharing table fellowship, healing the sick, and teaching about the kingdom. Jesus commands them, "Whenever you enter a town and they receive you, eat what is set before you; heal the sick in it and say to them, 'The kingdom of God has come near you'" (Luke 10:8–9). They are so fully enabled to act in Christ's name that Jesus can say to them, "He who hears you hears me, and he who rejects you rejects me, and he who rejects me rejects him who sent me" (Luke 10:16).

Did Jesus intend for this bestowal of the ability to act in his name to end with his death and resurrection, so that later generations would not possess a visible sign or "sacrament" enabling those who receive it to act uniquely in the person of Christ to teach, sanctify, and govern the flock? Certainly, Jesus intends that no office in the church should become a point of sinful pride for its holder: "Neither be called masters, for you have one master, the Christ. He who is greatest among you shall be your servant; whoever exalts himself will be humbled, and whoever humbles himself will be exalted" (Matt 23:10–12). Jesus commissions no one to take his (or the Father's) place, which would be the grossest sin of pride. Yet, after his resurrection he tells the eleven remaining disciples, "All authority in heaven and on earth has been given to me. Go therefore and make disciples of all nations, baptizing them in the name of the Father and of the Son and of the Holy Spirit, teaching them to observe all that I have commanded you; and lo, I am with you always, to the close of the age" (Matt 28:18–20). Making "disciples of all nations" takes time, and it seems appropriate to assume that in making this command, Jesus envisions the need to commission future generations of Christian leaders to act in his name.

The New Testament's depictions of the early church suggest that the apostles, while unique in their authority due to their intimate connection with Christ's earthly ministry, considered themselves able, through the power of the Spirit and by the visible sign of the laying on of hands, to pass on their ability to act in Christ's name in leading his church. In 1 Timothy 4:14, Paul commands Timothy, "Do not neglect the gift you have, which was given you by prophetic utterance when the elders laid their hands upon you." Paul describes the "office of bishop"—which certainly did not contain every element that we now associate with it—as tasked with the "care for God's church" (1 Tim 3:1, 5). This office has spiritual power that can only derive from Christ, since Paul compares it to the authority by which a man is able to "manage his own household" (1 Tim 3:5), and the church is in fact the "household of God" (Eph 2:19). In 2 Timothy, Paul speaks of "the gift of God that is within you [Timothy] through the laying on of my hands" (2 Tim 1:6), and he commands Timothy to hand on this gift to others: "You then, my son, be strong in the grace that is in Christ Jesus, and what you have heard from me before many witnesses entrust to faithful men who will be able to teach others also" (2 Tim 2:1–2). Paul makes clear that Timothy's authority in preaching the gospel has its roots both in "the laying on of . . . hands" and in the living Christ himself.

At the right hand of the Father, the Lord Jesus is alive and active. Through the visible sign or sacrament of the "laying on of . . . hands," he gives men the spiritual power to act in his name, not least in the liturgical celebration of the Eucharist. He continues today to commission laborers who share in a ministerial way in making present the saving power of his cross and resurrection, and he does this through the sacrament of holy orders.

The final sacrament at issue is the anointing of the sick (extreme unction). We have seen that when Jesus sends out the seventy, he commands them to "heal the sick" (Luke 10:9) and he gives them a share of his power. They return joyfully, proclaiming that they received power even over demons in Christ's name. Their authority "over all the power of the enemy" (Luke 10:19) includes the domain of illness and mortal disease, since it is precisely in this domain that Jesus himself performs many mighty works.

In the Gospel of Mark, when Jesus returns to his hometown of Nazareth, "he laid his hands upon a few sick people and healed them" (Mark 6:5). Immediately after this, Jesus "called to him the twelve, and began to send them out two by two, and gave them authority over the unclean spirits" (Mark 6:7). The instructions that Jesus gives the twelve disciples in Mark 6 are essentially identical to those which he gives the seventy in Luke 10. The twelve disciples "cast out many demons, and anointed with oil many that were sick and healed them" (Mark 6:13).

Clearly this healing—performed with the sign of anointing with oil—constitutes a sharing in the power of Jesus, which attains its fullness in his cross and resurrection by which he conquers sin and death. The healing communicates a participation in Jesus's overcoming of sin and death, and the twelve disciples receive the power to perform this sign. The question then is whether only the twelve disciples (and the seventy) who received a direct commission from Jesus in his earthly life have the power to perform this sign.

The letter of James indicates that the answer is no. James remarks, "Is any among you sick? Let him call for the elders of the church, and let them pray over him, anointing him with oil in the name of the Lord; and the prayer of faith will save the sick man, and the Lord will raise him up; and if he has committed sins, he will be forgiven" (Jas 5:14–15). The ascended Lord Jesus will work through the (sacramental) sign administered by "the elders of the church" so as either to cure the illness or to "save," raise up, and forgive the dying believer. In performing this sacramental sign, the "elders of the church" spread the saving power of Christ's cross and resurrection.[48]

Baptism and the Eucharist demonstrate that Christianity is a sacramental religion, since Jesus unites believers through visible signs to his saving work. In Jesus's ministry and in the apostolic period, we find that the ascended Jesus sends the Holy Spirit as part of the initiation of believers, and that the Spirit's strengthening is associated with a royal

---

48. See Jean-Claude Larchet, *The Theology of Illness*, trans. John and Michael Breck (Crestwood, NY: St. Vladimir's Seminary Press, 2002).

anointing. We find that Jesus, the bridegroom, makes marriage into a permanent sign that unites believers with his self-sacrificial love on the cross. We find that Jesus commissions men to share in Jesus's authority in communicating the saving power of the cross and resurrection, and that the apostles understood this to continue through the sign of the laying on of hands. Lastly, we find that Jesus commands his disciples to heal the sick and dying in his name, and that the apostles understood this to continue (in a manner extended to saving the dying from their sins) through the sign of anointing with oil. Jesus did not intend for these signs to come to an end prior to his coming in glory, even though they are not as fundamental as baptism and the Eucharist. They continue in the church through the sacraments of confirmation, marriage, ordination, and extreme unction.

CHAPTER 5

MONASTICISM

Numerous monasteries continue to flourish today within the Catholic Church, but the question is whether this befits the Christian gospel. Readers unfamiliar with the Catholic Church's teaching on monasticism should consult paragraphs 914–945 of the *Catechism of the Catholic Church*, as well as paragraphs 43–47 of Vatican II's *Lumen Gentium*. In my biblical reflection, I focus on Jesus's commendation of voluntary poverty and chaste celibacy (or singleness) for the sake of the kingdom, as well as on the significance of obedience for both Jesus and Paul. In laying out some biblical foundations of Catholic doctrine about monastic communities of believers who encourage each other in living out this vocation of poverty, chaste celibacy, and obedience for the sake of the kingdom, I cannot here recapitulate the experience of the living liturgical community in which, over the centuries, this path of discipleship emerged and received the church's approval. But I hope to show that the monastic life continues today in large part due to biblical reasoning.

LUTHER'S CONCERN

In his *Commentary on Galatians* (1531), Martin Luther negatively recalls his own experience as a monk. Over time, he notes, monks find that they do not become better; they remain embedded in certain patterns of sin which they struggle against fruitlessly. The very purpose of the monastic life is to become more holy, but they remain the same sinners they always were or even get worse. Given this situation, he suggests that the problem is with monasticism rather than with the monks. The problem with monasticism is that it seeks "righteousness and salvation by works."[1] We should instead take refuge simply in the free mercy of Christ, which is ours if we have faith.

It might seem that this account of faith produces presumption. In response, Luther observes that God is merciful "not to them that are hard-hearted and secure, but to such as repent and lay hold by faith upon Christ the mercy-seat."[2] Furthermore, Luther reports that the act of ceasing to rely upon oneself, and relying instead solely upon God's mercy in Christ to those who believe, itself overcomes the temptation of the flesh. Put succinctly, the Word of God does what all our works cannot do. As Luther states,

> I have suffered many and various passions, and the same also very vehement and great. But so soon as I have laid hold of any place of Scripture, and stayed myself upon it as upon my chief anchor-hold, straightways my temptations did vanish away: which without the Word it had been impossible for me to endure.[3]

When it comes to specific recommendations regarding the future of monasticism, we may turn to his 1520 treatise "An Appeal to the Ruling Class of German Nationality as to the Amelioration of the State of Christendom." He describes monks (Benedictines, Cistercians, and Augustinians, among others) and friars (Franciscans and Dominicans) as "the great multitudes who swear many vows, but keep few"—not through

---

1. Martin Luther, "A Commentary on St. Paul's Epistle to the Galatians, 1531 (Selections)," in *Martin Luther: Selections*, 99–165, at 150.
2. Ibid., 151.
3. Ibid., 155.

their own fault but due to the fallen human condition, which they seek to fight against as though works could save them.[4] Although he does not here reject monasticism *tout court*, he urges that no further houses for mendicant orders should be built and that no more begging should take place in Christian countries. He also observes that "the numerous sects and differences within the one Order should be abolished."[5] In the competition among and within orders, the problem is that minor things are receiving the bulk of attention, while faith itself atrophies despite being the one thing necessary. In Luther's view, therefore, the pope should forcibly reduce the number of the members of religious orders, because they are leading astray simple folk. Luther charges that "they only pay attention to works," although their original founders, now long gone, were filled with faith.[6] As he describes the situation, which he compares to the idolatry of Israel after the patriarchs had died, "the Orders, now lacking knowledge of the divine works and faith, only torment themselves pitiably, worrying and labouring about their own rules, laws, and customs, without ever reaching a true understanding of what constitutes a religious and virtuous life."[7] He reads 1 Timothy 3:5–7 as now applying, unfortunately, to the religious orders.

In his treatise, Luther offers further specific proposals for diminishing the religious orders. Noting the frequent dissension and competition for money between religious-order priests and diocesan priests, he suggests ways of preventing monks and friars from preaching and hearing confessions. He also suggests freeing all monks, friars, and nuns from their vows, and making continued stay in a monastery or religious house to be completely voluntary. Such a plan, he argues, would restore monasteries and priories "to the way in which they were regulated by the apostles and for a long time afterwards," since at the outset "monasteries and priories were only Christian schools to teach

4. Luther, "An Appeal to the Ruling Class of German Nationality as to the Amelioration of the State of Christendom," in *Martin Luther: Selections*, 403–85, at 445.
5. Ibid.
6. Ibid., 446.
7. Ibid.

Scripture and morals according to the Christian way," and people were therefore quite free to come and go.[8] It was only later that Christian freedom was impinged by vows, which turned the denizens of monasteries and priories "into permanent prisoners."[9] The negative effects of such vows do not solely harm those who make the vows. On the contrary, Christians in general have come to respect religious vows more than they respect baptismal vows, despite the fact that those who take religious vows do not and cannot live up to them, and despite the fact that Christ never commanded that his followers take such vows.

Luther goes on to say that there are many monks and nuns who have not been able to live up to their religious vow of sexual continence. Some sexual sins are among those "from which no friar is allowed to absolve his fellow" but that can only be absolved by the bishop or by an appointed confessor.[10] The result is that many monks and nuns refuse to confess or do not confess honestly, while continuing to receive the sacraments. Luther urges them to not worry about the rules laid down by the bishops or abbots/abbesses. They should privately confess their "secret sins" to anyone whom they choose.[11]

In his treatise, Luther does not call for an end to monasticism. He makes clear that he would close "the recent monasteries" but leave open the older ones, not least because the latter were founded so as to give a place for noblemen's children (those who could not inherit land or title) "to serve God, to study, to become scholarly people, and to help others to do so."[12] Nonetheless, Luther undermines the viability of monastic religious life by suggesting that the religious orders contribute to a spiritually dangerous focus on works; by his critique of the vows of obedience, stability, and continence; by his emphasis that religious begging should be outlawed; and by his view that monks and friars should not be able to preach or hear confessions.

---

8. Ibid., 447.
9. Ibid.
10. Ibid., 452.
11. Ibid.
12. Ibid., 462.

It is not surprising, then, that in his *Commentary on Galatians*, published eleven years after "An Appeal to the Ruling Class" and thus after the Reformation had begun to establish its own distinctive structures, Luther even more strongly connects monasticism with a works righteousness that destroys faith. Similarly, in his 1537 commentary on the Gospel of John, Luther condemns monasticism still more strongly. As he asks rhetorically, "In the devil's name, of what good is a holy order that does not make anyone holy? Or what other purpose do the orders serve than to wring vain admiration from the people and to hinder and divert them from recognizing and receiving the true holiness that is given by the Holy Spirit?"[13] The monastic orders, he concludes, are nothing more than the (ever-failing) effort to become righteous by our own works, and so they must be utterly rejected as "falsehood and fiction, and nothing but sin and stench in the eyes of God. . . . Whether I become a barefoot friar or a monk and work-righteous person of a different order, I remain a condemned sinner just as I was born from Adam."[14]

BIBLICAL REFLECTION

When Jesus is discussing marriage (and forbidding divorce and remarriage), he remarks in response to a challenge from his disciples: "Not all men can receive this precept, but only those to whom it is given. For there are eunuchs who have been so from birth, and there are eunuchs who have been made eunuchs by men, and there are eunuchs who have made themselves eunuchs for the sake of the kingdom of heaven. He who is able to receive this, let him receive it" (Matt 19:11–12). It is easy to understand what eunuchs from birth and from the hands of men are, but what does it mean to make oneself a eunuch "for the sake of the kingdom of heaven"?

---

13. Martin Luther, *Sermons on the Gospel of St. John: Chapters 14–16*, trans. Martin H. Bertram, *Luther's Works*, 24:169.
14. Ibid., 170.

It does not appear to mean literal castration; rather, it seems that Jesus is proposing voluntary chaste celibacy—abstinence from marriage and sexual intercourse—for some of his followers. Since he has just praised marriage, it is clear that he does not mean that all of his followers will take this path of voluntary celibacy "for the sake of the kingdom of heaven." Some will do so, however: namely, those who are "able to receive this."

Almost immediately thereafter in the Gospel of Matthew, Jesus has a conversation with a young man who wants to know "What good deed must I do, to have eternal life" (Matt 19:16). In response, Jesus tells him to "keep the commandments" (Matt 19:17), specifying that he means the Decalogue. The young man replies that he has kept the commandments. Yet, the young man feels that something is lacking, since he adds, "What do I still lack?" (Matt 19:20). Jesus then gives him an instruction for attaining Christian perfection. Jesus states, "If you would be perfect, go, sell what you possess and give to the poor, and you will have treasure in heaven; and come, follow me" (Matt 19:21).

Earlier in the Gospel of Matthew, in the Sermon on the Mount, Jesus emphasizes the need for perfection: "You, therefore, must be perfect, as your heavenly Father is perfect" (Matt 5:48). Does this mean that all Christians must sell all our possessions and follow Jesus without any property of our own? It might seem so, since Jesus proceeds to warn his disciples that "it will be hard for a rich man to enter the kingdom of heaven. Again I tell you, it is easier for a camel to go through the eye of a needle than for a rich man to enter the kingdom of God" (Matt 19:23–24). Furthermore, Jesus's twelve disciples emphasize that they themselves have abandoned their property and homes in order to follow him. As Peter says, "We have left everything and followed you. What then shall we have?" (Matt 19:27).

Just as Jesus praises marriage but says that some people will be called to be "eunuchs" for the kingdom's sake, so also Jesus calls some, *though not all*, to give away all their property and live in accordance with voluntary poverty.[15] In his Sermon on the Mount, Jesus teaches that "when you give alms, do not let your left hand know what your right hand is doing, so that your alms may be in secret; and your Father who sees in secret will reward you" (Matt 6:3–4). Once one has given away all one's property—an act that can hardly be kept secret—it logically follows that one can no longer give alms but must receive them. By contrast, Jesus anticipates that in general his followers will have sufficient property or wealth so as to be able to give alms. Yet some will be called to voluntarily renounce all their property.

As Jesus prepares his disciples and his other followers for his approaching crucifixion, he instructs them about the need to deny their own desires. In the Gospel of Mark, we read that Jesus "called to him the multitude with his disciples, and said to them, 'If any man would come after me, let him deny himself and take up his cross and follow me. For whoever would save his life will lose it; and whoever loses his life for my sake and the gospel's will save it'" (Mark 8:34–35). It is difficult, however, to "deny" oneself. The one who denies himself does not do his own will, but instead consents to experiencing some kind of suffering that otherwise he would seek to avoid. We are all tempted to do only what we wish to do. At Gethsemane, on the night before his crucifixion, Jesus models for us the attitude that we must have: "My Father, if it be possible, let this cup pass from me; nevertheless, not as I will, but as thou wilt" (Matt 26:39).

Jesus intends for his church to be marked by obedience. Consider the path by which he instructs believers to handle wrongdoing by fellow believers. The first two steps involve asking for an apology and substantiating one's claim: "If your brother sins against you, go and tell him his fault, between you and him alone. If he listens to you, you have gained your brother. But if he does not listen, take one or two others along with you, that every word may be confirmed by the

---

15. On this point see Gary A. Anderson's two books: *Sin: A History* (New Haven, CT: Yale University Press, 2009) and *Charity: The Place of the Poor in the Biblical Tradition* (New Haven, CT: Yale University Press, 2013).

evidence of two or three witnesses" (Matt 18:15–16). The third step adds a striking note of obedience: "If he refuses to listen to them, tell it to the church; and if he refuses to listen even to the church, let him be to you as a Gentile and a tax collector" (Matt 18:17). Jesus thereby mandates that we listen to and obey the decision of the church. The point for my purposes here is simply that obedience—consent to do what, if left on one's own, one would not necessarily will to do—is a constitutive element of Christian faith for all believers.

Allowing for different paths of self-renunciation, Jesus tells his twelve disciples that "every one who has left houses or brothers or sisters or father or mother or children or lands, for my name's sake, will receive a hundredfold, and inherit eternal life" (Matt 19:29). All are called to some form of self-renunciation, but some are called to a more radical self-renunciation. It is true that, as Jesus says, "whoever does the will of my Father in heaven is my brother, and sister, and mother" (Matt 12:50), but this certainly does not mean that all do the Father's will in the same way. Regarding the period between the inauguration of the kingdom and its consummation, Jesus teaches that "a man's foes will be those of his own household" and "he who loves son or daughter more than me is not worthy of me" (Matt 10:36–37). Thus, some people will take up their cross and follow Jesus within the context of their family or household. But in the Christian community there can also be people who form intentional households, not related by blood-ties, in which they relinquish their wills to their religious superiors so long as these superiors do not command them to do evil.

Monasticism involves voluntary poverty, chaste celibacy, and obedience, formalized in a vow to the Lord taken within a particular community whose purpose is to live in accord with this threefold way of radical discipleship.[16] When we turn to Paul, we find that

---

16. From an evangelical perspective, see Greg Peters, *The Story of Monasticism: Retrieving an Ancient Tradition for Contemporary Spirituality* (Grand Rapids, MI: Baker Academic, 2015); Dennis Okholm, *Monk Habits for Everyday People: Benedictine Spirituality for Protestants* (Grand Rapids, MI: Brazos, 2007).

he envisions distinct states of life in the church, even if he does not envision monasticism per se. For example, voluntary celibacy seems to Paul an appropriate way of bearing witness to the inbreaking of the kingdom, although Paul certainly does not require voluntary celibacy from his congregations. While observing that the person who marries "does not sin" in marrying (1 Cor 7:28), Paul compares the unmarried state favorably with the married one: "The unmarried man is anxious about the affairs of the Lord, how to please the Lord; but the married man is anxious about worldly affairs, how to please his wife, and his interests are divided" (1 Cor 7:32–34). For married people, Paul does not commend living without sexual intercourse. Rather, Paul says that in general "because of the temptation to immorality, each man should have his own wife and each woman her own husband. The husband should give to his wife her conjugal rights, and likewise the wife to her husband" (1 Cor 7:2–3). Nonetheless, Paul concludes that "he who marries his betrothed does well; and he who refrains from marriage will do better" (1 Cor 7:38). Paul praises the distinct states of life as the fruit of different divine gifts given to different members of the church. As he states, "Each has his own special gift from God, one of one kind and one of another" (1 Cor 7:7).

Paul makes clear that voluntary poverty does not mean laziness about working for one's food. He reminds the Thessalonian church that "when we were with you, we gave you this command: If any one will not work, let him not eat" (2 Thess 3:10). But he leaves room for members of the church, including himself, who work hard but voluntarily have little or no property. The earliest Christians, according to the book of Acts, sought to live without private possessions. We read that after the first Pentecost and the descent of the Holy Spirit, "all who believed were together and had all things in common; and they sold their possessions and goods and distributed them to all, as any had need" (Acts 2:44–45). But already in Paul's communities, Paul allows for private property even while insisting upon generous almsgiving. In urging the Corinthian church to donate to the church in Jerusalem, Paul makes clear that he does not ask the Corinthians to dispense with all their possessions. Rather, as he states, "I do not mean that others should be eased and you burdened, but that as a matter of equality your abundance at the present time should supply their want" (2 Cor 8:13–14).

Obedience has a central place in Paul's proclamation of the gospel. He states that Christ gave him "grace and apostleship to bring about the obedience of faith for the sake of his name among all the nations" (Rom 1:5). Likewise, he concludes the letter to the Romans by referring to "the revelation of the mystery which was kept secret for long ages but is now disclosed and through the prophetic writings is made known to all nations, according to the command of the eternal God, to bring about the obedience of faith" (Rom 16:25–26). He requires that his congregations obey his authority, although he exercises authority whenever possible by persuasion rather than by power. Likewise, though without any doubt about the outcome, he obediently submits his own apostolic call to the test of the apostles and elders in Jerusalem.

Paul recognizes that members of the church will live out their lives in different ways, since "there are varieties of gifts, but the same Spirit; and there are varieties of service, but the same Lord; and there are varieties of working, but it is the same God who inspires them all in every one" (1 Cor 12:4–6). In every case, the different ways of life are not for boasting, let alone for trying to save oneself by one's own strength, but are always "for the common good" (1 Cor 12:7) and under the rule of faith, hope, and love. As Paul observes in his paean to Christian love, "If I have prophetic powers, and understand all mysteries and all knowledge, and if I have all faith, so as to remove mountains, but have not love, I am nothing. If I give away all that I have, and if I deliver my body to be burned, but have not love, I gain nothing" (1 Cor 13:2–3).

Jesus proclaims that voluntary poverty and chaste celibacy will be the vocation of some of his followers, but not all of them. Jesus also makes clear the centrality of obedience. It makes sense, then, that the church should possess ways of living a distinctive religious life of radical poverty, chaste celibacy, and obedience—so long as the motivation for religious life is love and faith-filled desire to imitate Christ. Certainly this way of life can be abused, but all Christian ways of life can be abused. Monastic communities or households of men or women who voluntary vow to follow Christ during their lifetimes in poverty, chaste celibacy, and obedience belong to the church's embodiment of Christ's commandments under the guidance of the Holy Spirit.

CHAPTER 6

JUSTIFICATION AND MERIT

Although one of the most influential theological textbooks in use during Luther's youth, written by Gabriel Biel, was semi-Pelagian, the Catholic Church has consistently held that humans are saved by the utterly gracious mercy of God in Jesus Christ. For the Catholic Church's teaching on the subject today, the reader should see paragraphs 1987–2029 of the *Catechism of the Catholic Church*. The Catholic Church recognizes that no one can ever merit the utterly free gift of justification, and the Catholic Church also affirms that believers' final perseverance unto eternal life is God's free gift, to which the appropriate response will be gratitude to God for his mercy in Jesus Christ. Nonetheless, two issues remain contested in theological conversations about justification and merit. The first issue is whether the movement of grace that justifies the sinner also (at the same time) changes the heart of the sinner, so that at the moment of justification the justified person stands before God as holy; or whether justification only imputes Christ's righteousness to the sinner, without making the sinner holy in himself or herself due to the transformative power of the indwelling Holy Spirit. The second issue is whether, after the initial grace of justification and the gift of the indwelling Spirit, we can cooperate with grace and perform works of love that "merit" a divine reward because their primary agent is the divine Spirit dwelling within us. In my biblical reflection, I try to indicate some of the grounds of Catholic biblical reasoning on these subjects.[1]

LUTHER'S CONCERN

In Martin Luther's 1520 treatise *The Freedom of a Christian*, he cites Romans 10:9 and Romans 1:17, among other biblical texts, to show that "the Word of God cannot be received and cherished by any works whatever but only by faith. Therefore it is clear that, as the soul needs only the Word of God for its life and righteousness, so it is justified by faith alone and not any works."[2] With regard to justification, he compares the person who holds to both faith and works with a worshiper of Baal who also claims to worship the Lord. Citing two passages from Romans 3, he observes that "the moment you begin to have faith you learn that all things in you are altogether blameworthy, sinful, and damnable."[3] The person who has faith knows that he or she has need of Christ, because Christ alone is worthy of eternal life whereas

---

1. Contemporary Luther scholarship is divided on whether Luther, over the course of his career, granted that the movement of justification itself includes sanctification by the indwelling Spirit and the infusion of charity. See David S. Yeago, "Martin Luther on Renewal and Sanctification: *Simul Iustus et Peccator* Revisited," in *Sapere teologico e unità della fede. Studi in onore del Prof. Jared Wicks*, ed. María del Carmen Aparicio Valls, Carmelo Dotolo, and Gianluigi Pasquale (Rome: Gregorian University Press, 2004), 655–74. In the texts that I survey here (for the purposes of conveying Luther's concern about the Catholic position), Luther separates justification and sanctification rather strictly. In his 1536 "The Disputation Concerning Justification," Luther emphasizes that God cleanses us, even though arguably he still separates justification (by imputed righteousness) and sanctification: "[God] begins in reality to cleanse. For he first purifies by imputation, then he gives the Holy Spirit, through whom he purifies even in substance. Faith cleanses through the remission of sins, the Holy Spirit cleanses through the effect" ("The Disputation Concerning Justification," in *Luther's Works*, vol. 34, *Career of the Reformer IV*, trans. and ed. Lewis W. Spitz [Philadelphia: Muhlenberg, 1960], 147–96, at 168). If imputation or forensic justification simply means that "while we were yet sinners Christ died for us" (Rom 5:8), then I certainly agree. Here see Bruce D. Marshall, "*Beatus vir*: Aquinas, Romans 4, and the Role of 'Reckoning' in Justification," in *Reading Romans with St. Thomas Aquinas*, ed. Matthew Levering and Michael Dauphinais (Washington, DC: Catholic University of America Press, 2012), 216–37.

2. Martin Luther, "The Freedom of a Christian," in *Martin Luther: Selections*, 52–85, at 55.

3. Ibid., 55–56.

we sinners are not. Thus, Luther states that as soon as through faith we know how damnable and in need of Christ we are, we become just in God's eyes through faith in Christ. The key point is that we "are justified by the merits of another, namely, of Christ alone."[4]

Luther points out that the works of a sinful man cannot accomplish anything unto salvation. By contrast, faith's power is obvious. It unites us with the Savior, in whom and by whom we can be saved, if we cling to him in faith without trying to cling at the same time to any works of our own. Indeed, none of our works can touch our deepest need, which is to be purified in our "inner man." Faith is an action of the inner man that unites us with the only one who is pure, Jesus. Luther reasons,

> Since, therefore, this faith can rule only in the inner man, as Rom. 10[:10] says, 'For man believes with his heart and so is justified,' and since faith alone justifies, it is clear that the inner man cannot be justified, freed, or saved by any outer work or action at all, and that these works, whatever their character, have nothing to do with this inner man.[5]

Faith, clinging to Christ, is the key to everything, and we must avoid every path of thought or action that would undermine our faith by leading us to rely—even in the slightest bit—upon our own acts of love rather than purely upon Christ's act of mercy.

In his 1531 *Commentary on Galatians*, Luther underscores that in order to be righteous in God's eyes we need do nothing at all but believe in Jesus Christ. This righteousness, since it is Christ's, is not a mere earthly righteousness of the kind we might try (and fail) to obtain for ourselves. Rather, it is a "heavenly righteousness" because by faith we are united to Christ who is seated at the right hand of the Father, so that Christ is now "our high-priest intreating for us, and

---

4. Ibid., 56.
5. Ibid.

reigning over us and in us by grace."[6] We remain sinners in terms of our earthly righteousness, but in terms of our heavenly righteousness "no sin is perceived, no terror or remorse of conscience is felt; for in this heavenly righteousness sin can have no place: for there is no law, and where no law is, there can be no transgression."[7]

With regard to our heavenly righteousness, there is solely faith. Luther explains, "Although I am a sinner by the law, as touching the righteousness of the law, yet I despair not, yet I die not, because Christ liveth, who is both my righteousness and my everlasting and heavenly life."[8] To think otherwise would be to rely for salvation not upon Christ through faith, but rather upon ourselves through works. Since relying upon ourselves would mean death, given that we cannot make ourselves righteous by our own weak and sinful resources, it is no wonder that Luther insists that if this "article of justification be once lost, then is all true Christian doctrine lost. And as many as are in the world that hold not this doctrine, are either Jews, Turks, Papists or heretics."[9] Any reliance upon obedience to a law for salvation—whether Jewish law, Muslim law, or Christian (Papist) law—will fail to attain its goal and will stop far short of true "faith or Christian righteousness."[10]

Does not Jesus Christ himself, however, command his disciples to perform certain works of love? Luther gladly grants that Jesus does so, but Luther emphasizes that Jesus does not make such works the hinge of our righteousness in God's sight. Rather, Jesus simply admits that the law has a certain place, within its proper bounds. The commandments regarding works aim to keep "the flesh," namely our earthly desires, in check. This function is important, but we err deeply if we think that the necessary restrictions put upon the flesh—i.e., the requirement that believers perform certain works and avoid other works—are the

---

6. Luther, "A Commentary on St. Paul's Epistle to the Galatians, 1531 (Selections)," in *Martin Luther: Selections*, 105.
7. Ibid.
8. Ibid.
9. Ibid., 106.
10. Ibid., 107.

path by which we are righteous in God's sight. If good works were the path, then we would despair at finding that we continually fail to meet these requirements, as we do.

Fortunately, only faith is the true path of the heavenly righteousness to which Jesus calls us. In this regard Luther warns against the false notion of "the merit of congruence and worthiness," that is, the supposition that believers can truly be worthy (due to the indwelling Spirit and the infusion of charity) of divine reward rather than divine punishment. Luther urges that every Christian must be "humbled by the law, and brought to the knowledge of himself" as a sinner.[11] As St. Paul says, the law teaches that we are sinners; indeed, the whole world is perpetually guilty before God (cf. Rom 3:19; Rom 7:14; Rom 11:52). Faith alone can deliver us from this guilt, because in faith we cling to Jesus who has taken our guilt upon himself and imputed his own righteousness to us despite our sinfulness. When we recognize this truth, Luther argues, we will perceive that all the theological speculation "of the schoolmen touching the merit of congruence and worthiness, is nothing else but mere foolishness, and that by this means the whole Papacy falleth."[12]

However, is it possible to be united to Christ's righteousness while still being a sinner, indeed while still being as sinful as we ever were? Would not union with Christ involve love and a conversion of heart? Luther observes that by faith "we lay hold upon Christ" so that we come to possess "a quality and a formal righteousness in the heart."[13] Yet this "formal righteousness" is not charity but faith; our justification rests upon faith alone. Indeed, if our righteousness rested upon our own charity, then we would be turning Christ into "a judge and a tormentor," as he is wherever people imagine that they can attain "the merit of congruence and worthiness."[14]

---

11. Ibid., 109.
12. Ibid., 110.
13. Ibid.
14. Ibid.

Fortunately, we need not be worthy, let alone merit salvation congruently (i.e., as though in Christ we become truly worthy of it ourselves). All we need to do is cling to Christ in faith, since he "is no lawgiver, but a forgiver of sins and a saviour."[15] We need solely to rely upon Christ's perfectly congruent merit, since he alone is righteous and worthy of the reward that he receives for our sake. Faith perceives that Christ has accomplished "works and merits of congruence and worthiness abundantly."[16] How is it, though, that faith gives us a real share in these congruent merits, since we are and remain sinners? Luther explains that it is by "acceptation" or "imputation."[17] When we have faith in Christ, God accounts us righteous through Christ's merit.

Luther goes on to say that "this acceptation, or imputation, is very necessary" for two reasons.[18] First, no matter how good we become, we never are perfectly righteous, despite the ongoing purgative work of the Holy Spirit (a purgative activity that Luther fully grants so that believers are indeed able to do good works in gratitude to God). Second, we sometimes fall explicitly into sin.[19] At no point, then, can we rely upon our own good works, but we must always seize in faith upon the reality that "our sins are covered, and that God will not lay them to our charge" (cf. Romans 4).[20] Luther compares the sinner who trusts in Christ through faith, to the sinner who does not have faith in Christ but who instead (at best) attempts to bridge the gap by means of works.

> Sin is indeed always in us, and the godly do feel it, but it is covered, and is not imputed into us of God for Christ's sake; whom because we do apprehend by faith, all our sins are now no sins. But where Christ and faith be not, there is no remission or covering of sins, but mere imputation of sins and condemnation.[21]

---

15. Ibid.
16. Ibid.
17. Ibid., 111.
18. Ibid.
19. Ibid.
20. Ibid.
21. Ibid.

When we have faith, God imputes Christ's righteousness to us, rather than imputing our sins. This befits Christ's role as the sole "mediator and high priest" by whose "merit . . . we attain the remission of sins and righteousness."[22]

Luther emphasizes that this doctrine of justification by faith alone, a doctrine that brings "strong consolation to afflicted consciences in serious and inward terrors," is the very heart of Christianity and the very element by which salvation is gained.[23] Comparing the Church of Rome to Islam, Luther notes that since Muslims rely upon the laws contained in the Qur'an they cannot find salvation, and the same goes for the church under the pope. The pope "is condemned with all his kingdom, because he so walketh and teacheth (with all his religious rabble of sophisters and schoolmen), that by the merit of congruence we must come to grace, and that afterward by the merit of worthiness we are received into heaven."[24] Luther responds to these notions of merit by remarking that Christians, knowing themselves to be sinners, could not dare to hope that their works prior to grace could congruently merit the gift of grace. Nor could self-aware Christians imagine that by their works after grace they could make themselves truly worthy to obtain the gift of eternal life. The only reasonable path to salvation, then, is by faith alone: "To him that believeth in Christ, sin is pardoned and righteousness imputed. . . . Through faith in Christ therefore all things are given to us, grace, peace, forgiveness of sins, salvation and everlasting life."[25] For emphasis, Luther adds here that these things certainly do not come to us through "the merit of congruence and worthiness."[26] He concludes that the church under the pope, along with its theological guild, has taught false doctrine and indeed continues to do so, thereby taking on the role of the "false teachers" prophesied in 2 Peter 2:1. Indeed, for Luther the whole system of the church under the

---

22. Ibid.
23. Ibid., 112.
24. Ibid., 113.
25. Ibid.
26. Ibid.

pope, including its "ceremonies, masses, and infinite foundations of the papistical kingdom," stand upon the doctrine of salvation through merit and therefore stand against the real saving power of Jesus Christ.[27]

Luther hammers home his point by means of some rather strong passages against the errors of the church under the pope. The key error is claiming for ourselves what belongs only to Christ. The gift of righteousness and righteousness in and of itself belong to Christ. By contrast, the church under the pope insists "that we are able to obtain these things apart from Christ by the merits of congruence and worthiness."[28] This insistence puts the church under the pope in a terrible and tragic position, which Luther sums up as follows: "By these means they deny Christ, tread his blood under their feet, blaspheme the Holy Ghost, and despise the grace of God. Wherefore no man can sufficiently conceive how horrible the idolatry of the Papists is."[29] What the church under the pope teaches about merit leads, furthermore, to a whole system of false teaching involving "the difference of days, meats and persons, vows, invocation of saints, pilgrimages, purgatory, and such like," so that Luther finds himself compelled to conclude that "in these fantastical opinions the Papists are so misled, that it is impossible for them to understand one syllable of the Gospel, of faith, or of Christ."[30]

Turning from these broader charges regarding "the merit of congruence and worthiness" and its baneful fruits, Luther specifies that the scholastic theologians, who fight against the doctrine of justification by faith alone, claim that faith justifies us only when joined to "charity and good works."[31] The key point for such thinkers is that faith does not justify "except it be formed and furnished with charity."[32] If this were actually the case, Luther responds, then faith would not justify

---

27. Ibid.
28. Ibid., 114.
29. Ibid.
30. Ibid.
31. Ibid.
32. Ibid.

us at all; charity alone would be what justifies us. Faith would then be "in vain and unprofitable," since only charity would make us right with God if in fact it were true that "except faith be formed and beautified with charity, it is nothing."[33] Luther notes that these thinkers appeal to 1 Corinthians 13:2 for biblical support, which declares, "If I have all faith, so as to remove mountains, but have not love, I am nothing." To this position, Luther replies that for Paul, faith alone justifies, and "we must not attribute the power of justifying to that form [charity] which maketh a man acceptable unto God, but we must attribute it to faith."[34] Indeed, "without and before charity," faith justifies us, because faith alone successfully unites us to Christ's saving righteousness.[35] Charity has its place, but its place is not that of justification.

It is not our charity or works but faith alone that opens eternal life to us. Otherwise, Luther observes, Paul could not emphasize repeatedly that works of the law have no role in salvation, so that "a man is justified by faith apart from works of the law" (Rom 3:28). The removal of our sin is accomplished not by our charity but "by Christ crucified; upon whose shoulders lie all the evils and miseries of mankind, the law, sin, death, the devil and hell."[36] Luther emphasizes, therefore, that just as "neither the law nor any work thereof is offered unto us, but Christ alone: so nothing is required of us but faith alone, whereby we apprehend Christ, and believe that our sins and our death are condemned and abolished in the sin and death of Christ."[37]

BIBLICAL REFLECTION

In the third chapter of Romans, Paul begins a lengthy discourse on justification. Paul states that "all have sinned and fall short of the glory of God" (Rom 3:23). Since this is so, we cannot accomplish our own

---

33. Ibid.
34. Ibid., 116.
35. Ibid.
36. Ibid., 121.
37. Ibid.

restoration to right relationship with God. As sinners, we cannot justify ourselves. We cannot remove the guilt of our sins, and in our sinful condition, we cannot love God and neighbor as we ought. Paul clarifies that what pious Jews learn from trying to obey the Torah is that they "are under the power of sin" (Rom 3:9), as Gentiles also are. Thus, Paul argues that "no human being will be justified in his [God's] sight by works of the law, since through the law comes knowledge of sin" (Rom 3:20).[38]

How then can Israel and the Gentiles be restored to a just relationship with God, a relationship in which humans are not alienated by sin and guilt from the holy God? Paul proclaims that "the righteousness of God has been manifested apart from the law, although the law and the prophets bear witness to it" (Rom 3:21). This righteousness of God is manifested in Jesus, the Messiah to whom the law and the prophets bear witness. The righteousness of God is available to all people if they believe in Jesus. Paul explains that all believers "are justified by his grace as a gift, through the redemption which is in Christ Jesus, whom God put forward as an expiation by his blood, to be received by faith" (Rom 3:24–25). We are united to Christ's saving work (his work of redemption or expiation on the cross) by an act of faith. United to Christ by faith, we are justified in relation to God, because Christ has paid the penalty of our sins for us and has cleansed us from guilt. As Paul sums up, God "justifies him who has faith in Jesus" (Rom 3:26).

Paul emphasizes the fact that this justification is a gift. No "works" or "works of the law" justify us in the sight of God or merit the gift of justification. It is simply God's gift. We must get away from thinking that if we do X or Y, we will be just in God's sight. Rather, we can only be just in God's sight when by faith we are united to Christ, since Christ

---

38. See Simon J. Gathercole, *Where Is Boasting? Early Jewish Soteriology and Paul's Response in Romans 1–5* (Grand Rapids, MI: Eerdmans, 2002). Along similar lines, critical of the "new perspective on Paul," see Michael Bird, *The Saving Righteousness of God: Studies on Paul, Justification, and the New Perspective* (Eugene, OR: Wipf & Stock, 2007). For a historical overview of the debate, siding with the "old perspective" in a nuanced fashion, see Stephen Westerholm, *Perspectives Old and New on Paul: The "Lutheran" Paul and His Critics* (Grand Rapids, MI: Eerdmans, 2004). See also most recently John M. G. Barclay, *Paul and the Gift* (Grand Rapids, MI: Eerdmans, 2015).

alone pays the penalty of our sin and cleanses our guilt. Paul emphasizes that just as God ultimately manifested his righteousness through Christ (rather than through the Torah), so also our righteousness depends upon union with Christ rather than upon practicing Torah. This union comes about through faith, not through any works: "A man is justified by faith apart from works of the law" (Rom 3:28).

In Paul's view, the Torah itself testifies to the fact that justification comes not from obeying Torah but from God's sheer gift to the one who has faith. Thus, the man from whom God's covenantal people descends, Abraham, "believed God, and it was reckoned to him as righteousness" (Rom 4:3; cf. Gen 15:6). Abraham was made just in relation to God by an act of faith in God's promises. All Abraham had to do was to believe God. God did not owe Abraham anything, and yet when Abraham believed, God accepted Abraham as just in the sight of God. Paul spells out the implications of this fact for our understanding of justification: "Now to one who works, his wages are not reckoned as a gift but as his due. And to one who does not work but trusts him who justifies the ungodly, his faith is reckoned as righteousness" (Rom 4:4–5). Abraham simply trusts or believes the promises of God, and that suffices for the forgiveness of sins and for being reckoned righteous in the sight of God.

Why is it that God has chosen to accomplish the justification of his people through faith in Christ rather than by enabling them to obey the Torah perfectly on their own? Paul answers that it is God's desire to underscore justification's nature as a pure gift (or grace), rather than something that humans can accomplish without God. Paul emphasizes that the center of this gifting is Christ: "Therefore, since we are justified by faith, we have peace with God through our Lord Jesus Christ. Through him we have obtained access to this grace in which we stand, and we rejoice in our hope of sharing the glory of God" (Rom 5:1–2). Paul goes on to observe that Christ did not redeem us due to any worthiness of our own, but rather redeemed us as a sheer gift of divine love: "God shows his love for us in that while we were yet sinners Christ died for us" (Rom 5:8).

Does anything change in us when we are justified by faith? We are no longer enemies of God. Christ's death has reconciled all humans to God, and in faith we embrace our new status of friends of God. Are we still "sinners"? If the meaning of "sinners" is "humans not related justly to God," then we are no longer sinners, since in Christ we are related justly to God. But Paul says more than this, because he indicates that the justified person has been transformed by the indwelling Holy Spirit. He states that "God's love has been poured into our hearts through the Holy Spirit who has been given to us" (Rom 5:5). Paul argues that although our justification is unmerited, in Christ we have "died to sin" (Rom 6:2) and have been "freed from sin" (Rom 6:7). Paul knows that we will still be tempted to sin, but he argues that "sin will have no dominion" over us, since we live "under grace" (Rom 6:14). He goes on to tell believers that "you are not in the flesh [enslaved to the passions of the flesh], you are in the Spirit, if the Spirit of God really dwells in you. Any one who does not have the Spirit of Christ does not belong to him" (Rom 8:9). Since the Spirit dwells in us, we are headed toward eternal life in and with Christ rather than toward death (which is "the wages of sin" [Rom 6:23]). As Paul explains, "Now that you have been set free from sin and have become slaves of God, the return you get is sanctification and its end, eternal life" (Rom 6:22). Paul insists that we "have received the spirit of sonship" that makes us "children of God, and if children, then heirs, heirs of God and fellow heirs with Christ, provided we suffer with him in order that we may also be glorified with him" (Rom 8:15–17).

For our purposes here, the fundamental theological question consists in how to understand the relationship between being "justified by faith," being "set free from sin," receiving "the spirit of sonship," and receiving "the Holy Spirit who has been given to us." Granted that justification comes through faith and is God's utterly free gift to sinners rather than something that we can merit, does the movement of justification change our hearts so that, due to the indwelling Spirit who fills us with love, we are made truly just and not merely imputed to be just?

In the Old Testament, God promises that he will change the hearts of his people, Israel. Through the prophet Ezekiel, the Lord promises,

> I will sprinkle clean water upon you, and you shall be clean from all your uncleannesses, and from all your idols I will cleanse you. A new heart I will give you, and a new spirit I will put within you; and I will take out of your flesh the heart of stone and give you a heart of flesh. And I will put my spirit within you, and cause you to walk in my statutes. (Ezek 36:25–27)

This passage suggests that God's act of justifying his people, of cleansing them from their sins, will transform their hearts and interiorly change them. Similarly, in promising through Jeremiah the "new covenant" (Jer 31:31), in which God "will forgive" the people's sins (Jer 31:34), the Lord says of the renewed Israel, "They shall be my people, and I will be their God. I will give them one heart and one way, that they may fear me for ever, for their own good and the good of their children after them" (Jer 32:38–39). Here too we find the transformation of the heart linked with God's justifying gift of the forgiveness of sins.

Among the first Christians, we see a strong connection between faith, justification, and interior transformation of the heart. The sprinkling with "clean water" prophesied by Ezekiel now takes concrete shape. Those who have been "justified by faith" have become "sons of God," since "as many of you as were baptized into Christ have put on Christ" (Gal 3:24, 26–27). This is the case even though the New Testament makes clear that the temptation to sin still plagues Christians. Just as we would expect from the promise of Jeremiah 31–32, of "one heart and one way," we read in the book of Acts that "the company of those who believed were of one heart and soul" (Acts 4:32) and their love was so strong that "there was not a needy person among them" (Acts 4:34). Similarly, when Barnabas visited the church of Antioch, he "saw the grace of God" embodied in believers who are "faithful to the Lord" (Acts 11:23).

If justification through "one Lord, one faith, one baptism" (Eph 4:5) were not accompanied by the Holy Spirit turning our sinful "hearts of stone" into love-filled "hearts of flesh," then Jesus's vision of judgment day would be deeply troubling. In a parable recorded in the Gospel of Matthew, Jesus portrays his coming in glory and the final judgment, in which he will separate the "sheep" from the "goats." The sheep are those who have done works of love. Jesus portrays himself as telling the sheep,

> Come, O blessed of my Father, inherit the kingdom prepared for you from the foundation of the world; for I was hungry and you gave me food, I was thirsty and you gave me drink, I was a stranger and you welcomed me, I was naked and you clothed me, I was sick and you visited me, I was in prison and you came to me. (Matt 25:34–36)

If we pair this judgment scene with the risen Jesus's statement in the Gospel of Mark that "he who believes and is baptized will be saved; but he who does not believe will be condemned" (Mark 16:16), it seems clear that justification transforms our hearts so that we are able to undertake works of self-giving love for the poor and oppressed of this world.

In Jesus's Sermon on the Mount, we find the same expectation that justification brings about interior transformation, with the result that justified believers perform works of love. Jesus speaks not solely of faith but of works: "Enter by the narrow gate; for the gate is wide and the way is easy, that leads to destruction, and those who enter by it are many. For the gate is narrow and the way is hard, that leads to life, and those who find it are few" (Matt 7:13). Employing an analogy to fruit trees, he makes clear that those who truly believe in him will do works like his: "Every sound tree bears good fruit, but the bad tree bears evil fruit. A sound tree cannot bear evil fruit, nor can a bad tree bear good fruit. Every tree that does not bear good fruit is cut down and thrown into the fire" (Matt 7:17–19). Even more specifically, he indicates that the profession of faith—even when accompanied by mighty works—will not suffice for salvation, if those who profess faith do not perform works of love: "Not every one who says to me, 'Lord, Lord,' shall enter the kingdom of heaven, but he who does the will of my Father who is in heaven" (Matt 7:21). In faith, we must not only be baptized "in the name of the Father and of the Son and of the Holy Spirit" but also obey all that Jesus has commanded us to do (Matt 28:19–20).

In the Gospel of John, Jesus makes a similar connection between faith's assent and the interior transformation of heart that enables the believer to love. The Gospel of John makes clear both that we do not merit justification—we receive it in faith as a sheer gift—and that justification transforms us from sinners into true children of God. The evangelist states that "to all who received him [Christ], who believed in his name, he gave power to become children of God; who were born, not of blood nor of the will of the flesh nor of the will of man, but of God" (John 1:12–13). Later in the Gospel of John, John the Baptist connects belief with obedience, and thereby connects faith with interior transformation (love): "He who believes in the Son has eternal life; he who does not obey the Son shall not see life" (John 3:36). Those who believe and obey are those who are "born of water and the Spirit" (John 3:5). Newness of life is linked to faith in Jesus's word; for instance, Jesus tells the official whose child is dying, "Go; your son will live," and the official "believed the word that Jesus spoke to him and went his way" (John 4:50).

Like John the Baptist, Jesus in the Gospel of John draws together faith and salvation: "He who hears my word and believes him who sent me, has eternal life; he does not come into judgment, but has passed from death to life" (John 5:24). Yet Jesus clarifies that faith without love is insufficient for a salvific relationship to God. Jesus does so by commanding his disciples not only to "believe . . . in me" (John 14:1) but also to obey his "new commandment" (John 13:34). Jesus tells his disciples, "A new commandment I give to you, that you love one another;

even as I have loved you, that you also love one another" (John 13:34). The love that Jesus's disciples possess comes from God's transformative power for those who believe, not from their own resources. But Jesus insists that "he who believes in me will also do the works that I do" (John 14:12). This is only possible if when we believe in Jesus, our hearts are transformed by the indwelling Spirit so that we love. Indeed, if we do not obey Jesus's command to "keep my words" (John 14:24) by love, we do not truly have the Spirit dwelling within us.

At various points in Paul's epistles, the fact that a right relationship with God, rooted in faith, is not possible without love is made clear. This is what Paul means by stating, "If I have all faith, so as to remove mountains, but have not love, I am nothing" (1 Cor 13:2).[39] The point here is that justifying faith transforms one's heart. Similarly, James's insistence upon the unity of justifying faith and interior transformation fits with what Paul is saying in both 1 Corinthians and Romans. After insisting that believers must follow the commandment to love one's neighbor as oneself, James bluntly states,

> What does it profit, my brethren, if a man says he has faith but has not works? Can his faith save him? If a brother or sister is ill-clad and in lack of daily food, and one of you says to them, "Go in peace, be warmed and filled," without giving them the things needed for the body, what does it profit? So faith by itself, if it has no works, is dead. (Jas 2:14–17)

The right relationship to God given by faith in Jesus Christ includes the indwelling Spirit and the transformation of the heart so that we do works of love. James is quite clear. We cannot be justified—in right relationship to God—if we lack the Spirit's promised transformation of

---

39. See Scot McKnight and Joseph B. Modica, eds., *The Apostle Paul and the Christian Life: Ethical and Missional Implications of the New Perspective*, (Grand Rapids, MI: Baker Academic, 2016); Michael J. Gorman, *Becoming the Gospel: Paul, Participation, and Mission* (Grand Rapids, MI: Eerdmans, 2015); Gorman, *Cruciformity: Paul's Narrative Spirituality of the Cross* (Grand Rapids, MI: Eerdmans, 2001).

our hearts: "For as the body apart from the spirit is dead, so faith apart from works is dead" (Jas 2:26). Abraham's faith, by which he believed God, involved the interior transformation of his heart by which he cleaved to God even above his only son, the son of the covenant (Isaac). Only because of this interior transformation can Abraham be "called the friend of God" (Jas 2:23). James could not be clearer about what is at stake: "You see that a man is justified by works and not by faith alone" (Jas 2:24). This does not mean that faith and justification are not the unmerited gifts of God; of course they are. It means only that, as the Lord foretold through the prophets, the cleansing from sin would be accompanied by a new "heart of flesh." As Paul puts it, "If any one is in Christ, he is a new creation" (2 Cor 5:17).

When we have justifying faith in Christ, the indwelling Spirit is a principle (or cause) of our actions, although our will also remains a principle of our actions. One graced human action can have two principles because the transcendent God is not a competitive cause on the same ontological level as human beings. When we are united to Christ, we receive a share of his Spirit. Paul remarks that "it is no longer I who live, but Christ who lives in me; and the life I now live in the flesh I live by faith in the Son of God, who loved me and gave himself for me" (Gal 2:20). Christ living in us does not mean that our actions become less our own. Rather, it means that our graced actions are both fully ours and fully the Spirit's, who acts through us. As Paul puts it, "Work out your own salvation with fear and trembling; for God is at work in you, both to will and to work for his good pleasure" (Phil 2:12–13). Paul notes elsewhere that "where the Spirit of the Lord is, there is freedom" (2 Cor 3:17), because the Spirit frees us from slavery to sin and draws us into eternal life. Our very body is "a temple of the Holy Spirit" (1 Cor 6:19), who indwells us and enables us to "glorify God" (1 Cor 6:20) by our actions. The Holy Spirit directs our action without thereby depriving us of freedom. In prayer and in our other activities, "the Spirit helps us in our weakness" (Rom 8:26). Paul comments that "in Christ Jesus neither circumcision nor uncircumcision is of any avail, but faith working through love" (Gal 5:6), and Paul adds that "if you are led by the Spirit you are not under the law" (Gal 5:18).

Those who are "in Christ Jesus" and "led by the Spirit," insofar as the Spirit is the source of their acts of love, perform acts that are good and that justly deserve a reward; God rewards his own grace in us.[40] In his Sermon on the Mount, Jesus repeatedly describes such meriting. He states, for example, that "when you fast, anoint your head and wash your face, that your fasting may not be seen by men but by your Father who is in secret; and your Father who sees in secret will reward you" (Matt 6:17–18). Likewise, he speaks of a reward for almsgiving and prayer, and in both cases, he concludes that "your Father who sees in secret will reward you" (Matt 6:4, 6). Jesus teaches that if we endure reviling and persecution for his name's sake, our "reward" will be "great in heaven" (Matt 5:12). If we love our enemies, we will likewise have a "reward" (Matt 5:46). Similarly, welcoming prophets and righteous men merits the reward of a prophet and righteous man, and giving a drink of water to one of Jesus's disciples merits a reward (see Matt 10:41–42).[41]

Paul too envisions "wages" given to those who labor for Christ, in proportion to their labor (1 Cor 3:8). He anticipates that each person will "appear before the judgment seat of Christ, so that each one may receive good or evil, according to what he has done in the body" (2 Cor 5:10). This does not mean that Paul thinks that anyone should put "confidence in the flesh" (Phil 3:3), as though worldly status meant anything. It means simply that Paul, justified by faith through the Spirit moving within him, undertakes his labors of love so that he

---

40. On this point see Charles Raith II, *Aquinas and Calvin on Romans: God's Justification and Our Participation* (Oxford: Oxford University Press, 2014); Raith, "Calvin's Critique of Merit, and Why Aquinas (Mostly) Agrees," *Pro Ecclesia* 20 (2011): 135–53; Raith, "Aquinas and Calvin on Merit, Part II: Condignity and Participation," *Pro Ecclesia* 21 (2012): 195–210. For the view that thinking of eternal life in terms of "reward" is ultimately distortive, since all is grace (as indeed it is!), see Scot McKnight, *The Heaven Promise: Engaging the Bible's Truth about Life to Come* (Colorado Springs, CO: WaterBrook, 2015).

41. See Nathan Eubank, *Wages of Cross-Bearing and Debt of Sin: The Economy of Heaven in Matthew's Gospel* (Berlin: Walter de Gruyter, 2013); Gary A. Anderson, *Sin: A History* (New Haven, CT: Yale University Press, 2009).

might attain the true reward, namely "the prize of the upward call of God in Christ Jesus" (Phil 3:14). In faith, Paul knows that his works of love—accomplished in Christ and through the indwelling Spirit— merit a reward from God. He describes this reward in exalted terms in 2 Timothy 4:7–8, as he approaches his death: "I have fought the good fight, I have finished the race, I have kept the faith. Henceforth there is laid up for me the crown of righteousness, which the Lord, the righteous judge, will award to me on that Day, and not only to me but also to all who have loved his appearing." The "crown of righteousness," eternal life, is given as a reward by "the righteous judge" to those who "have fought the good fight." The eternal reward that Paul expects, the reward that Paul thinks he deserves or merits, is due to him in justice because the indwelling Spirit has acted through him thanks to the atoning blood of Christ in whom Paul has faith.

From certain passages in Romans where Paul is insisting that practicing the Torah cannot justify us, one can see how a strong separation between justifying faith and interior transformation (love) arises. With Paul, I affirm that the grace of justification—the gift of justifying faith—is utterly unmerited and comes as a sheer gift. I affirm that we need do nothing but "repent, and be baptized . . . in the name of Jesus Christ" in order to be justified or forgiven in God's sight (Acts 2:38). Yet, intrinsic to the grace of justification is the indwelling Spirit and an interior transformation in charity that enables the believer at the very moment of justification to share truly in Christ's righteousness. In addition, the indwelling Spirit acts as a principle of the free actions of the person who depends in faith upon the crucified Christ for salvation. Thus, Paul can affirm that he expects to be given an eternal reward due to him in justice from "the righteous judge" because he has fought the good fight by God's grace. In this sense, due to the indwelling Spirit of Christ, Paul can merit eternal life, not as a reward corresponding to merely human acts but as a reward corresponding to the Spirit's action in and through the believer who is being configured to Christ. In the body of Christ, God crowns his own gifts: all gratitude and praise are owed to God.

CHAPTER 7

PURGATORY

The Reformation sought to redirect Christian piety away from a de facto concentration upon purgatory and prayers for the dead, and toward the ultimate purpose for which God made humans—eternal life with God in the new creation, which we can fail to obtain if we reject God's mercy. In their renewal of Christian piety, the Reformers rejected purgatory as both unnecessary and unbiblical. Readers unacquainted with the Catholic Church's teaching on purgatory and indulgences should consult paragraphs 1030–1032 and 1471–1479. In my biblical reflection, I explore biblical reasoning about the intermediate state, namely the separated soul's existence after death but prior to the general resurrection. I argue for the existence of a communion between all conscious believers, who are united in the body of Christ through their love for Christ and love for each other. I also identify biblical texts that make plausible the view that we undergo purification in the intermediate state, a purification that enables those who love Christ (but who are still weighed down by the effects of vice) to fully slough off sin and enter into perfect love.

LUTHER'S CONCERN

In his "Disputation on the Power and Efficacy of Indulgences"—the famous Ninety-Five Theses posted on the Castle Church in Wittenberg on All Saints' (or perhaps All Souls') Eve 1517—Martin Luther criticizes the doctrine of purgatory alongside associated practices, such as having Masses celebrated for the benefit of souls in purgatory or undertaking additional sacrifices for the remission of the purgative punishments for those who die without being in a state of perfect charity. Luther's criticism focuses mainly upon the monetary sacrifice of purchasing papal "indulgences," granted by the pope as a participation in the church's treasury of merits, to which the pope has the "keys" (cf. Matt 16:19).

Luther points out that the church's "penitential canons apply only to men who are still alive" (thesis 8).[1] Since this is so, it follows that "it is a wrongful act, due to ignorance, when priests retain the canonical penalties on the dead in purgatory."[2] The dead in purgatory have been released from all of the church's canonical penalties. The absurdity of the church's teaching on purgatory appears even more clearly when the church changes its canonical penalties, and then applies them in their new form to the dead in purgatory. For Luther, it is obvious that the "claims of the church," not least when they are changed, cannot and do not apply to the dead (thesis 13).[3]

Luther also suggests that people likely experience their purgatory while dying, although he does not explicitly rule out the existence of purgatory as traditionally understood. He reasons that if people have defects in their faith or love, they will inevitably be horrified at the prospect of death and will even come close to despair. This experience of horror and fear surely suffices "to constitute the pain of purgatory" (thesis 15).[4] Purgatory, then, would appear to best describe not a state of punishment that most people undergo after death, but rather what people of weak faith undergo during the dying process.

This intuition is strengthened by the further point that purgatory

---

1. Martin Luther, "The Ninety-five Theses," in *Martin Luther: Selections*, 490–500, at 491.
2. Ibid.
3. Ibid.
4. Ibid.

would seem to involve "uncertainty," as the middle ground between hell, which involves despair, and heaven, which involves assurance (thesis 16).[5] Once dying is over, it would seem that there could be no more uncertainty: we will know immediately whether we are going to be with God for eternity. If we find that we are going to be with God, then surely we would be flooded with joy and assurance, rather than suffering the middle ground of purgatory. And if I understand thesis 17 correctly, Luther also suggests that the knowledge that we are to live eternally with God would surely increase our love for God, thereby abating "the pains of souls in purgatory."[6]

Furthermore, Luther points out that the church knows next to nothing about the state of souls in purgatory, and thus any speculations about purgatory have little or no basis. In thesis 18, he remarks that "it does not seem proved, on any grounds of reason or Scripture, that these souls are outside the state of merit, or unable to grow in grace." In thesis 19, he adds, "Nor does it seem proved to be always the case that they are certain and assured of salvation, even if we are very certain of it ourselves."[7] The point is that divine revelation teaches us about heaven and hell, but it does not teach us about the purgatorial state. Since we do not really know anything about the state of imperfect souls after death, how can we make claims about their condition? If there is a middle ground between heaven and hell, how do we know that all souls in this middle ground go to heaven, and how do we know that they cannot do further works of love in this middle ground (so as ostensibly to merit a higher place in heaven than their works on earth merited)? As another example of the problem of our lack of revealed knowledge about this state, Luther poses a difficult question: "Who knows whether all souls in purgatory wish to be redeemed in view of what is said of St. Severinus and St. Paschal?" (thesis 29).[8]

---

5. Ibid.
6. Ibid., 492.
7. Ibid.
8. Ibid., 493.

Those two saints—a seventh-century pope and a ninth-century pope, respectively—were known in popular piety for their desire to endure purgatorial pains for others, rather than going directly to heaven. But if such could be the case—if saints could prefer to be in purgatory than in heaven—then the very distinction between purgatory and heaven seems to be undermined. Behind this point is, again, an emphasis on our ignorance about the state of purgatory.

Turning to the logic of indulgences issued by the pope, Luther notes that the papal claim to offer a "plenary remission of all [purgatorial] penalties" can surely only mean penalties that the pope himself has imposed, since the pope has no efficacious authority over God's penalties (thesis 20).[9] Putting this point more bluntly and colorfully, thesis 27 states: "There is no divine authority for preaching that the soul flies out of purgatory immediately [i.e., as soon as] the money clinks in the bottom of the chest."[10]

Luther's contention here is that the pope uses the sale of indulgences to fleece his frightened flock out of their money. The sale of indulgences, however, touches upon even deeper problems, including not only whether the church knows anything about purgatory but also whether the church under the pope has been deceiving the faithful on central matters of salvation. The latter question is implied by thesis 33: "We should be most carefully on our guard against those who say that the papal indulgences are an inestimable divine gift, and that a man is reconciled to God by them."[11] Why should the pope be thought to possess "keys" to a supposed treasury of merits through which the purgatorial punishment of sins can be lessened, when in fact if a Christian—living or dead—simply repents, surely God in Christ Jesus gives that Christian nothing less than "plenary remission from penalty and guilt, and this is given him without letters of indulgence"

---

9. Ibid., 492.
10. Ibid., 493. This is a slogan that was likely used by the Dominican indulgence preacher Johann Tetzel. It should also be noted that Luther is responding to a particular document (the "Summary Instruction"), which makes specific claims about indulgences.
11. Ibid.

(thesis 36)?[12] Christians should seek to be truly contrite for their sins. If they are so, as shown by works of mercy such as almsgiving, then they are forgiven by God and have no need of papal indulgences (theses 39–45).[13] Far from removing purgatorial punishment, purchasing indulgences for oneself while one's poor brother needs food and clothing incurs a greater punishment.

When Luther turns in the Ninety-Five Theses to the church's treasuries of merit, he makes his position clear both directly and by way of irony. He observes that "the treasures of the church, out of which the pope dispenses indulgences, are not sufficiently spoken of or known among the people of Christ" (thesis 56).[14] But the true treasures of the church, of which Luther here speaks, are not what the pope has in view in giving indulgences. Rather, Luther notes that "the true treasure of the church is the Holy Gospel of the glory and the grace of God" (thesis 62).[15] It is specifically the gospel of God's grace that is "not sufficiently spoken of or known among the people of Christ." One reason that the gospel of grace is not known is because the preaching of the gospel has been shamefully exchanged for preaching that promotes the purchase of indulgences, generally for the purpose of enhancing the Vatican's coffers.

As Luther continues, he clarifies his position on the claim that the pope holds the keys to the treasury of merits amassed by Christ and the saints, and shared in by the whole mystical body. He states that the "treasures of the church, out of which the pope dispenses indulgences," cannot be "the merits of Christ and the saints, because, even apart from the pope, these merits are always working grace in the inner man, and working the cross, death, and hell in the outer man" (thesis 58).[16] This aspect of how we relate to Christ's merits will be developed further in

---

12. Ibid., 494.
13. Ibid. At this early stage Luther is still extolling "works of love," and he takes care not to condemn papal indulgences per se.
14. Ibid., 496.
15. Ibid.
16. Ibid.

Luther's later theology. Here Luther's main point is that when people speak about "the treasures of the church" or "the keys of the church" that "are bestowed by the merits of Christ" (thesis 60), these "treasures" and "keys" can mean nothing other than the free grace that Christ gives all people, without needing the pope to issue an indulgence, let alone needing someone to purchase an indulgence.[17]

It follows that the pope must not get in the way of Christ or try to take the place of Christ. Luther thinks that the focus on indulgences is absurd, given that indulgences are utterly nothing in comparison to the graces that Christians truly possess from Christ (*not* from the pope, although the pope too can receive these graces). Among these graces are "the gospel, spiritual powers, gifts of healing, etc., as is declared in I Corinthians 12" (thesis 78).[18] Indulgences introduce monetary gain into what should be the free gift of God's grace, and therefore are an offense to the very meaning of grace. Luther makes this point in a delicate fashion by asking a rhetorical question that shows the problem with indulgences.

> Why does not the pope liberate everyone from purgatory for the sake of love (a most holy thing) and because of the supreme necessity of their souls? This would be morally the best of all reasons. Meanwhile he redeems innumerable souls for money, a most perishable thing, with which to build St. Peter's church, a very minor purpose. (thesis 82)[19]

For the pope to be willing to dispense the grace of Christ, money should hardly be needed. If the pope actually could liberate everyone from purgatory by granting indulgences, he should just go ahead and liberate everyone out of pure love for all his flock.

In later writings, Luther teaches explicitly that there is no purgatory.

---

17. Ibid.
18. Ibid., 498.
19. Ibid.

His 1537 commentary on the Gospel of John stands as a representative example. Luther observes that the enmity of the pope and his followers against Luther and his followers "is due to our refusal to believe what they want us to believe. It all revolves about matters of faith, the Word, and the Sacrament."[20] Far from inventing anything and far from being the source of their own faith, Luther and his followers have received everything not from the church under the pope but from Christ himself: "The Gospel which we preach and also the Baptism and Sacrament which we receive and administer are, after all, not ours but our Lord Christ's. We did not invent these, nor did we create and institute them; but they were revealed to us by God, ordained and given to us through Christ, in whom we are baptized and called and in whom we believe,"[21] By contrast, the church under the pope has invented monasticism, purgatory, salvation by works, and other such things. Luther explains that "the Holy Spirit sometimes lets His Christians fall, err, stumble, and sin," and the church under the pope has erred gravely, even being so "brazen and foolish enough to conclude that the church ranks higher than the Holy Spirit and Christ Himself with His Gospel."[22]

Even when "the doctrines which the Holy Spirit promulgated through Christ are at variance with the teachings of the church," the church under the pope has consistently insisted that "what the church says stands and must be obeyed without any argument."[23] In making this claim, the church under the pope has shown that it is not really the true Christian church. Luther states in this regard, "They take the words 'Holy Spirit' and 'church' and apply them to their trumpery. . . . They brashly determine and formulate whatever doctrines they themselves choose and then allege that this is the work of the Holy Spirit."[24] For Luther, the true church is where "Christ and His Word" are, that is

20. Luther, *Sermons on the Gospel of St. John: Chapters 14–16*, in *Luther's Works*, 24:274.
21. Ibid.
22. Ibid., 172.
23. Ibid., 172–73.
24. Ibid., 174.

to say "wherever Christ is understood, known, and believed; wherever His Baptism and the office of the ministry are administered."[25]

Thus, when Luther's teachings elicit the condemnation and hatred of the church under the pope, it is because Luther (and his followers) have been chosen by Christ "out of the world" (John 15:19). Luther defends his preaching of the true gospel: "If this displeases the pope, or if he is harmed by it, if the sale of indulgences drops, if purgatory is extinguished—how can I help it? Why did the pope build such things on his lies, apart from and even in opposition to God's Word and yet on the pretext and under the name of God's Word?"[26] The nonexistence of purgatory should not surprise anyone, since God's Word does not testify to it. As Luther concludes,

> They have brought it about that everything the pope has been able to decree, dream up, and put on parade—even open deception, such as indulgences, purgatory, pilgrimages, cowls, tonsures, the veneration of saints, etc.—is declared to have come from the Holy Spirit, even though they themselves have to admit that this is not found in the Gospel and that Christ has said nothing about it.[27]

BIBLICAL REFLECTION

Paul boldly remarks to his Corinthian congregation that he "would rather be away from the body and at home with the Lord" (2 Cor 5:8). In Paul's view, it would seem, Christians are "at home with the Lord" and "away from the body" for a period prior to the general resurrection. Such a state, for Paul, is preferable even to earthly life. Since in earthly life the great thing for Paul is to be in conscious communion with Christ, being "at home with the Lord" in the period prior to

---

25. Ibid., 174–75.
26. Ibid., 275.
27. Ibid., 356.

the general resurrection cannot be less than conscious communion with Christ.[28]

In Philippians 1:21, Paul similarly affirms that "to me to live is Christ, and to die is gain." Death can only be "gain" if it brings him into a more intimate relationship with Christ. Paul says that his "desire is to depart and be with Christ, for that is far better" (Phil 1:23). He compares this with remaining "in the flesh" (Phil 1:24). It is not the case that Paul expects to die and to immediately possess his risen body while his corpse molders in the tomb. Rather, as Paul states in 1 Thessalonians, "those who have fallen asleep" (1 Thess 4:15)—namely those who have died in Christ—will obtain their risen body only at the general resurrection. The general resurrection does not take place immediately after a person dies, but rather it will occur when "the Lord himself will descend from heaven with a cry of command, with the archangel's call, and with the sound of the trumpet of God" (1 Thess 4:16). When this happens, the earthly world as we know it will come to an end and be transformed. Paul envisions that "the dead in Christ will rise first; then we who are alive, who are left, shall be caught up together with them in the clouds to meet the Lord in the air; and so we shall always be with the Lord" (1 Thess 4:16–17).[29]

The reference to "those who have fallen asleep" signifies the same existential situation as Paul describes when he describes being "at home with the Lord" and when he calls this situation a "gain" and "far better" than earthly life. "Sleep" here means a nonannihilating death. It is a euphemism, not a description of an unconscious intermediate state between death and the general resurrection. Paul expects to be consciously united to Christ, while being "away from the body," prior to the general resurrection.

In the Gospel of Luke, Jesus prophesies the end time through a series

---

28. On the conscious intermediate state, see N. T. Wright, *Surprised by Hope*, 171. For doubts about the existence of an intermediate state, see J. Richard Middleton, *A New Heaven and a New Earth: Reclaiming Biblical Eschatology* (Grand Rapids, MI: Baker Academic, 2014), 227–37.

29. For discussion of this passage see Middleton, *A New Heaven and a New Earth*, 222–25.

of images. He makes clear that the end time, the final judgment, will come upon humanity unexpectedly. He explains in this regard, "As it was in the days of Noah, so will it be in the days of the Son of man. They ate, they drank, they married, they were given in marriage, until the day when Noah entered the ark, and the flood came and destroyed them all" (Luke 17:26–27). In a sense this "day" has already come about through the inauguration of the kingdom by Jesus's cross and the outpouring of the Spirit, but the "day" of consummation has not yet come. Since the general resurrection will only occur on the day of consummation, Christians who die before the final judgment will be alive with Christ but will not immediately possess their glorified bodies. In the Gospel of Luke, Jesus tells one such believer, the good thief who is crucified by his side, that "today you will be with me in Paradise" (Luke 23:43). This "Paradise" is the intermediate state.

During this period prior to the general resurrection, the dead who are alive with Jesus are numerous. Jesus, therefore, is never without his friends. An instructive example of encountering Jesus with his (dead but alive) friends occurs at the Transfiguration. We read that "after six days Jesus took with him Peter and James and John, and led them up a high mountain apart by themselves; and he was transfigured before them" (Mark 9:2). His dazzling garments express his divinity, and he is not alone in this state, since "there appeared to them Elijah with Moses; and they were talking to Jesus" (Mark 9:4). Although Elijah's condition remains biblically mysterious—he was taken "up to heaven by a whirlwind" (2 Kgs 2:1)—we know that Moses "died . . . in the land of Moab" and was buried "in the valley in the land of Moab opposite Beth-pe'or" (Deut 34:5–6). There is no need to suppose that the transfiguration, which was a vision, required Moses already to possess his risen body prior to the general resurrection. But Peter, James, and John see Jesus shining and standing in dazzling light with his friends Moses and Elijah.

That there is an intermediate state in which Jesus's friends are "away from the body" but "at home with the Lord" is further indicated by the book of Revelation, in which the seer (John) perceives "under the altar the souls of those who had been slain for the word of God and for the witness they had borne" (Rev 6:9). The seer recounts that in his mystical vision, after they had cried out for justice, the souls "were each given a white robe and told to rest a little longer, until the number of their fellow servants and their brethren should be complete, who were to be killed as they themselves had been" (Rev 6:11). The "white robe" is an image of baptismal purity and victory. These souls "rest" from their sufferings, but they are not asleep or else they could not be "told" anything.

The book of Revelation makes clear that Christian worship on earth is in communion with the worship that the angels and (dead) saints offer to Christ in "Paradise" prior to the general resurrection, the final judgment, and the new creation. Thus, John the seer "looked, and . . . heard around the throne [of God] and the living creatures and the elders the voice of many angels, numbering myriads of myriads and thousands of thousands, saying with a loud voice, 'Worthy is the Lamb who was slain, to receive power and wealth and wisdom and might and honor and glory and blessing!'" (Rev 5:11–12). The human "elders" and angels are joined in this praise by creatures from every realm, including earth: "I heard every creature in heaven and on earth and under the earth and in the sea, and all therein, saying, 'To him who sits upon the throne and to the Lamb be blessing and honor and glory and might for ever and ever!'" (Rev 5:13).

All persons who are possessed of faith and charity—all conscious believers who are in a state of charity—are in spiritual communion with each other. In this regard, Paul states, "I rejoice in my sufferings for your sake, and in my flesh I complete what is lacking in Christ's afflictions for the sake of his body, that is, the church" (Col 1:24). As Paul recognizes, Christ "is the head of the body" (Col 1:18), and Christ has reconciled "to himself all things, whether on earth or in heaven, making peace by the blood of his cross" (Col 1:20). In this ecclesial body of Christ, then, Paul's sufferings are "for the sake of his [Christ's] body." The whole church gains from Paul's sufferings; in Christ, Paul's sufferings serve the upbuilding of the whole church in love. Each member of the church, following the path of Christ, does everything "for the sake of" the whole church and indeed for the sake of everyone who is called to be a member of the church. Since "all were made to drink of one Spirit" (1 Cor 12:13), all members of the body are in relationship with each other. Paul therefore remarks, "If one member suffers, all suffer together; if one member is honored, all rejoice together" (1 Cor 12:26).

We should not take in a strictly individualistic sense the great promise of Jesus to reward those who suffer for his sake. Jesus proclaims, "Blessed are you when men hate you, and when they exclude you and revile you, and cast out your name as evil, on account of the Son of man! Rejoice in that day, and leap for joy, for behold, your reward is great in heaven" (Luke 6:22–23). The "reward" is not solely for the individual, but overflows to the members of the body of Christ; just as Christ's own reward is ordered to his members. Thus, everything Paul does is for the whole church and not simply for his own "reward" or his own "crown of righteousness, which the Lord, the righteous judge, will award to me on that Day" (2 Tim 4:8). He receives this "reward," but at the same time, as his Christlike life shows, love impels him to pour out everything that he has (including his "reward") upon all God's people: "Our mouth is open to you, Corinthians; our heart is wide" (2 Cor 6:11).

At present, of course, Paul dwells "away from the body" and "at home with the Lord," but he cannot thereby cease to love Christ's whole body with a wide heart. His heart is configured fully to "the grace of our Lord Jesus Christ," who "though he was rich, yet for your sake he became poor, so that by his poverty you might become rich" (2 Cor 8:9). Paul, who is now already enjoying his "reward" and his "crown," cannot become self-centered: as a member of Christ's body, he must pour out everything he has out of love for God's people. As he says in the context of his earthly ministry, "Who is weak, and I am not weak? Who is made to fall, and I am not indignant?" (2 Cor 11:29). All the saints who are configured to Christ are united to Christ's prayer at the right hand of the Father for the whole people of God, that he might "prepare a place" for us (John 14:2) and "that he might fill all things" (Eph 4:10), since Christ "always lives to make intercession" for us (Heb 7:25). All who are united to Christ in the intermediate state continue, like Christ himself, to desire to share with the whole body of Christ the "reward" that, due to the grace of the Holy Spirit, they earned in their earthly lives. As Paul says, "None of us lives to himself, and none of us dies to himself. If we live, we live to the Lord, and if we die, we die to the Lord; so then, whether we live or whether we die, we are the Lord's" (Rom 14:7–8). Having died, Paul remains the Lord's and does not live "to himself." On the contrary, Paul overflows even more perfectly with Christ's love.

Indeed, the "reward" and the "crown of righteousness" attained by Paul and other followers of Christ consist fundamentally in Christ's love. To be in "Paradise" with the Lord means to shine with life and love as he does, so that one can fully say that "to live is Christ" (Phil 1:21). This is the great "treasure in heaven" (Luke 18:22; cf. Matt 6:21) that Christ has to offer, since "God is love" (1 John 4:8) and "love never ends" (1 Cor 13:8). The treasures of the body of Christ, the church, are none other than Christ, who pours out his Spirit and unites us to his Father. This treasure flows through the whole church. In the Gospel of Matthew, Jesus establishes Peter as steward of his church, in the sense that Peter receives "the keys of the kingdom of heaven" (Matt 16:19). The "keys" open the church's treasury, and what is there are the "rewards" of the saints who have been "faithful unto death" and have received "the crown of life" (Rev 2:10). In the body of Christ, these treasures are not greedily stored up or kept to oneself, but rather are fully shared and poured out in the service of all those who are united to Christ by faith, repentance, and love. Those who are "at home with the Lord" not only "rejoice always" but also, in Christ, "pray constantly" so that "the word of the Lord may speed on and triumph" (1 Thess 5:16–17;

2 Thess 3:1). The whole body of Christ is a communion of prayer and worship, in which Christ and his members intercede for the whole world, asking that God's will—love—"be done, on earth as it is in heaven" (Matt 6:10).

In his first letter to the Corinthians, Paul emphasizes that only what is built upon the foundation of Christ (love) can endure in the world to come: "For no other foundation can any one lay than that which is laid, which is Jesus Christ. Now if any one builds on the foundation with gold, silver, precious stones, wood, hay, stubble—each man's work will become manifest; for the Day will disclose it" (1 Cor 3:11–13). In one sense, this "Day" is the final judgment. When we die, however, we immediately encounter Christ and undergo personal judgment; if this were not so, then Paul could not hope to be "at home with the Lord" prior to the final judgment. Thus, it is important to appreciate Paul's insistence that "each man's work . . . will be revealed with fire, and the fire will test what sort of work each one has done" (1 Cor 3:13). This "fire" is an image of purification, an image that indicates that suffering may be involved even for those who are united to Christ in love, insofar as they have built with "hay" rather than with "gold." Paul states, "If the work which any man has built on the foundation survives, he will receive a reward. If any man's work is burned up, he will suffer loss, though he himself will be saved, but only as through fire" (1 Cor 3:14–15).

Christ has paid the penalty of sin and has perfectly forgiven us, but we nonetheless must go through the penitential experience of suffering and death so as to be fully configured to him in love. His love liberates us from our vices, but breaking free from our vices involves suffering, as we know from experience. As forgiven sinners, we must "suffer with him [Christ] in order that we may also be glorified with him" (Rom 8:17). Paul notes that "the whole creation has been groaning in travail together until now; and not only the creation, but we ourselves who have the first fruits of the Spirit groan inwardly as we wait for adoption as sons, the redemption of our bodies" (Rom 8:22–23).

For those who have lived lives of wonderful charity and who have been fully configured in their earthly lives to the cruciform Lord, this "groaning in travail" need not continue in any negative sense in the intermediate state prior to the general resurrection, other than in the sense of praying for the final consummation. But for the souls of those who are united to Christ in repentance and love but who are still united imperfectly due to vices, this "groaning in travail" will include some suffering so that they may "be glorified with him [Christ]." When the "Day" comes for each of us that discloses "what sort of work each one has done" (1 Cor 3:13)—a disclosure that occurs immediately after death in the individual judgment that consists in our encounter with Christ—some persons will find that much of their work on earth must be "burned up." They "will be saved, but only as through fire"—an image of purification.[30] It is the Spirit of Christ, dwelling within us, who purifies believers both now and in the intermediate state, as "beholding the glory of the Lord, [we] are being changed into his likeness from one degree of glory to another" (2 Cor 3:18).

Living fully in Christ who "lives to make intercession" for us (Heb 7:25), believers such as Paul who are fully "at home with the Lord" intercede with Christ for Christ's members on earth and for Christ's members who are undergoing purification through the indwelling Spirit of Christ so as to fully attain in Christ "the city which is to come" (Heb 13:14). Since the intermediate state is a conscious one, as a "gain" that involves a radical deepening of intimacy with the Lord, the church is a constant communion of prayer and mutual assistance in every way, including assistance during the period of penitential purifying, whether in this life or after death in the intermediate state

---

30. For criticism of any notion of "purgatory," see Wright, *Surprised by Hope*, 166–71; McKnight, *The Heaven Promise*, 179–82. For an appreciative presentation of the notion of "purgatory" from an evangelical perspective, see Jerry L. Walls, *Heaven, Hell, and Purgatory: Rethinking the Things That Matter Most* (Grand Rapids, MI: Brazos, 2015). Walls draws upon C. S. Lewis's belief in purgatory, a belief that manifests itself in a number of Lewis's works. For criticisms of Walls's position, see *Four Views on Hell*, ed. Preston Sprinkle (Grand Rapids, MI: Zondervan, 2016); as well as, from a different perspective, Mats Wahlberg's review of Walls's book: Wahlberg, "Last Things," *First Things* no. 264 (June/July 2016): 59–61.

(for whatever amount of "time" that purifying might take). All things are indeed at the service of those who love Christ: "So let no one boast of men. For all things are yours, whether Paul or Apollos or Cephas or the world or life or death or the present or the future, all are yours; and you are Christ's; and Christ is God's" (1 Cor 3:21–23).

CHAPTER 8

SAINTS

Paul refers to all believers as "saints," which they are. The Catholic Church identifies certain persons (after their deaths) as saints in a particular sense, however, since the church recognizes them to be now perfectly united with Christ in love due to the extraordinary charity they manifested in their lives, a charity that continues after their deaths and that stirs them to intercede with Christ for the needs of Christ's people here on earth. The Catholic Church encourages believers to ask for the help and prayers of all the saints, both fellow believers on earth and those who presently dwell as separated souls in the intermediate state. According to the Reformers, the Catholic Church's understanding of the saints in the intermediate state is unbiblical and has resulted in the grave distortion of Christian piety. For readers unacquainted with the Catholic Church's teachings on the saints in the intermediate state, I recommend paragraphs 828, 946–962, and 2683 of the *Catechism of the Catholic Church*. In my biblical reflection, I begin with the heroes of biblical Israel and then reflect upon the conscious presence of Paul and others in the intermediate state. Without being able to do justice here to the interplay of the various biblically warranted modes of biblical reasoning about the saints in the intermediate state, I suggest some biblical paths for approaching the Catholic understanding of the communion of saints.

LUTHER'S CONCERN

In his 1537 commentary on the Gospel of John, Martin Luther has this to say about his theological outlook as a young monk and priest under the church led by the pope:

> We knew nothing and were taught nothing of the righteousness of Christ inherent in His going to the Father. Instead, we directed the people away from Christ straight to themselves. . . . Yes, in addition, we made of Christ a terrible Judge, whom we had to propitiate with our works and with the intercession of Mary and the saints.[1]

All this was a complete error, since Christ forgives us and freely offers his own righteousness to us if we will just accept it with faith, without attempting to obtain it as our own work. His mercy is available to us without the need of any assistance from Christians who have died. Christ is not "a terrible Judge." He only seems that way to those who imagine righteousness as a precondition for approaching Christ. For such people is Christ a terrible Judge, only because they have not apprehended the gospel of grace.

Not only do we not need the intercession of the saints, but also the undue emphasis on dead Christians dangerously diverts our mind from where the Holy Spirit is actually to be found—here on earth. With regard to seeking the Holy Spirit where he actually is, Luther comments that when he was "steeped in . . . monkery and unbelief," he and his fellow monks were constantly thinking about "the deceased saints and blessed ones in heaven, even though in Scripture the word 'holy' is always applied to those living here on earth."[2] For St. Paul, however, the "saints" are his fellow living Christians, and Luther emphasizes that this usage should still be employed. In describing ourselves as saints, we are describing what Christ has done for us through "His

---

1. Luther, *Sermons on the Gospel of St. John: Chapters 14–16*, in *Luther's Works*, 24:348.
2. Ibid., 170.

Baptism, Word, grace, and Spirit"; we are not describing "our stinking work-righteousness," since in this regard we are still sinners.[3] When we think of the "saints," therefore, we must think of our fellow living Christians, whose sins have been covered by Christ, so that they "are accounted entirely pure and holy before God."[4] This focus enables us to meet the Holy Spirit in the church of Christ in this world, in the preaching of the Word and in the sacraments. As Luther says, "We are members of a holy fraternity in Wittenberg, in Rome, in Jerusalem, and wherever holy Baptism and the Gospel are."[5] Since the Holy Spirit has truly come upon us if we receive the gospel in faith, we are "saints of God" and we must not "gape upward . . . as though He [the Holy Spirit] were flitting about up there among the deceased saints, apostles, martyrs, virgins, etc."[6]

According to Luther, then, the church under the pope has greatly misled people by giving the name "saints" only to certain Christians who have died—in Luther's words, "to the deceased souls and to their positions and orders."[7] The result has been, first of all, a denial of the creed's affirmation that the church is the "communion of saints." Second, the result has been "pilgrimages" and "the worship of the saints."[8] At more than one point in his commentary on John, Luther criticizes such things, which in his view divert attention from Christ and the gospel of grace. He suggests that the devil has made great gains by means of "pilgrimages and the idolatrous adoration of saints, at one place with the Sacred Blood, at another with this or that Mary."[9] Put simply, the devil leads people into idolatry by playing them for fools, so that their devotion will go to someone other than Christ. Luther provides an example: "I have heard of a lad who had been lying submerged in water for two days; but when his parents took him and

---

3. Ibid., 171.
4. Ibid.
5. Ibid.
6. Ibid.
7. Ibid.
8. Ibid., 172.
9. Ibid., 74.

pledged him to St. Anne, he was restored to life."[10] Far from being a miracle, this is the work of the devil to get people to focus on St. Anne rather than on Christ. The devil has the power to trick people into thinking that someone is dead, so that when the supposedly dead person is resuscitated, people worship the saint (who supposedly interceded) instead of Christ. Luther concludes, "If anyone directs you to any help other than the doctrine and the works of the Lord Christ, you can conclude freely that this is the devil's work and his false miracles, by means of which he deceives and misguides you, just as he has done so far under the name of Mary and the saints where Christ was never known or taught aright."[11]

In his 1528 "Preface to the Psalms," Luther redirects devotion to the saints. He proposes that those who wish to look for saints, should look to the great figures of the Bible, and should look to their inward thoughts rather than to outward works. Of all the books in the Bible, he proposes that the book of Psalms stands as the best replacement for the popular legends of the saints. He observes in this regard, "No books of moral tales and no legends of saints which have been written, or ever will be written, are to my mind as noble as the book of Psalms; and if my purpose were to choose the best of all the edificatory books, legends of saints, or moral stories . . . my choice would inevitably fall on our present Book [i.e. the Psalms]."[12] But what makes Psalms so great a choice, since it seems to contain hymns and prayers but no (or almost no) legends or stories about saints? For Luther, the answer is that in Psalms: "We find, not what this or that saint did, but what the chief of all saints did, and what all saints still do."[13] Namely, we find constant prayer to God, and we find a record of sufferings and behavior amid life's struggles. Above all, we find a clear promise of "the death and resurrection of Christ" and of Christ's "kingdom, and the nature

---

10. Ibid., 75.
11. Ibid., 75–76.
12. Martin Luther, "Preface to the Psalms," in *Martin Luther: Selections*, 37–41, at 37.
13. Ibid.

and standing of all Christian people."[14] Psalms directs our attention to Christ and, in a secondary and related way, to the church on earth comprised of God's saints. The authors of the Psalms are these saints (as are all today who receive the gospel in faith), and the book of Psalms "presents us with saints alive and in the round."[15]

Luther goes on to say that in the nonbiblical legends of the saints, many strange and miraculous deeds appear, but the focus is on the works of the saints. By contrast, Psalms focuses on the words of the saints, and thus the focus is on their interior lives rather than their outward works. Their interior lives were profound indeed. As Luther remarks, Psalms records "their deepest and noblest utterances, those which they used when speaking in full earnest and all urgency to God."[16] Not that their works are absent from the Psalms, but their words and faith inevitably have the central place because they lay "bare their hearts and the deepest treasures hidden in their souls," so that we can see their hearts and learn their unguarded thoughts.[17] Contrasting the Psalms with the popular legends of the saints, Luther points out that mere legends, written after the event and by others, cannot and do not convey the souls of their subjects. Since a pure interior life is better than all miracles or works, he praises the Psalms for taking us into the very core of the lives of the saints, a place that the popular legends of saints fail to attain.

The book of Psalms also has the advantage of being composed during very stormy times in the lives of its authors. These disturbances enable the authors to speak plainly and urgently to God about the things that really matter, rather than being complacently attached to the things of the world. We thereby find a true example of interior faith, both in praising God and in penitence and sorrow. As Luther says regarding the psalms of praise, "In them you can see into the

---

14. Ibid., 38.
15. Ibid.
16. Ibid.
17. Ibid., 39.

hearts of all the saints as if you were looking at a lovely pleasure-garden, or were gazing into heaven."[18] Since this is so, whenever we get the urge to gaze into heaven where the blessed are now, we should simply read the psalms of praise. Likewise, if we wish to know what hell or separation from God is like, we should read the sorrowful psalms: "In these, you see into the hearts of all the saints as if you were looking at death or gazing into hell, so dark and obscure is the scene rendered by the changing shadows of the wrath of God."[19]

In Luther's view, the Psalms should take the place of legends of the saints for another reason as well. Namely, the saints whose lives are so popular were themselves enamored by the Psalms. Indeed, all Christian saints—all true believers in Christ—treasure the Psalms in a special way. The reason is that Christ speaks to us through the Psalms, and it is also as though we are speaking to him. Luther states that "every man on every occasion can find . . . Psalms which fit his needs, which he feels to be as appropriate as if they had been set there just for his sake. In no other book can he find words to equal them, nor better words. Nor does he wish it."[20] The implication is that if he does wish it and reverts back to the popular legends of the saints, then there is some problem. After all, in the Psalms, Christian saints today hear words that meet their needs and thereby find themselves "in the company of the saints," insofar as "all of them join in singing a little song with him, since he can use their words to talk with God as they did."[21] Obviously, this use of the Psalms is only open to those who have faith and who can perceive Christ and the church in the Psalms.

Luther offers a final reason not to pay attention to the legends of the saints, but instead to read the Psalms. Anyone who reads the legends of the saints will discover works that not only cannot be imitated, but in fact should not be imitated. Luther notes that the works in these

---

18. Ibid.
19. Ibid., 40.
20. Ibid.
21. Ibid.

legends "are, in most cases, the beginnings of sects and factions, that lead and even drag one away from the fellowship of the saints"—perhaps because they produce strong devotion to one saint or another rather than devotion to Jesus (Luther is not explicit here).[22] The very opposite effect comes from reading the Psalms. The Psalms do not promote extraordinary works of devotion to this or that person, but rather urge us to endure the storms of life with a spiritual equanimity in "the fellowship of the saints; for, whether in joy, fear, hope, or sorrow, it teaches you to be equable in mind and calm in word, as were all the saints."[23] Luther thus retains space for an appreciation for celebrating the lives of Christians through the centuries who have been faithful to God, so long as we recognize that the "saints" include all who believe in the true gospel and who persevere in Christ's grace. All such can learn how to pray and how to act from the Psalms, without recourse to the wild legendary tales of miraculous works. Luther concludes by hearkening back to the times, not long ago, when Germans had no access to the truth of the gospel and could not understand the Psalms, which were concealed in Latin: "For of old, in the dark times, what a treasure it would have been held to be, if a man could have rightly understood one single Psalm, and could have read or heard it in simple German. To-day, however, blessed are the eyes that see what we see and the ears that hear what we hear."[24]

BIBLICAL REFLECTION

In the period of Second Temple Judaism, we find a deep appreciation for the holy persons of Israel's past, who were understood to be mediators and exemplars of God's covenantal relationship with Israel. In the Wisdom of Solomon, for example, the personified figure of Wisdom appears as the interior protector and strengthener of these holy persons.

---

22. Ibid.
23. Ibid.
24. Ibid., 41.

Wisdom gave Adam, after his fall, the "strength to rule all things" (Wis 10:2). In the time of Noah, Wisdom saved the human race, "steering the righteous man [Noah] by a paltry piece of wood" (Wis 10:4). Wisdom recognized Abraham as a "righteous man" and "preserved him blameless before God," even in the crisis of his near-sacrifice of Isaac (Wis 10:5). Wisdom saved Job from destruction, and guided Jacob "on straight paths" so as to teach him that "godliness is more powerful than anything" (Wis 10:10). Wisdom stayed by the side of Joseph and "brought him the scepter of a kingdom and authority over his masters" (Wis 10:14). At the time of Moses, Wisdom delivered "a holy people and blameless race" out of the hands of "a nation of oppressors" (Wis 10:15).

With a similar appreciation for the holy persons of Israel's past, Sirach 44 exhorts, "Let us now praise famous men, and our fathers in their generations. The Lord apportioned to them great glory, his majesty from the beginning" (Sir 44:1–2). Sirach praises holy Jews from a wide array of walks of life, beginning with rulers and leaders: "There were those who ruled in their kingdoms, and were men renowned for their power, giving counsel by their understanding, and proclaiming prophecies; leaders of the people in their deliberations and in understanding of learning for the people, wise in their words of instruction" (Sir 44:3–4). Among the holy ones of Israel who have been remembered, Sirach names Enoch as "an example of repentance to all generations" (Sir 44:16); Noah as "perfect and righteous" (Sir 44:17); Abraham as unique "in glory" and as "faithful" (Sir 44:19–20); Isaac and Jacob as blessed for the sake of Abraham; Moses as "a man of mercy, who found favor in the sight of all flesh and was beloved by God and man" (Sir 45:1); Aaron as chosen "out of all the living to offer sacrifice to the Lord" (Sir 45:16); Phinehas as "zealous in the fear of the Lord" (Sir 45:23); Joshua as "a great savior of God's elect" (Sir 46:1); Caleb as an exemplar of how good it is "to follow the Lord" (Sir 46:10); Samuel as "beloved by his Lord" (Sir 46:13); David as the recipient of "the covenant of kings and a throne of glory in Israel" (Sir 47:11); Solomon as a man of peace and wisdom in his youth; Elijah as "ready at the appointed time . . . to restore the tribes of Jacob" (Sir 48:1, 19); Hezekiah as doing "what was pleasing to the Lord" (Sir 48:22); Isaiah as comforting "those who mourned in Zion" (Sir 48:24); Josiah as taking "away the abominations of iniquity" (Sir 49:2); Jeremiah as "consecrated in the womb as prophet" (Sir 49:7); Ezekiel as seeing "the vision of glory which God showed him above the chariot of the cherubim" (Sir 49:8); Zerubbabel and Jeshua as building "a temple holy to the Lord, prepared for everlasting glory" (Sir 49:12); Nehemiah as rebuilding Jerusalem; and "Simon the high priest, son of Onias, who . . . in his time fortified the temple" (Sir 50:1).

In this same vein of praising famous men, the letter to the Hebrews praises the holy "cloud of witnesses" who led and taught God's people. Hebrews emphasizes that the holiness of these exemplars derived from their faith in God: by faith "the men of old received divine approval" (Heb 11:2). The first person praised in Hebrews 11 is Abel. Abel "received approval as righteous," and although "he died," nonetheless "through his faith he is still speaking" (Heb 11:4). Enoch's faith was such that he not only "pleased God" but also did "not see death" (Heb 11:5). Noah believed God, detached himself from the sinful worldliness of his contemporaries, and "became an heir of the righteousness which comes by faith" (Heb 11:7). Since these exemplars yearned for the "heavenly" homeland promised by God, "God is not ashamed to be called their God, for he has prepared for them a city" (Heb 11:16).

After Noah, Hebrews praises Abraham and Sarah. Both are exemplars of saving faith. Abraham "obeyed" God and "looked forward to the city which has foundations, whose builder and maker is God" (Heb 11:8, 10), while Sarah "considered him [God] faithful who had promised" that she would bear a son (Heb 11:11). As shown by the (near) sacrifice of Isaac, Abraham even had faith "that God was able to raise men even from the dead; hence did he receive him [Isaac] back" (Heb 11:19). Isaac, Jacob, and Joseph all receive mention in the list of holy Israelites. Moses "considered abuse suffered for the Christ greater wealth than the treasures of Egypt, for he looked to the reward," namely, eternal life (Heb 11:26). In the midst of trials, he kept his eyes focused on God "who is invisible" (Heb 11:27). The whole people of Israel, in their crossing of the Red Sea and their conquest of Jericho, exemplified the power of faith. Hebrews 11 goes on to mention more recent leaders of Israel: "Gideon, Barak, Samson, Jephthah, . . . David and Samuel and the prophets" (Heb 11:32). These exemplars "through faith conquered kingdoms, enforced justice, received promises, stopped the mouths of lions, quenched raging fire, escaped the edge of the sword, won strength out of weakness, became mighty in war, put foreign enemies to flight" (Heb 11:33–34). Lest all this sound unrealistically triumphant in temporal ways, Hebrews 11 adds that some Israelites chose to be martyred so "that they might rise again to a better life" (Heb 11:35), and "others suffered mocking and scourging, and even chains and imprisonment. They were stoned, they were sawn in two, they were killed with the sword; they went about in skins of sheep and goats, destitute, afflicted, ill-treated—of whom the world was not worthy—wandering over deserts and mountains, and in dens and caves of the earth" (Heb 11:36–38).

In forming a covenantal people and in sending his Son for the restoration of that people and the inauguration of his eschatological kingdom, God intends for believers to identify actively with holy fellow believers who have gone before them and who are now alive with God. At the transfiguration, Jesus is not seen *alone* in his glorified state; he is with Moses and Elijah, who represent the rulers and prophets of Israel. When Paul encounters the ascended Jesus on the road to Damascus, Jesus tells him, "I am Jesus, whom you are persecuting" (Acts 9:5). By persecuting the members of Jesus's body (such as Stephen), Paul had been persecuting Jesus himself. Jesus surrounds himself with his friends. Jesus's friends will be recognizable in that they "bear much fruit" (John 15:8) and thereby glorify his Father; Jesus's friends will be distinguished from the world because they receive Jesus's Spirit and embody his love. The Spirit-filled followers of Jesus will also receive the indwelling Father and Son (see John 14:23) so that they can lead holy lives of love.

Testifying to the truth of the general resurrection of the dead, Jesus asks, "Have you not read what was said to you by God, 'I am the God of Abraham, and the God of Isaac, and the God of Jacob'? He is not God of the dead, but of the living" (Matt 22:31–32). Having died, Abraham, Isaac, and Jacob departed earthly life; but for them, as Paul says of himself, it was true that "to die is gain" (Phil 1:21). They are now "with Christ, for that is far better" (Phil 1:23). They are consciously and joyfully "at home with the Lord" (2 Cor 5:8), and they are filled with love, since their faith configured them to the love of Christ. At home with Christ, they share in his selfless love and his intercessory prayer for the whole world. Recall how Moses interceded with God for the people in the golden calf incident: "Turn from thy fierce wrath, and repent of this evil against thy people" (Exod 32.12). In response "the Lord repented of the evil which he thought to do to his people" (Exod 32:14). In Christ, Moses shares even today in Christ's living "to make intercession" for his people (Heb 7:25). Christ, the one Mediator, involves all members of his body in his mission of merciful "intercession," through the power of his salvific cross, to our loving Father.

In the Gospel of John, Jesus states that "he who believes in me will also do the works that I do; and greater works than these will he do, because I go to the Father" (John 14:12). This applies explicitly to believers in Jesus during their earthly lives, but it also applies to the holy people in the intermediate state, since as we have seen they remain consciously alive and "to live is Christ, and to die is gain" by being even more fully "with Christ" (Phil 1:21, 23). To live "with Christ" means to be fully united to Christ's prayer that God's "will be done, on earth as it is in heaven" (Matt 6:10) and to Christ's prayer that believers "may become perfectly one, so that the world may know that thou hast sent me and hast loved them even as thou hast loved me" (John 17:23). If they are "with Christ," then surely his prayer will be theirs too, just as it is for believers on earth. Otherwise dying would not be "gain."

The holy people in the intermediate state take part in the "body of

Christ" (1 Cor 12:27), dwelling as it were "under the altar" (Rev 6:9) and sharing in the worship of the slain and risen Lamb (Rev 4–5), a worship marked by self-sacrificial love for the whole church. They are at "rest" (Rev 6:11) in the way that the risen and ascended Jesus is at rest. Namely, they are at peace, filled with joyous happiness, and praying with Christ for the perfect consummation of his work of justice and love. With Christ and the "innumerable angels" (Heb 12:22), the "spirits of just men made perfect" (Heb 12:23) are contributing, through their prayers, to the coming of the kingdom of their Head.

At the end of the letter to the Romans, Paul provides a list of all those to whom he wishes to send greetings. First on the list is Phoebe, "a deaconess" who "has been a helper of many and of myself as well" (Rom 16:1–2). Then follow Prisca and Aquila, "my fellow workers in Christ Jesus, who risked their necks for my life," Epaenetus, Mary, Andronicus, Junias, Ampliatus, Urbanus, Stachys, Apelles, the family of Aristobulus, Herodion, the family of Narcissus, Tryphaena and Tryphosa, Persis, Rufus and his mother, Asyncritus, Phlegon, Hermes, Patrobas, Hermas, Philologus, Julia, Nereus and his sister, Olympas, "and all the saints who are with them" (Rom 16:3–4, 15). Surely all or most of these "saints," holy persons who collaborated with Paul, are now "at home with the Lord." They have gained by becoming actively and fully united to Christ. They now zealously love Christ's whole body. Thus we cannot forget them, no more than Israel could forget its heroes of faith. Certainly they do not forget us or fail to beseech God that his plan for our salvation be fulfilled.

Over the generations, Jesus has been building up a holy eschatological people that unites Israel and the nations in his own "body" (1 Cor 12:12). Such saints, during their earthly lives and after their deaths, do not compete with Christ. Rather, they are the reason Christ came. Christ does not encounter us by himself as a lone individual, but with and through his friends. During his public ministry, he is usually found in the company of his disciples. Christ's friends "will also do the works" that Christ does (John 14:12). When we see Christ's friends loving each other as Christ has loved us, we come to believe that God has sent Christ (see John 14:21).

Jesus tells his disciples in the Gospel of John, "By this my Father is glorified, that you bear much fruit, and so prove to be my disciples" (John 15:8). As Jesus says earlier, "A new commandment I give to you, that you love one another; even as I have loved you, that you also love one another. By this all men will know that you are my disciples, if you have love for one another" (John 13:34–35). Jesus has inaugurated the kingdom by his cruciform love, and Jesus expects to be encountered in and through his friends who manifest their cruciform love. We must not forget those who have gone before us over the centuries and who today live in Christ, not because of any importance that they had or have due to their own resources, but because of the indwelling Spirit that united them with Christ in their lives and that unites them far more perfectly now to Christ's active love for his whole body (including us).

It is because we encounter Christ in and through believers that Paul can say: "Be imitators of me, as I am of Christ" (1 Cor 11:1). Again, Paul does not thereby get in the way of Christ. Rather, both during his life and now that he is "at home with the Lord," Paul allows Christ to shine through him, since as Paul says, "It is no longer I who live, but Christ who lives in me" (Gal 2:20). At the transfiguration, Jesus shows that Moses and Elijah are still assisting in Jesus's work. It follows that just as the angels minister to us, so also the holy dead serve Christ and us through their prayer. The holy dead are conscious, and we are united to them in the body of Christ, in which every member lives to serve the whole body in accordance with Christ's saving love.

The significance of almost two thousand years of saints who have explicitly followed Christ in faith and holiness, including but hardly limited to those who are alive on earth today, is to enact what it means to be in Christ, overflowing with love for all his people. Were we to forget to call the saints blessed (Luke 1:48), to greet them in Christ (Rom 16:3, 10), and to implore the prayers they offer both during their earthly lives and from "under the altar," we would not truly recognize the extent and power of the inaugurated kingdom. The saints today can "do the works" that Christ does, and even "greater works than these," because Christ sustains and strengthens the whole church so that each saint, whether "at home in the body" or "at home with the Lord" (2 Cor 5:6, 8), "may be able to comfort those who are in any affliction, with the comfort with which we ourselves are comforted by God" (2 Cor 1:4).

When Paul looks forward to the "gain" of being "at home with the Lord," he does not mean that then he will finally be able to forget about or not pray for the brother "for whom Christ died" (Rom 14:15). The intermediate state is not a place where each contented soul "lives to himself," since in fact Christ is "Lord both of the dead and of the living" (Rom 14:7, 9). As I have emphasized, Christ now "lives to make intercession" (Heb 7:25) for people who are currently alive on earth. How could it be that those who are consciously united to Christ in the intermediate state, and who "live to the Lord" (Rom 14:8) in a state of overflowing self-giving love, desire no share or receive no share in the intercession for which Christ now lives? Recall the paralytic healed by Jesus in Capernaum. When the paralytic's four friends could not reach Jesus due to the crowd, "they removed the roof above him [Jesus]; and when they had made an opening, they let down the pallet on which the paralytic lay" (Mark 2:4). Moved by "*their* faith" (Mark 2:5; emphasis added), Jesus forgives the sins of the paralytic.

This active participation in Christ's work does not put the members of Christ's body in competition with the perfect and unique efficacy of Christ's intercession. Rather, it is simply that conscious union with Christ means that "Christ . . . lives in me" (Gal 2:20) and enables me to share in his concrete love and prayer for sinners. Both on earth and in the intermediate state, the inaugurated kingdom is precisely this divine gift of overflowing communion in the love of God, by which God constantly runs to embrace sinners (Luke 15:20). Christ includes the angels and the saints in the intermediate state, as well as his holy people alive today on earth, in his life and in his rejoicing (see Luke 15:10).

When Christ's saints are no longer perceived as icons of Christ but instead are invoked as though they had autonomous power of their own, then they are profoundly misunderstood and the communion that unites the body of Christ no longer functions. But abuse of the saints (or of the angels, for that matter) does not mean that their ongoing mission is outside Christ's purposes. Those who are dead in Christ are alive: God "is not the God of the dead, but of the living" (Matt 22:32). Admittedly, the full and perfect communion of heaven and earth awaits the consummation of all things, when there will no longer be any separation between the members of Christ's body. But to lack appreciation for and relationship with the saints—the holy men and women who have gone before us and also the holy men and women who are alive on earth today and whose prayers we covet[25]—weakens our appreciation for the church as the people of God and body of Christ. To love the saints and to ask regularly for their prayers is to love Christ and the Father who sent him, since "by this all men will know that you are my disciples, if you have love for one another."

---

25. With regard to the latter, see Philip Graham Ryken, ed., *The Communion of Saints: Living in Fellowship with the People of God* (Phillipsburg, NJ: P&R, 2001).

CHAPTER 9

PAPACY

In this final chapter, I examine the papacy, which is one of the ways in which the church's ability to make unified doctrinal judgments is assured. The Reformers confronted a terribly corrupted recent history of the papacy, with popes living in Avignon, fighting over who was the true pope, greedily soaking up money from the faithful, living in ostentatious pomp, leading oppressive armies, and carrying on sexual affairs. Readers who do not know what the Catholic Church teaches about the papacy should consult paragraphs 874–896 of the *Catechism of the Catholic Church*, as well as paragraphs 18–29 of Vatican II's *Lumen Gentium*. In my biblical reflection, I examine biblical texts pertaining to the mission of Peter as an instrument of unity in the church. These texts indicate that the Catholic position on the papacy flows from biblical reasoning and serves Christ's will for his church.

LUTHER'S CONCERN

In Luther's 1520 epistle "An Open Letter to Pope Leo X," which serves as a preface to his "The Freedom of a Christian," Luther tells the pope that he (Luther) has "spoken only good and honorable words concerning you whenever I have thought of you."[1] He argues that it is the members

---

1. Martin Luther, "An Open Letter to Pope Leo X," in *Martin Luther: Selections*, 43–52, at 44.

of the Roman Curia who have received his opprobrium. Pope Leo X, Luther suggests, is an honorable man who has become the figurehead of a dishonorable See, the "Roman church."[2] The pope presides over "the most licentious den of thieves [Matt. 21:13], the most shameless of all brothels, the kingdom of sin, death, and hell," a kingdom that "even Antichrist himself, if he should come, could think of nothing to add to its wickedness."[3] Although the person of Leo need not be rejected, the Roman Church and Curia must be rejected.

Luther then makes clear the terms on which dialogue between him (and his followers) and the Roman Church must proceed. These terms include the following: (1) "In all other matters I will yield to any man whatsoever; but I have neither the power nor the will to deny the Word of God"; (2) "I acknowledge no fixed rules for the interpretation of the Word of God, since the Word of God, which teaches freedom in all other matters, must not be bound [II Tim. 2:9]"; and (3) "A man is a vicar only when his superior is absent. If the pope rules, while Christ is absent and does not dwell in his heart, what else is he but a vicar of Christ? What is the church under such a vicar but a mass of people without Christ? Indeed, what is such a vicar but an antichrist and an idol?"[4]

For Luther, Pope Leo may be a good man, but he is operating under a powerful and dangerous confusion. Neither Pope Leo nor the church can set "fixed rules for the interpretation of the Word of God." Since we must always be free to follow Scripture where it leads rather than "to deny the Word of God," Pope Leo has no authority to set bounds for doctrinal teaching. Nor can Pope Leo claim to be a vicar or representative of Christ in any unique or authoritative sense; rather, the living Christ is himself present in the church, and it is only to this living Christ (and to those imbued with the presence and wisdom of the living Christ) that believers should listen. The office of pope or

---

2. Ibid., 45.
3. Ibid., 46.
4. Ibid., 46, 50–51.

bishop of Rome gives no authority. It is only the possession of Christ through true faith that gives authority, and only one who has this true faith can be a teacher in the church.

Luther therefore warns Pope Leo: "Be not deceived by those who pretend that you are lord of the world, allow no one to be considered a Christian unless he accepts your authority, and prate that you have power over heaven, hell, and purgatory. . . . They err who ascribe to you alone the right of interpreting Scripture."[5] Christians do not need to accept the pope's pastoral or doctrinal authority, and Christians must not imagine that papal excommunication has any bearing upon the final judgment. It is the living Christ and his Word (Scripture) that have authority, and no mere human or group of humans can bind God's Word to a particular interpretation. Luther tells Pope Leo that "they err who exalt you above a council and the church universal," and Luther does not grant that either councils or the "church universal" have authority to interpret Scripture in a binding fashion.[6]

The critique of the papacy is extended and developed in another treatise Luther wrote in 1520, "The Babylonian Captivity of the Church." In discussing baptism, which should be a sign of our faith in the power of Christ's death and resurrection, he suggests that the pope's misunderstanding of baptism shows the falseness of papal claims. He writes, "Our splendid freedom, and our proper understanding of baptism, are in shackles to-day, and the blame can be laid at the door of the autocratic pontiff of Rome. . . . The pontiff's only concern is with oppressing us with his decrees and laws, and in ensnaring and keeping us captive under his absolute authority."[7] This "absolute authority" is based upon a misreading of certain New Testament texts. In making this case, Luther insists upon the freedom of Christians: "I declare that neither pope, nor bishop, nor any one else, has the right to impose so

---

5. Ibid., 51.
6. Ibid.
7. Luther, "The Babylonian Captivity of the Church," in *Martin Luther: Selections*, 248–359, at 304.

much as a single syllable of obligation upon a Christian man without his own consent."[8]

Among the biblical texts often cited in favor of the papacy, Luther mentions Luke 10:16, John 10:27, Matthew 16:19, and Matthew 18:15–17. Regarding the power of the keys to bind and to loose (Matthew 16:19), Luther observes that the popes have claimed that the power of the keys gives them the ability to dispense from solemn vows. But in fact the keys have only to do with the forgiveness of sin, and in this regard "the keys belong to all," since all can and should forgive.[9] In Matthew 16:19 Jesus "was not giving authority to take the whole church into captivity and oppress it by any laws."[10] Regarding Luke 10:16, "He who hears you hears me," Luther observes that this applies solely to preachers of the gospel, and so it only applies to the pope "when he is teaching the gospel and proclaiming Christ."[11] We should no more obey the pope than we should obey anyone who preaches Christ, and the true preaching of the gospel can be known because it does not deprive anyone of his Christian freedom. Faith is "the freest of all things."[12]

Luther's 1520 "An Appeal to the Ruling Class of German Nationality as to the Amelioration of the State of Christendom" is also helpful in elucidating his view of the papacy. After first observing how the popes had shamefully treated many German emperors over the years, Luther argues that the papacy has long defended itself from real reform by means of "three walls." The first wall consists in the papacy's argument that secular states have no jurisdiction over the papacy's acts; the second wall, in the claim that only the pope can interpret Scripture definitively; and the third wall, in the claim that no church council can be called or approved without the consent of the pope, thereby rendering impossible "a truly free council."[13]

---

8. Ibid.
9. Ibid., 312.
10. Ibid., 305.
11. Ibid.
12. Ibid.
13. Luther, "An Appeal to the Ruling Class of German Nationality as to the Amelioration of the State of Christendom," in *Martin Luther: Selections*, 403–85, at 407.

In response to these three walls, Luther points out that all Christian people are equally Christian, and furthermore, given 1 Peter 2:9 and Revelation 5:9, that all Christians are equally priests. It is not consecration by a pope or a bishop, then, that makes the fundamental difference, but rather it is true profession of Christian faith. He gives the hypothetical example of what if "a small group of earnest Christian laymen were taken prisoner and settled in the middle of a desert without any episcopally ordained priest among them"; these laymen could ordain a priest from among their number as well as (or better than) could any pope or bishop.[14] The key point is that because it is only being a true Christian that matters (all else being simply a difference in function or office), "all have spiritual status, and all are truly priests, bishops, and popes."[15]

When popes fail to rightly "expound the word of God and administer the sacraments," they have failed in their office and should be punished by the secular authorities, forced to follow "that understanding of the Scriptures which we possess as believers," and deprived of their ability to summon or approve a council.[16] Luther appeals to common sense: "It can never be the pope alone who is in the right, if the creed is correct in the article, 'I believe in one, holy, Christian church'; or should the confession take the form: 'I believe in the pope of Rome'?"[17] Luther calls for a "genuinely free council" that would truly build up the church by underscoring that "no Christian authority is valid when exercised contrary to Christ."[18] Given the strivings of the papacy against the true gospel and the true sacraments, Luther can only conclude that the popes "belong to the community of Antichrist and the devil, and have nothing in common with Christ except the name."[19]

---

14. Ibid., 408.
15. Ibid., 409.
16. Ibid., 409–10, 414.
17. Ibid., 414.
18. Ibid., 416–17.
19. Ibid., 417.

BIBLICAL REFLECTION

When Jesus Christ prepared to inaugurate the kingdom of God by enduring the tribulation of the cross (thereby bringing about the restoration of Israel and the forgiveness of sins), he began his public ministry by choosing twelve disciples. Just as the people of Israel were constituted by the Lord around the twelve sons of Jacob/Israel and so around the twelve tribes, the messianic people of God were constituted by Jesus around his twelve disciples. In the Gospel of Luke, the first disciple that Jesus calls is Simon (Peter). Jesus commands Simon to "put out into the deep and let down your nets for a catch" (Luke 5:4) and when Simon obeys, the result is a catch that fills two boats with fish. Simon recognizes his lack of human worthiness before Jesus: "Depart from me, for I am a sinful man, O Lord" (Luke 5:8). But Jesus reassures him: "Do not be afraid; henceforth you will be catching men" (Luke 5:10).

Jesus's gathering of the twelve, with Simon Peter at the forefront, is an eschatological action that flows from Jesus's prayer. The evangelist Luke reports that prior to making his final selection of the twelve from among the larger number of his disciples, Jesus "went out into the hills to pray; and all night he continued in prayer to God. And when it was day, he called his disciples, and chose from them twelve, whom he named apostles" (Luke 6:12–13). Among these disciples/apostles, Luke lists Simon Peter first.

Simon has a distinctive role among the twelve. Matthew, Luke, and John signal his unique authority among the twelve in specific ways. Matthew reports that it is Simon Peter who answers correctly when Jesus asks his disciples who they think he is: "You are the Christ, the Son of the living God" (Matt 16:16). This leads Jesus to proclaim Simon especially blessed and to give him the central leadership role in the church: "I tell you, you are Peter ['Rock'], and on this rock I will build my church, and the powers of death shall not prevail against it. I will give you the keys of the kingdom of heaven, and whatever you bind on earth shall be bound in heaven, and whatever you loose on earth shall be loosed in heaven" (Matt 16:18–19).[20] Luke reports that at the Last Supper, after Jesus has instituted the eschatologically new Passover and new manna, Jesus tells his disciples that they will "eat and drink at my table in my kingdom, and sit on thrones judging the twelve tribes of Israel" (Luke 22:30). Regarding the period between his inauguration of the kingdom and its final consummation, Jesus gives a unique command to Simon. He states, "Simon, Simon, behold, Satan demanded to have you, that he might sift you like wheat, but I have prayed for you that your faith may not fail; and when you have turned again, strengthen your brethren" (Luke 22:31–32). This statement refers to Peter's coming denial of Jesus, and it also makes clear Peter's unique role in strengthening the followers of Jesus during the period prior to the consummation of the kingdom. Peter is presented as the leader (under Jesus) of the eschatological people that will share in Jesus's kingdom.

In the Gospel of John, Peter receives from the risen Lord a threefold commission—answering to his threefold denial—that none of the other disciples/apostles receive. At the dawn of the inaugurated kingdom, the risen Jesus comes and breakfasts with the disciples. He first enables them to draw in a miraculous catch of fish. He then asks Peter three times whether Peter loves him, and three times he adds, "Feed my lambs" (or the cognate statements "Tend my sheep" and "Feed my sheep" [John 21:15–17]). When the Lord reigns at the right hand of the Father, Peter will be entrusted in a unique way with tending and feeding the flock of the Lord.

The Lord Jesus himself, of course, is "the shepherd of the sheep," the "good shepherd" who "lays down his life for the sheep" (John 10:2, 11). In fulfillment of Ezekiel's prophecies, Jesus has already promised that "there shall be one flock, one shepherd" (John 10:16). Since Jesus is the

20. For a historical-critical analysis that differs sharply from my position, see Robert H. Gundry, *Peter: False Disciple and Apostate according to Saint Matthew* (Grand Rapids, MI: Eerdmans, 2015). For a position closer to mine, see Martin Hengel, *Saint Peter: The Underestimated Apostle*, trans. Thomas H. Trapp (Grand Rapids, MI: Eerdmans, 2010). See also Markus Bockmuehl, *Simon Peter in Scripture and Memory: The New Testament Apostle in the Early Church* (Grand Rapids, MI: Baker Academic, 2012).

shepherd, why is there any need for Peter to perform the shepherd's role of tending and feeding the sheep? The answer is that Jesus gives Peter a unique participation in Jesus's authority in the eschatological church.

In 1 Corinthians 15, the preeminent role of Peter receives further confirmation. In his list of eyewitnesses of the risen Jesus, Paul states that Jesus "appeared to Cephas [Peter], then to the twelve" (1 Cor 15:5). No one else is named before Peter, and Peter is named before "the twelve" as a whole. Likewise, in recounting what he did after his conversion to Christ, Paul states that "after three years I went up to Jerusalem to visit Cephas, and remained with him fifteen days" (Gal 1:18). He visited Cephas (Peter), but he saw no other apostles "except James the Lord's brother" (Gal 1:19).

In the same letter, Paul reports having to oppose Peter "to his face, because he stood condemned" (Gal 2:11). If Peter did not possess a central leadership role, it would hardly have mattered that "he stood condemned" or that Paul dared to oppose him. Paul does not mention any conflicts that he may have had with others of the original twelve. Paul's authority is evidenced by the fact that he was able to correct Peter and that Peter, in his leadership role, accepted Paul's correction. According to Paul, Peter retained the primary mission of preaching "the gospel to the circumcised" (Gal 2:7), while Paul was given the primary mission of preaching the gospel to the Gentiles.

Paul also names Peter alongside James and John as the "pillars" who approve his ministry by extending to him "the right hand of fellowship" (Gal 2:9). Whether the James of Galatians 2:9 is the brother of John or (as seems to be the case) the brother of Jesus, the identification of three "pillars" fits with what the Gospels describe. During his earthly ministry, Jesus often takes Peter, James, and John with him at crucial moments, including the transfiguration and the garden of Gethsemane. In every instance, Jesus acknowledges Peter as the leader of this group of three.

In the book of Acts, when the apostles are gathered in the upper room in Olivet (near Jerusalem), Peter is named first among the assembled apostles and other followers of Jesus. Peter leads the assembled community in the task of replacing Judas among the twelve. On the day of Pentecost, when the outpouring of the Holy Spirit takes place among Christ's eschatological people, Peter is the one who authoritatively interprets what is happening. He delivers a speech to the devout Jews who are amazed by what they are seeing. Inspired by his speech, they say "to Peter and the rest of the apostles, 'Brethren, what shall we do?'" (Acts 2:37). Peter responds, "Repent, and be baptized everyone one of you in the name of Jesus Christ for the forgiveness of your sins; and you shall receive the gift of the Holy Spirit" (Acts 2:38). Peter goes on to perform a miracle of healing in the name of Jesus Christ (see Acts 3:6–10), and he then gives another powerful speech. His leadership role continues to be accentuated through his arrest, his bold speech to the Jewish leaders, his condemnation (on behalf of Jesus and the Spirit) of Ananias and Sapphira, his escape from prison, his condemnation of Simon Magus, his healing of the paralyzed man Aeneas, his raising of the dead woman Tabitha, his authoritative dream in which the Lord declared all foods clean, and his welcoming of the Gentile Cornelius (and his family) into the community of the baptized.

Although in Acts 13 Paul becomes the focus of the remainder of the book of Acts, Paul's insistence that the Gentiles do not need to be circumcised or to practice Torah causes a controversy that leads to a council of "the apostles and the elders" (Acts 15:4) in Jerusalem. After the issue had been debated for a while, the first to speak authoritatively on the issue is Peter. Peter recalls his own experience in the conversion of the Gentiles and makes the fundamental theological point regarding salvation by faith in Christ: "Now therefore why do you make trial of God by putting a yoke upon the neck of the disciples which neither our fathers nor we have been able to bear? But we believe that we shall be saved through the grace of the Lord Jesus, just as they will" (Acts 15:10–11).

All the above can be read simply as Peter receiving a leadership role among the first Christians. Jesus, however, established his eschatological community not only for the first generation. Jesus's foresight did not end with the death of Peter, which, according to the Gospel of John, he foresaw: "Truly, truly, I say to you, when you were young, you girded yourself and walked where you would; but when you are old, you will stretch out your hands, and another will gird you and carry you where you do not wish to go. (This he said to show by what death he was to glorify God)" (John 21:18–19). Jesus made preparations for an extended interim period in which the new covenant, the inaugurated kingdom, would be lived out both well and badly. Thus, during his earthly ministry, he informs his disciples that "the secret of the kingdom of God" (Mark 4:11) can be perceived in the parable of the sower. He explains that when "the sower sows the word," there will be a variety of responses: some will fall away immediately, some will fall away during tribulation, some will fall away due to being caught up in worldly pursuits, and finally some will "hear the word and accept it and bear fruit, thirtyfold and sixtyfold and a hundredfold" (Mark 4:14, 20). This has been the actual situation of the church over the centuries. Many nominal believers have lost interest and gone through the motions at best (and caused deep scandal at worst), but those who have held onto the Word of God faithfully have indeed born great fruit in the world. Jesus foresees the period between the inauguration and consummation of the kingdom as one of sufficient length that he can ask, "When the Son of man comes, will he find faith on the earth?" (Luke 18:8).

In preparing for his own ascension to the right hand of the Father, the risen Jesus commanded Peter to perform the role of shepherd under Jesus (who is the "good shepherd"): Peter is to tend the flock and feed the lambs, and Peter is to strengthen his brethren. We saw in Matthew 16:19 that Peter receives "the keys of the kingdom of heaven." In the prophecy of Isaiah 22, the Lord states that he will overthrow one "steward" (Isa 22:15) and install another:

> In that day I will call my servant Eliakim the son of Hilkiah, and I will clothe him with your robe, and will bind your girdle on him, and will commit your authority to his hand; and he shall be a father to the inhabitants of Jerusalem and to the house of Judah. And I

will place on his shoulder the key of the house of David; he shall open, and none shall shut; and he shall shut, and none shall open. (Isa 22:20–22)

A "steward" in this sense stands in the place of the king; even though he is not the king, he has the power to open or shut gates to outsiders/insiders and to keep or free people in prison, and is respected by the people of the king. In light of this prophecy, Jesus's promise about the keys suggests that the "steward" of the ascended and reigning King, Jesus Christ, is to be Peter. The Isaianic prophecy continues with the Lord saying, "I will fasten him like a peg in a sure place, and he will become a throne of honor to his father's house. And they will hang on him the whole weight of his father's house, the offspring and issue, every small vessel, from the cups to all the flagons" (Isa 22:23–24). Here the steward will have no small role in the ongoing eschatological household of the Lord, but at the same time his role will be that of a "servant," under the lordship of the King and serving the people of God until the King comes in glory.

Peter is that steward in the eschatological household of the Lord. I have suggested, however, that Jesus can see farther than the limits of Peter's lifetime. In inaugurating the kingdom, Jesus does not proclaim (even to his disciples) the hour of its consummation: "But of that day and hour no one knows, not even the angels of heaven, nor the Son, but the Father only" (Matt 24:36). Jesus tells us that the hour will sneak up on us. We will be engaged in our routine activities, not knowing that the final consummation is upon us. He states in his eschatological discourse, "As were the days of Noah, so will be the coming of the Son of man. For as in those days before the flood they were eating and drinking, marrying and giving in marriage, until the day when Noah entered the ark . . . so will be the coming of the Son of man" (Matt 24:37–39). Since the consummation will come "at an hour you do not expect" (Matt 24:44), it is clear that Jesus (according to the Gospel of Matthew) does not teach that the consummation is imminent. When

Jesus establishes Peter as steward of the inaugurated kingdom, he already has in view Peter's death and the post-apostolic generations.

God gave Israel leaders to assist them in staying together in true worship, even though division was never far from them. Recall that Israel's true king is YHWH, the Lord, and so when the people of Israel demand a king, the prophet Samuel rebukes them: "You have this day rejected your God, who saves you from all your calamities and your distresses; and you have said, 'No! but set a king over us'" (1 Sam 10:19). Yet God has a plan for the kingship, and so God commands Samuel, "Hearken to their voice, and make them a king" (1 Sam 8:22). Going further back, remember that God raises up Moses and Aaron to lead the twelve tribes. God instructs Moses about his brother Aaron: "You shall speak to him and put the words in his mouth; and I will be with your mouth and with his mouth, and will teach you what you shall do. He shall speak for you to the people; and he shall be a mouth for you, and you shall be to him as God" (Exod 4:15–16). God designates Aaron as the high priest of the people, and God commands that "Aaron shall bear the names of the sons of Israel in the breastpiece of judgment upon his heart, when he goes into the holy place, to bring them to continual remembrance before the LORD" (Exod 28:29). When Korah, Dathan, and Abiram (and their followers, all leading men of Israel) rise up against Moses and Aaron during the exodus journey, they accuse Moses and Aaron: "You have gone too far! For all the congregation is holy, every one of them; why then do you exalt yourselves above the assembly of the LORD?" (Num 16:3).

During the same exodus journey, the people threaten to break apart at numerous junctures; there is civil war (see Exodus 32:26–29) and an apparent effort by one tribe to break away from the others (see Numbers 32). The people threaten to disintegrate in various ways during the period of the judges, and the northern ten tribes split from the southern two tribes after the reign of Solomon. They even divide with respect to worship. Solomon obediently makes a "house for the name of the LORD, the God of Israel" (1 Kgs 8:20) in Jerusalem, but after the rebellion of the northern ten tribes, Jeroboam (the new king of the north) fears that "'if this people go up to offer sacrifices in the house of the LORD at Jerusalem, then the heart of this people will turn again to their lord, to Rehobo'am king of Judah.' So the king took counsel, and made two calves of gold. And he said to the people, 'You have gone up to Jerusalem long enough. Behold your gods, O Israel, who brought you up out of the land of Egypt'" (1 Kgs 12:27–28).

When Jesus, in preparation for the period between the inauguration and consummation of the kingdom of God, gives the "keys" to Peter and commands Peter to tend his flock, Jesus is preparing his messianic people for dissensions and divisions. He knows full well that, as he says in the Gospel of Matthew, "the kingdom of heaven is like a net which was thrown into the sea and gathered fish of every kind; when it was full, men drew it ashore and sat down and sorted the good into vessels but threw away the bad. So it will be at the close of the age" (Matt 13:47–49). Even his disciples become deeply jealous of each other—for example, when James and John ask Jesus for the privilege of sitting at his right and left hands in his kingdom, and "the ten heard it, they began to be indignant at James and John" (Mark 10:41). Jesus teaches them—and teaches Peter in many other instances—that the only true way to lead the eschatological community is to imitate Jesus's servanthood and willingness to die for the people out of love. As Jesus says to his jealous disciples, "You know that those who are supposed to rule over the Gentiles lord it over them, and their great men exercise authority over them. But it shall not be so among you; but whoever would be great among you must be your servant, and whoever would be first among you must be slave of all" (Mark 10:42–44). Jesus knows that Peter, even when he is commissioned as steward and has become an apostle filled with the Spirit, will fail at this and will need criticism (which Paul gives to him). Yet Jesus still gives the "keys" to Peter, because Jesus knows that his church, in order to stay together as much as possible and to interpret and perform the gospel rightly in the course of proclaiming it to the whole world, needs a "steward" or shepherd (under the "Good Shepherd") who serves the visible unity of the church, not least by playing a leadership role in its councils and its definitive proclamation of the gospel.

Jesus cares a lot about the unity of his eschatological people. In his farewell discourse in the Gospel of John, he prays to the Father that the apostles and all "those who believe in me through their word" (John 17:20), across the generations, will

> all be one; even as thou, Father, art in me, and I in thee, that they also may be in us, so that the world may believe that thou hast sent me. The glory which thou hast given me I have given to them, that they may be one even as we are one, I in them and thou in me, that they may become perfectly one, so that the world may know that thou hast sent me and hast loved them even as thou hast loved me. (John 17:21–23)

In the face of the terrible difficulties that the people of Israel had in staying together, Jesus provides his messianic people with an apostolic structure (fulfilling that of the twelve tribes) and with one leader among the apostles who has the unique role of steward and shepherd under Jesus. It is in this sense that Peter is the "rock" upon which Jesus will build his "church, and the powers of death shall not prevail against it" (Matt 16:18). Peter must remain humble and accept suffering. Jesus rebukes Peter sharply for failing to do this (see Matthew 16:21–23), but he never gives up on Peter.

In his prayer for unity and in his words to Peter, Jesus has in mind not only the lifetime of Peter, but also the whole time of the ongoing eschatological community, which will last until the kingdom that Jesus inaugurates by his cross and resurrection is consummated by Jesus's coming in glory. Jesus will continue to reign over the church—"Lo, I am with you always, to the close of the age" (Matt 28:20)—and so his arrangements regarding the church's leadership allow both for human sinfulness and for the gradual historical unfolding of what is contained in Scripture. With regard to unity, Jesus is no more starry-eyed than is Paul, who in the book of Acts warns the elders of the church in Ephesus:

> Take heed to yourselves and to all the flock, in which the Holy Spirit has made you guardians, to feed the church of the Lord which he obtained with his own blood. I know that after my departure fierce wolves will come in among you, not sparing the flock; and from among your own selves will arise men speaking perverse things, to draw away the disciples after them. (Acts 20:28–30)

Popes are not preserved from becoming "fierce wolves" who betray Jesus in certain terrible ways (just as Peter did), but they are preserved from corrupting the gospel and making its true proclamation no longer possible in the church. Jesus promises his disciples that "when the Spirit of truth comes, he will guide you into all the truth" (John 16:13), and he also takes care to commission Peter, despite Peter's sins, to lead the Spirit-filled flock (John 21:15–17). Under Christ, an active principle of unity in interpreting and performing the gospel is appropriate, given the centrifugal forces that afflict an institution that exists across a broad span of time and space.

The form that this Petrine ministry takes in the church develops over time under the guidance of the Spirit, and at certain periods of the church's history sinful men have gravely abused the Petrine office. The Roman "Curia" or Vatican bureaucracy, which exists to support the ministry of the successors of Peter, has also at times been the site of abuses, since the church on earth bears within its visible domain many who fall into grievous sin. But Jesus's promise that his church, built upon the "rock" of Peter, will not be overcome by the "powers of death" (Matt 16:18) endures, not because of any human strength on the part of the papacy but because of the power of Jesus's prayer (Luke 22:32) and because of the power of Jesus's sending (despite the fact that those whom he sends are free and fallen): "As the Father has sent me, even so I send you" (John 20:21).

CONCLUSION

The Catholic Church's biblical reasoning has been formed over the centuries in the process of handing down the gospel, proclaiming it liturgically, preaching it, living it, and resolving doctrinal controversies. In the Christian life of faith and love, biblically warranted reasoning about biblical realities includes liturgical proclamation and interpretation, investigation of the plain sense of Scripture, biblical typologies and typological reasoning, historical-critical study, apostolic authority and the Petrine ministry, canonical exegesis, and church councils. In the present book, I have not been able to display the fuller context of Catholic biblical reasoning, since I have only had space to set forth (rather sparely) some interconnected biblical texts that bear upon the disputed doctrines. For each disputed Catholic doctrine, there are biblical texts that have taught the church in its process of formulating a doctrinal judgment. I have done my best to present these texts in the present book, since my intended audience is Bible-believing Christians who deem the disputed Catholic doctrines to be biblically mistaken.

The fuller context of Catholic biblical reasoning has been well described by Khaled Anatolios in his work on the fourth-century Trinitarian controversies. While arguing that "doctrine is essentially a demonstration precisely of the 'sufficiency' of Scripture," he points out that Scripture's "sufficiency" also includes its ability to ensure "a continuity in the transmission (*traditio*) of scriptural truth."[1] In this respect, he emphasizes that the church's doctrine arises not merely from abstract logic applied to Scripture, but from Scripture as lived out in "the entirety of Christian faith and life," including the liturgy, prayer, the moral life, and so forth.[2]

It needs to be said emphatically that awareness of the range of biblically warranted modes of biblical reasoning in doctrinal development is not by any means limited to Catholics. On the contrary, one sees it in the Methodist exegete Richard Hays's insistence that "to read Scripture well, we must bid farewell to plodding literalism and rationalism" and must interpret Scripture as people who are "standing *within* the still-unfolding narrative trajectory of Israel's covenantal relationship with the God of Abraham, Isaac, and Jacob."[3] One sees it, too, in the Reformed theologian Peter Leithart's emphasis on the significance of typology and tropology for the Reformers and his careful argument that biblical "interpretation is a communal activity."[4] Again, one sees it in the Lutheran theologian Karlfried Froehlich's insistence that neither the Bible nor the interpreter "has ever existed outside a community of faith" and his recognition that "paying attention to the 'principles' of biblical interpretation means taking into account the articulated faith and hope of the interpreters as well as of the communities they served."[5] Many other such scholars could be named.

All too briefly, the present book has addressed nine issues that have proven to be church-dividing for the past five hundred years: Scripture (and its interpretation), Mary, the Eucharist, the seven sacraments, monasticism, justification and merit, purgatory, saints, and the papacy.

1. Khaled Anatolios, *Retrieving Nicaea: The Development and Meaning of Trinitarian Doctrine* (Grand Rapids, MI: Baker Academic, 2011), 283–84.

2. Ibid., 7.

3. Richard B. Hays, *Reading Backwards: Figural Christology and the Fourfold Gospel Witness* (Waco, TX: Baylor University Press, 2014), 105–6.

4. Peter J. Leithart, *Deep Exegesis: The Mystery of Reading Scripture* (Waco, TX: Baylor University Press, 2009), 14–15, 208–9.

5. Karlfried Froehlich, *Sensing the Scriptures: Aminadab's Chariot and the Predicament of Biblical Interpretation* (Grand Rapids, MI: Eerdmans, 2014), 3, 19.

At the outset of the Reformation, Luther argued that on each of these matters the Catholic Church had strayed from the proper "standard of teaching" or rule of faith (Rom 6:17). Most Protestants today continue to hold on biblical grounds that the Catholic Church is wrong about its doctrinal judgments in these nine areas (or at least most of them). In this book, I have not been able to advance full-scale arguments in favor of Catholic doctrinal judgments, since to do so would require attending to how particular doctrinal interpretations of Scripture arise from within "the entirety of Christian faith and life," the entirety of the biblically warranted modes of biblical reasoning. By and large, I have only been able to set forth some biblical texts that in my view show that the church-dividing controversies between Catholics and Protestants cannot be a matter of one side holding that the other side is simply unbiblical.

In his 2003 book *The Heart of Christianity: Rediscovering a Life of Faith*, the late biblical scholar Marcus Borg asks: "What is the heart of Christianity? What does it mean to be a Christian today?"[6] He contrasts an older answer to this question with the answer that he himself gives. The older answer, he observes, "sees Christianity as grounded in divine authority," so that "the Bible is true *because* it comes from God."[7] The answer that Borg himself gives, which he calls "the emerging paradigm" and which is also known as liberal Christianity (which has Protestant and Catholic forms), is that Christianity is a human construct in response to experiences of the sacred. For Borg, we cannot now know the "flesh-and-blood Jesus" who lived and died in ancient Israel, but we can affirm that "Jesus continued to be experienced by his followers after his death as a divine reality of the present, and that such experiences continue to happen today."[8] In my view, by contrast, the gospel of Jesus Christ, who speaks to us authoritatively and mercifully

---

6. Marcus J. Borg, *The Heart of Christianity: Rediscovering a Life of Faith* (New York: HarperCollins, 2003), xi.
7. Ibid., 7–8.
8. Ibid., 82.

in Scripture as proclaimed in worship, is radically different from the human spirituality that Borg proposes.

I mention Borg, whose approach is replicated by numerous liberal Catholic and Protestant theologians today, in order to indicate why I consider it so important to work together with Protestants who, sharing my commitment to divine revelation and the Holy Spirit's inspiration of Scripture, seek modes of biblical reasoning that are rooted in the truth that the God of Israel, the Creator, has "sent the Son into the world, not to condemn the world, but that the world might be saved through him" (John 3:17). If Protestants who agree with the teaching of the early church on Christ and the Trinity find my biblical reflections unhelpful, then perhaps they reject my account of the range of biblically warranted modes of biblical reasoning; or perhaps they do not think that the biblical texts I cite in my biblical reflections apply sufficient pressure in the direction of the doctrinal judgments that Catholics affirm. But so long as we share a view of the gospel as divine revelation rather than solely a human construct, we can discuss together what modes of biblical reasoning and associated biblical texts *are* warranted by Scripture for the task of the church's doctrinal teaching.

In the meantime, as we seek to hear "the Spirit of truth" (John 16:13) with an ever greater faith, hope, and love, let us urgently and with repentance proclaim the gospel of Jesus Christ to our Christian communities and our world, broken by sin and death, and in deep need of the everlasting beauty and wisdom of "Emmanuel . . . God with us" (Matt 1:23).

A MERE PROTESTANT RESPONSE

Kevin J. Vanhoozer

INTRODUCTION: ON THE ROAD TO EMMAUS

It is a pleasure and honor to offer response to Matthew Levering's challenging answer to the question, "Was the Reformation a mistake?" I write as a "mere Protestant"[1]—one who celebrates what Protestants have in common—and I can think of no better Roman Catholic conversation partner than Saint Matthew. I say "saint" in all seriousness, in the Pauline sense of fellow believing Christian, a person set apart through faith in Christ to express the heart and mind of Christ by speaking the truth in love and loving the truth we speak.

I hope Matthew will not mind my canonizing him. The *Catechism of the Catholic Church* paragraph 828 associates canonization with proclaiming a saint's "heroic virtue," and to my mind Matt is indeed set apart not only as a prodigious scholar but a saint who embodies the intellectual

---

1. For a fuller explanation, see my *Biblical Authority after Babel: Retrieving the Solas in the Spirit of Mere Protestant Christianity* (Grand Rapids, MI: Brazos, 2016).

and spiritual virtues: honesty, charity, and, most importantly, humility. These qualities are rare in academia, especially as concerns long-standing differences between theological traditions. Five hundred years ago, Protestants and Roman Catholics pronounced mutual anathemas on one another, launched H-bombs (accusations of heresy) at one another and followed up with literal conflagrations (burnings at the stake).

Matthew epitomizes the best kind of interlocutor: one who listens before he speaks. It is telling that he devotes almost half of his book to listening to Luther. This is entirely in character. As a longtime member of Evangelicals and Catholics Together, he has listened patiently for years. For the past ten years alongside Hans Boersma, he has codirected the Center for Catholic-Evangelical Dialogue (now the Paradosis Center) and, in addition, is part of the steering committee of the Chicago Theological Initiative, which similarly works to create opportunities for dialogue between evangelical Protestants and Roman Catholics on a variety of doctrinal topics and theological themes. It has been my privilege to talk with him, as a fellow pilgrim on the Emmaus road, about those things that happened to Jesus in Jerusalem (Luke 24:13–14).

I have the utmost respect for anyone who is able to listen charitably to other viewpoints and to present arguments for his own position, especially when he presents those arguments as offering for critical review. Such is the case here. Matthew did not have to ask me to provide a response, much less give me the last word! Most authors do not want a critical voice pointing out their every flaw and fallacy (not that such is my intent). Academics suffer from status anxiety too. Yet, "perfect love casts out fear" (1 John 4:18). In the present context, I take this to mean that perfect love of truth casts out or overrides fear of criticism. There is no better test for truth than to submit your opinion to critical examination in open dialogue. All this to say that, when I use the moniker, "Saint Matthew," I mean it.

In the present work, Levering (henceforth I resort to the conventional academic nomenclature) does more than answer his title question about whether the Reformation was a mistake. Where we might have expected a

simple yes or no, he instead gives us something more nuanced: a "No, but..."
and a series of arguments about nine doctrinal matters, each an ingredient in
his cumulative case for viewing Roman Catholicism as "not unbiblical." It is
worth reflecting for a moment on the unspoken connection between his title
and the subtitle. How does showing that Catholic doctrine is not unbiblical
address the question of whether the Reformation was a mistake? Well, if the
Protestant protest can be boiled down to Luther's famous complaint—"I ask
for Scriptures and Eck [and Roman Catholics in general] offers me the
Fathers. I ask for the sun, and he shows me his lanterns. I ask: 'Where is
your Scripture proof?' and he adduces Ambrose and Cyril"—then one way
to say that the Reformers were mistaken in their critique of Rome would
be to give Luther what he wanted. This is what Levering attempts here: he
wants to show that the very same doctrines that the Reformers dismissed as
unbiblical do indeed have biblical legs to stand on.

Not to put too fine (or militaristic) a point on it, but Levering here
uses the Protestants' secret weapon—Scripture—against the Reformers.
This, at least, is how I read his book. He is winsomely engaging evangelicals on their own turf, so to speak, with a view to persuade them
not necessarily to cross the Tiber, but to suggest that doing so may be a
legitimate evangelical option. My response concentrates on what I take
to be the three distinguishing marks of Levering's proposal: its charming
catholic spirit, daring *Protestant strategy*, yet enduring *Roman substance*.[2]

THE REFORMATION AS MISTAKE
OR TRAGIC NECESSITY:
LEVERING'S CATHOLIC SPIRIT

Levering's catholic spirit—by which I mean his irenic and inclusive
tone and desire to converse with the universal church—is evident
right from the start, when he says that he agreed to accept the risk of
answering the question "Was the Reformation a mistake?" because he

---

2. In what follows, I use "Catholic" (with a capital "C") as shorthand for the Roman Catholic
Church, and "catholic" (with a lowercase "c") to mean "universal" or "in keeping with the whole."

wanted to "show appreciation for the love of the Word of God that has been manifested to me by numerous Protestant friends and colleagues" (p. 11). Yes, he has Protestant friends (recall his dedicating this book to Todd Billings, a Reformed theologian) and family members, and it is these that first come to mind when he thinks of the Reformation, which is why he refuses simply to call the Reformation "a mistake."

A Tragic Necessity?

In light of Jesus's prayer for his disciples "that they may all be one" (John 17:21) Levering considers the ecclesial and doctrinal disagreements that divide Roman Catholic and Protestant Christians—and therefore his extended family—to be indeed "tragic" (p. 15). How else should one react to our inability to share the Lord's Supper, especially in light of our common proclamation "one Lord, one faith, one baptism" (Eph 4:5)?

It was the church historian Jaroslav Pelikan who first coined the term "tragic necessity" to describe the Reformation, as a chapter title for his book *The Riddle of Roman Catholicism*.[3] Pelikan wrote the book before Vatican II, before Matthew Levering was even born. Here is how Pelikan explained the tragic necessity: "Roman Catholics agree that it was tragic, because it separated many millions from the true church; but they cannot see that it was really necessary. Protestants agree that it was necessary, because the Roman Church was so corrupt; but they cannot see that it was such a tragedy after all."[4] More recently, Protestant historians Thomas Albert Howard and Mark A. Noll have written, "In the light of 2017, it seems to us that Protestants are duty-bound to try to understand the tragic dimensions of the Reformation. . . . At the same time, Catholics should make the same effort to grasp why Protestants, then and now, felt that the Reformation was necessary."[5]

Diarmaid MacCulloch describes the Reformation somewhat differ-

---

3. Pelikan, *The Riddle of Roman Catholicism* (Nashville: Abingdon, 1959).
4. Ibid., 46.
5. Howard and Noll, eds., *Protestantism after 500 Years*, (New York: Oxford University Press, 2016), 17.

ently in his prize-winning history of the sixteenth century, *Reformation: Europe's House Divided; 1490–1700.*[6] *House divided* is already tragic, but the rhetoric gets worse in his more recent work: "If you study the sixteenth century, you are inevitably present at something like the aftermath of a particularly disastrous car-crash. All around are half-demolished structures, debris, people figuring out how to make sense of lives that have suddenly been transformed."[7] We are living not in the sixteenth but the twenty-first century, however, and probably more has happened in the last fifty years to reshape the Roman Catholic/Protestant division than in the entire four hundred and fifty years that preceded it. For example, since Vatican II there has been a new openness in Rome to non-Catholics and a new concern for biblical interpretation.

In 2005, Mark Noll and Carolyn Nystrom wrote a book that posed the question, *Is the Reformation Over?* They begin by taking stock of how radically the situation has changed since the sixteenth century in their opening chapter, "Things Are Not the Way They Used to Be."[8] One of the big changes, prompted in part by Vatican II, is the renewed interest among Roman Catholics in biblical interpretation. If the Reformation was primarily about being biblical (i.e., *sola scriptura*), does Levering's claim that Catholic doctrine is not unbiblical finally put to rest the issue that prompted Luther's protest? Is the Reformation over, or are we simply over the Reformation and its divisive concern for establishing doctrines biblically? In any case, the pertinent question is not simply historical ("*Was* the Reformation a mistake?") but contemporary (*Is* reformation ongoing and *still* necessary?). We shall return to this question in due course.

Keeping Up with the Catholics

Protestant theologians have sometimes struggled to keep up with all the changes, and Levering's new work may well send them back to

6. MacCulloch, *Reformation: Europe's House Divided; 1490–1700* (New York: Penguin, 2004).

7. Diarmaid MacCulloch, *All Things Made New: The Reformation and Its Legacy* (Oxford: Oxford University Press, 2016), 1.

8. Mark A. Noll and Carolyn Nystrom, *Is the Reformation Over? An Evangelical Assessment of Contemporary Roman Catholicism* (Grand Rapids, MI: Baker Academic, 2005).

the drawing board again, not least in search of new metaphors with which to describe the current situation. G. C. Berkouwer, a Protestant observer at Vatican II, started the ball rolling by describing the "new Catholicism" and its call for *ressourcement*, a return to and appropriation of patristic theology and modes of biblical interpretation.[9]

About the same time, the North American evangelical theologian David Wells wrote his incisive and insightful study *Revolution in Rome*.[10] Wells found himself trying to get his mind around what he came to see was the "divided mind" of Vatican II. On several points, Wells discovered conflicting perspectives, even "mutually incompatible theologies,"[11] the one conservative, the other liberal. Vatican II encouraged not either-or but both-and thinking. Though Wells didn't put it this way, we can: the tension is between a centripetal force that makes everything gravitate towards a Roman center and a centrifugal force that opens out towards a Catholic circumference. To observers like me, then, the burning question is "How far will the *Catholic* Church stay *Roman?*"

A few years later, in the UK, Herbert Carson published his *Dawn or Twilight? A Study of Contemporary Roman Catholicism*.[12] Unlike Wells, Carson read the documents coming out of Vatican II with a certain hermeneutic of suspicion, arguing that the appearance of change hid an underlying unchanging reality. In a later work, he framed his concern in this way: "The tone may be friendlier, and the presentation more acceptable to late twentieth-century readers, yet the decrees of Trent are still there."[13]

A few evangelicals did not simply write about Roman Catholicism

---

9. See Berkouwer, *The Second Vatican Council and the New Catholicism* (Grand Rapids, MI: Eerdmans 1965).

10. Wells, *Revolution in Rome* (Downers Grove, IL: InterVarsity, 1972). Coincidentally, Carlos Eire describes the sixteenth-century Reformation as a "revolution," that is, a paradigm shift, a change in conceptual worldview, a transitional moment when a people's thinking changes irreversibly (Eire, *Reformations: The Early Modern World, 1450–1650* [New Haven, CT: Yale University Press, 2016], 744).

11. Wells, *Revolution in Rome*, 27.

12. Carson, *Dawn or Twilight? A Study of Contemporary Roman Catholicism* (Leicester: InterVarsity, 1976).

13. Carson, *The Faith of the Vatican* (Darlington, UK: Evangelical, 1996), 13.

but engaged it. For seven years John Stott and others participated in ERCDOM and produced a book, *The Evangelical Roman Catholic Dialogue on Mission, 1977–1984*.[14] The goal was not to bring about organic or structural unity but to exchange views in order to increase mutual understanding, discover common theological ground and, where possible, promote common witness.[15] The participants experienced disagreements, yet they insist that "the walls of our separation do not reach to heaven."[16] Significantly, they acknowledge, "We see in one another 'the fruit of the Spirit'" and thus "between us an initial if incomplete unity."[17] Finally, they insist that by dialogue they mean not a diluting of differences but "a frank and serious conversation . . . in which each side is prepared to listen respectfully to the other, with a view to increased understanding on the part of both."[18]

One of the lesser known but most interesting voices currently engaging Roman Catholicism is that of the Italian evangelical Leonardo De Chirico.[19] His is a cautionary voice that urges evangelicals not to focus on particular points of doctrinal difference only, for to do this is to lose sight of the theological forest for the trees. This is significant, for Levering asks us to do exactly that, by focusing his attention on nine doctrinal trees in particular. The forest—the fundamental structure of the "system" of Roman Catholicism, specifically the way they relate Scripture, church, and tradition in the pattern of theological authority—remains offstage, out of sight.[20]

---

14. Basil Meeking and John Stott, eds., *The Evangelical Roman-Catholic Dialogue on Mission, 1977–1984: A Report* (Exeter, UK: Paternoster, 1986).

15. Ibid., 81–82.

16. Ibid., 81.

17. Ibid., 82.

18. Ibid., 86.

19. See esp. De Chirico's doctoral dissertation, now published as *Evangelical Theological Perspectives on Post-Vatican II Roman Catholicism*, Religions and Discourse vol. 19 (Bern, Switzerland: Peter Lang, 2003).

20. De Chirico himself suggests that the real differences are to be found at the structural level, and he identifies two in particular: the way Roman Catholics construe the relationship of nature and grace and the mediatorial role of the institutional Church. Gregg Allison uses this bifocal lens as the hermeneutical framework for his own assessment of Roman Catholicism (see Allison, *Roman Catholic Theology and Practice: An Evangelical Assessment* (Wheaton, IL: Crossway: 2014), 43–66).

If I belabor the point, it is primarily to locate my response to Levering as simply the most recent in a long line of Protestant theologians trying to grapple with the fact of our division, what kind of division it is, and how necessary continuing division is.[21] In particular, the most difficult and painful question concerns the necessity of the ongoing division that prevents Protestants and Roman Catholics from enjoying table fellowship.[22] The apostle Paul appealed to the Corinthian Christians "that there be no divisions among you" (1 Cor 1:10). However, like the Corinthians, present-day Christians are likely to say, "I follow Peter (and his papal successors)," or "I follow Luther," or "I follow Calvin"—to which the only appropriate question is Paul's: "Is Christ divided?" (1 Cor 1:13).

A Catholic Spirit

A catholic spirit marks Levering's work, an admirable openness to friendship with and learning from Christians in other traditions than his own. I take the term "catholic spirit" from John Wesley's sermon of the same name. It reflects his conviction, expressed in *The Character of a Methodist*, that "as to all opinions *which do not strike at the root of Christianity*, we think and let think."[23] In the sermon, Wesley observes that though we each believe our opinions to be true, we cannot be certain that all our opinions are true. He here evinces what one contemporary philosopher terms *epistemic conscientiousness*: "When I am conscientious I will come to believe that other normal, mature

---

21. Perhaps the closest "authorized" evangelical response to Roman Catholicism after Vatican II is the 1986 World Evangelical Fellowship document "Evangelical Perspectives on Roman Catholicism," *Evangelical Review of Theology* 10, no. 4 (1986): 354–64. This document focuses on particular areas of doctrinal disagreement (e.g., Mary; purgatory) and has now been superseded by Gregg Allison's comprehensive *Roman Catholic Theology and Practice* and a book Allison coauthored with Chris Castaldo, *The Unfinished Reformation: What Unites and Divides Catholics and Protestants after 500 Years* (Grand Rapids, MI: Zondervan, 2016).

22. See the policy stated in the *Catechism of the Catholic Church*, 2nd ed. (New York: Doubleday, 1995): "Ecclesial communities derived from the Reformation and separated from the Catholic Church, 'have not preserved the proper reality of the Eucharistic mystery in its fullness, especially because of the absence of the sacrament of Holy Orders.' It is for this reason that, for the Catholic Church, Eucharistic intercommunion with these communities is not possible" (para. 1400).

23. Cited in Albert C. Outler, ed., *John Wesley* (New York: Oxford University Press, 1964), 92.

humans have the same natural desire for truth and the same general powers and capacities that I have."[24] An epistemically conscientious Protestant will include Roman Catholics in the set of "other normal, mature humans" (and vice versa). Wesley appears to be working with a distinction between having saving faith on the one hand and being able adequately to conceptualize it on the other. The main objective of his sermon, however, is to press home the importance of a catholic spirituality: "Though we cannot think alike, may we not love alike? May we not be of one heart, though we are not of one opinion?"[25]

We should not infer that Wesley did not care about sound doctrine, only that he distinguished between essential beliefs and nonessential opinions.[26] This is clear in his remarkable "Letter to a Roman Catholic," written in 1749 to Irish Catholics, where he sets out what true Protestants believe in a kind of expanded version of the Apostles' Creed, and then asks, "Now, do not you yourself approve of this?"[27] Later in the letter he tells his recipients, "I hope to see *you* in heaven" and suggests that if they search their consciences, they will feel the same way about him.[28]

Wesley affirms the importance of individual conscience and the freedom of religion on the grounds that no one can prescribe a particular faith for another. We love God with all our hearts, yet no human can command the heart of another. Doctrine nevertheless matters, because the most important thing is to have one's heart right with God, and no one can please God unless they believe in the Lord Jesus Christ, and certain things about him (Rom 10:9–10; 1 Thess 2:4; Heb 11:6; 1 John 4:15).

What then is a catholic spirit? Wesley insists, first, that it "is not

---

24. Linda Trinkhaus Zagzebski, *Epistemic Authority: A Theory of Trust, Authority, and Autonomy in Belief* (Oxford: Oxford University Press, 2012), 55.

25. Wesley, "Catholic Spirit," in Outler, *John Wesley*, 93.

26. For example, Wesley believes in episcopal church government, but he commends those who in good conscience think the presbyterian form to be better because it is more biblical ("Catholic Spirit," 99).

27. Wesley, "A Letter to a Roman Catholic," in Outler, *John Wesley*, 496.

28. Ibid., 498.

an indifference to *all* opinions."[29] Indeed, unsettledness of thought "is a great curse, not a blessing."[30] Second, it is not indifference as to the form of public worship. Indeed, we are to worship "in spirit and truth" (John 4:24). Stated positively, Wesley's "catholic spirit" is his generosity of spirit to all Christians who have hearts right with God. It is easy to hold opinions; it is far harder to love one's enemies: "Anyone who does not love does not know God, because God is love" (1 John 4:8). The challenge for Roman Catholic/Protestant dialogue is to love one another without becoming indifferent to the truth.

Why This Conversation Feels Different

Luther, Calvin, and Wesley all engaged Roman Catholics in dialogue. In one respect, then, there is nothing new about my Protestant response to Levering. Of course, the historical situation has changed dramatically after five hundred years. These days, Protestants and Roman Catholics are not competing for Western Christianity but allies in the struggle to preserve it from various forces and ideologies like secularization and globalization. When it comes to the big questions of life and worldview—the dignity of human beings, the sanctity of marriage, the ultimacy of the triune God—conservative evangelicals have more in common with orthodox Roman Catholics than with liberal Protestants or, for that matter, health-and-wealth evangelicals who have exchanged the truth of the cross for the lie of worldly prosperity.

In Levering's words, "Luther and Catholics (then and now) are largely playing on the same side" (p. 34). This is certainly true regarding broad worldview issues as well as core orthodox doctrines like the Trinity. Even as it concerns the proclamation of the gospel, confessional Protestant evangelicals are often closer to Roman Catholics than to liberal Protestants or even to some whom profess evangelical faith but teach another (e.g., prosperity) gospel.

In addition to agreement over issues of substance, there also appears

---

29. Wesley, "Catholic Spirit," in Outler, *John Wesley*, 101.
30. Ibid., 102.

to be a move towards the methodological middle. Post–Vatican II Roman Catholics, especially those like Henri de Lubac who want to retrieve patristic modes of biblical interpretation, have rediscovered Scripture as the soul of theology, while evangelicals like Timothy George and Alister McGrath have stressed the importance of reclaiming the great Christian tradition. The result of the new Roman Catholic interest in biblical interpretation is on full display in the present book.

And yet, for reasons that I trust will become apparent in the next section, this conversation feels different from the kind of conversations evangelicals typically have in various *Three Views* or *Four Views* books. I am not convinced that the positions that Levering presents as "not unbiblical" are indeed options for evangelicals. Why not? It has to do less with the particular evidence Levering adduces and the way he handles it than the overarching pattern of theological authority to which he makes tacit appeal. The burden is now on me to explain why "not unbiblical" is not necessarily equivalent to "biblical." Just as two wrongs don't make a right, so a double negative may not necessarily make a positive.

BIBLICAL VS. NOT UNBIBLICAL: LEVERING'S PROTESTANT STRATEGY

We now come to the heart of Levering's proposal: his apparently Protestant strategy to show why Catholic doctrine is not unbiblical. It is important to remember that Levering does not say the Reformation was a mistake, only that the Reformers made mistakes in judging certain Catholic doctrines to be unbiblical.

There is not space in my response to offer a full-orbed response to each of Levering's nine chapters. I could not hope to do each of the issues justice. However, as mentioned previously, I am more interested in the theological forest than I am the particular doctrinal trees. I will not therefore try to respond to each and every chapter. Instead, I want to concentrate on his underlying assumptions and overall approach, namely, his theological method—the way he appeals to Scripture, church, and church tradition to develop and defend doctrinal arguments. If there is a dispute between Protestants and Roman Catholics over Scripture, it primarily concerns not its nature but its proper use and place in the doing of theology. For as we shall see, the real issue is not whether Roman Catholics use the Bible to do theology (they do) or accord it authority (they do), but rather whether they accord Scripture supreme authority in its own interpretation (they don't).

We will begin by examining what Levering says in chapter 1 about who has the authority to say what the Bible means. We then return to the introduction to consider what Levering means by biblical reasoning. This will put us in a better position to evaluate his use of Scripture in arguing for a Catholic understanding of Mary in chapter 2. My consistent aim throughout will be to encourage readers to attend to the way in which Levering appeals to the Bible as one thread in a larger theological tapestry. In this spirit, I conclude my examination of his Protestant strategy with some thoughts on the relationship between being "not unbiblical" and *sola scriptura*. The goal is to clarify his use of Scripture as an element in a broader pattern of theological authority. It is this general pattern of use, not particular interpretations, that Protestants primarily protest.

Who Interprets Scripture according to Scripture and with What Kind of Authority?

Do Protestants and Roman Catholics agree on the doctrine of Scripture? As Levering notes, both agree "that Scripture is God's authoritative Word," though he does not mention that they disagree as to which books ought to be acknowledged as canonical. Roman Catholics include seven more Old Testament books (collectively referred to as the Apocrypha) in the canon than Protestants, a fact borne out by their respective lists of biblical books in confessional and catechetical documents. Levering appeals to two apocryphal books—the Wisdom of Solomon and Sirach—in the "biblical reflection" portion of his chapter on purgatory, perhaps forgetting that such appeals to extracanonical books will fall on deaf Protestant ears.

I nevertheless agree with Levering: the real dispute pertains to the status and interpretation of the Bible in the church. I also agree with his claim that "Scripture teaches that the church is the faithful interpreter of Scripture under the guidance of the Holy Spirit" (p. 35), although we disagree about the referent of "church," the manner of the Spirit's guidance (i.e., does the Spirit primarily guide the bishops or, more narrowly, the magisterium or, more broadly, the whole company of the faithful?), and about the consistency of the church's faithfulness. I wonder, then, whether we disagree about the nature of Scripture in more areas than the canon. Luther affirmed the clarity and sufficiency of Scripture, as Levering rightly points out.

Levering begins his biblical reflection on Scripture with biblical examples of God's people disagreeing about the meaning of God's Word. No argument here: that people disagree about the meaning of God's Word is a tragic phenomenon as old as Eden (Gen 3:1–5). Levering then considers the dissent in the church at Corinth, observing that Paul appeals to his apostolic authority to settle internal disputes. However, as we know from 2 Peter 3:16, even Paul can sometimes be difficult to understand, so unless we are willing to descend into interpretive chaos, *somebody* must be able to articulate the right interpretation of God's Word. Somebody must have say-so (i.e., interpretive authority).

Levering here turns to Acts 15, the famous episode of the Jerusalem Council, where the leaders at the Jerusalem church, led by the Spirit, issue an authoritative decree resolving an issue on which there had been "no small dissension and debate" (Acts 15:2), namely, whether to require the circumcision of Gentile converts. Both Protestants and Roman Catholics acknowledge the canonical status of Acts 15, but they derive different morals from it. Levering concludes that "it is clear that God does not intend for Scripture to function without the ability of the church's leaders to determine authoritatively what Scripture means on a disputed point" (p. 51). It is not entirely clear to me how he gets there. After all, Acts 15 is narrative description, not doctrinal prescription. Not everything that happens in the narratives of Acts is necessarily authoritative for the church today (e.g., speaking in tongues in Acts 2). Furthermore, even if it was authoritative, Acts 15:6 indicates that the result was a joint decision of the apostles and the elders, and 15:22 adds "with the whole church" (interestingly, the NRSV translates the phrase "with the consent of the whole church"). In short, Acts 15 provides clearer support for the kind of conciliarism that the Reformers supported than it does for the Roman magisterium.[31]

For Levering, what stands out in the pattern of interpretive authority is the role of the church leaders, whose interpretations "are binding for the whole people of God under the guidance of the Holy Spirit" (p. 52). As it stands, the claim is underdetermined because Levering does not say who those church leaders are. Some Protestant denominations ordain bishops too. However, though Paul teaches that the ascended Christ appoints pastors and teachers as gifts to the church for its edification (Eph 4:11–12), it is not clear that it is the leaders rather than the whole church whom the Spirit is leading into all truth (John 16:13). Again, Acts 15 mentions elders and "the whole church" as well as the apostles.

I agree with Levering that the risen Christ appoints pastors who have a certain authority to lead the church, but I do not think he has made a biblical case for either apostolic succession in general or for identifying the right line of succession with Roman Catholic bishops only. Nor has he made a biblical case that the office of apostle continues after the first generation of apostles (for Protestants "apostolic authority" refers to the writing of the apostles in the New Testament, not a continuing teaching office). There are Methodist, Lutheran, and Anglican bishops in Protestant churches, and the Orthodox Church claims a pedigree as

---

31. On the Reformers' positive perspective on the role of church councils in the pattern of interpretive authority, see my *Biblical Authority after Babel*, 132–36. Note, too, that it is James rather than Peter that casts what appears to be the deciding vote at the Jerusalem Council (Acts 15:13–21).

ancient as that of the Roman Catholic Church. Levering has therefore not convinced me that the teaching authority subsists in the Roman line of bishops alone. In sum, the idea that interpretive authority has been vouchsafed to the Roman Catholic Church only is not biblical.

Protestants appeal to Acts 15 to argue that biblical interpretation is the privilege and responsibility of the whole church, guided by the Holy Spirit and instructed by those whom the church recognizes as having the gifts commensurate with the offices of pastor, elder, bishop, and teacher. I shall return towards the end of my response to the admittedly difficult question about the locus of interpretive authority, often thought to be the Achilles' heel of Protestantism.

Being Biblical and Reasoning Biblically

For years now I have asked myself the question, what does it mean to be biblical? Now, thanks to Levering's spirited defense of Catholic doctrine, I need to ask, what does it mean *not* to be *un*biblical? It's an odd construction: "not unbiblical." In terms of formal logic, to be "not un-*p*" is equivalent to being *p*. Yet again I must ask, does being biblical merely mean being not unbiblical? Protestants want to say something more positive and robust.

Let me therefore suggest, as a preliminary definition, that being biblical means doing theology "according to" or "in accordance with" (Gk. *kata* plus the accusative) the Scriptures (1 Cor 15:3). To speak "in accordance with" Scripture involves more than simply using it. As is well known, the heretics in the early church all had their preferred "proof texts"—particular verses that seemed to support their false teaching. Being biblical in the sense I intend therefore involves more than simply using the text, particularly if by "using" we mean putting the text to work for one's own purposes rather than the text's!

We should also distinguish between what we might name—after the two principles of worship—the "normative" and the "regulative" principle of being biblical. According to the normative principle, a teaching is biblical as long as it is not explicitly prohibited by Scripture.

According to the regulative principle, a teaching is biblical only if it is explicitly taught in Scripture. I take it then when Levering says, "not unbiblical," he has the normative principle in mind, insofar as he is arguing that Catholic doctrine is allowed (not forbidden) by Scripture, not that it is required. This is the thrust of his biblical reflections: that the doctrine under consideration has enough biblical grounds for being judged *not contrary* to Scripture. I note in passing that those who set the bar low have a better chance of clearing it.[32]

Protestants typically set the biblical bar higher, adopting something like the regulative principle by asking, "Where stands it written?" That it is written, or that it can be deduced from what has been written, stands as a *sine qua non* in Protestant theology. While Protestant exegetes are happy to use extrabiblical evidence to understand the context of the biblical authors, Protestant theologians resist using extrabiblical sources to supplement what Scripture says, and they are particularly loath to view any extrabiblical sources, even if they come from the apostles themselves, as revelatory. Put differently, Protestants deny that tradition is a source of supplementary revealed teaching. It does not follow, however, that there is no place for tradition in the Protestant pattern of authority. As we shall see below, there is.[33]

Everything depends on what Levering means by Catholic "modes of biblical reasoning." Thankfully, he tells us. Moreover, he rightly identifies the sticking point, namely, "what counts as biblical evidence for a doctrinal judgment of truth" (p. 20). The central claim Levering

---

32. It is worth noting that the Roman Catholic Church goes further, insisting that its interpretation of Scripture is not simply one option among many but the correct and authoritative reading. This mistakenly confuses what Christians *may* believe on the basis of Scripture (albeit sometimes with slim scriptural evidence) with what they *must* believe. It is a costly category mistake.

33. Heiko A. Oberman distinguishes the position that there is a second source of authoritative revelation ("Tradition II") from the view of most church fathers that apostolic tradition transmits the same revelatory content as contained in Scripture ("Tradition I"). See Oberman, *Forerunners of the Reformation: The Shape of Late Medieval Thought*, trans. Paul L. Nyhus (London: Lutterworth, 1967), 58. Anthony N. S. Lane further distinguishes between a "coincidence" view that assumes tradition always gets it right (what I call "strong" Tradition I) and an "ancillary view" that treats tradition as a helpful external guide (Tradition I) in Lane, "Scripture, Tradition, and Church: An Historical Survey," *Vox Evangelica* 9 (1975), 37–55. My own position, similar to that of the Reformers, is the ancillary view.

makes about the way Catholics are biblical is this: "Catholic doctrine arises from Scripture, but it does so through a liturgically inflected and communal process of 'thinking with' Scripture in ways that cannot be reduced to an appeal to biblical texts" (p. 20) By implication, Levering suggests that Protestants "think about" Scripture apart from this liturgically inflected and communal process, as if the paradigm Protestant interpreter was an individual at home in his or her study. Note that he doesn't say this about Protestants (he is far too polite), but he doesn't have to—even many Protestants think about the priesthood of the believer in something like this fashion.

Levering's key point is that biblical reasoning involves more than making sense of the text's language and literature, as if one could isolate the Bible as a textbook from the community in which it lives and moves and has its being, the church. It is a most important point, which even Protestants have made. For example, Stanley Hauerwas denies "that the text of the Scripture makes sense separate from a Church that gives it sense."[34] However, it is one thing to say that the Bible makes sense in the *context* of the believing community, quite another to say that the community *gives* the Bible its sense, and something else again to insist that the Bible makes sense *only in communities that are in communion with the Church of Rome.* I affirm the first option, not the second or third.

Levering is entirely correct to call attention to the importance of reading Scripture in the context of the believing and worshiping community of believers. Here too, however, everything depends on how we describe the church's interpretive activity. For example, is it more appropriate to describe the church as a people of the book (i.e., Luther's "creature of the Word") or Scripture as the book of the people (i.e., creature of the church)? Will the real authorizing agency please stand up?

Levering adduces several biblical examples of the people of God learning about the Word of God in community—from Ezra and Nehemiah to the Jerusalem Council and the disciples at Emmaus. But

---

34. Hauerwas, *Unleashing the Scriptures: Freeing the Bible from Captivity to America* (Nashville: Abingdon, 1993), 27.

this does not mean that the people of God are the "living 'subjects' of God's Word in history" (p. 25). From a Protestant perspective, the active subjects and communicative agents in handing on God's Word are first and foremost the Son and Spirit. The church is an element in this economy of light; it is not the primary filament. As Levering himself acknowledges, it is the Spirit who guides the church into all truth. Just "what" or "who" the church is remains the real contentious issue.

Back to biblical reasoning. For Levering, the salient point is that the way the church read Scripture in the past is often out of sync with the way modern biblical scholars read Scripture today. Perhaps he thinks the modern grammatical-historical way of reading the Bible for its literal sense ultimately derives from the Reformers. Hence his contrast between reading the Bible to find historical or logical proofs (the Protestant way?) and participating in the "living liturgical community" (p. 28, 111) that receives and ponders the Word of God.[35] It is by participating in this liturgical community, Levering suggests, that the church discerns the mystery behind the history, that is, the figural significance of biblical texts. It is this liturgical mode of reasoning (also known as doctrinal development) that, for Levering, renders Catholic doctrine "not unbiblical."[36]

A Case Study in Biblical Reasoning: Marian Dogma

I turn now from describing Levering's mode of biblical reasoning in the abstract to examining its operation as it is manifest in his chapter on Mary. What does it mean to be biblical when it comes to the study of Mary (Mariology)? In particular, how does the Catholic mode of biblical reasoning move from the biblical account of Mary to the dogmas of her immaculate conception (1854) and bodily assumption (1950)?

---

35. To be fair, he acknowledges that Protestants value communal modes of reasoning too.
36. Of course, just as Protestants must deal with the reality of rival biblical interpretations, Roman Catholics must deal with the reality of rival liturgical traditions (e.g., Orthodox, Lutheran, Reformed, etc.).

Levering has authored an entire book on the latter doctrine and is familiar with the typical Protestant objections, whether these be from the Reformers themselves, or Karl Barth, or present-day evangelicals.[37] Levering points out that the difference of opinion cannot be reduced to Scripture vs. Tradition.[38] For most post–Vatican II Catholics, Tradition is not a second *source* of revelation as much as the *stream* of Scripture's legitimate interpretation as it has flowed through time in the church: "The key questions, then, have to do not so much with Tradition per se but rather with the ways in which the Bible can be legitimately interpreted, what counts as biblical evidence, and the role of the Holy Spirit in the Church."[39] This is the key point for Levering: Tradition is itself the mode of biblical reasoning. For Protestants, the crucial question is whether Scripture can trump the Tradition of its ecclesial interpretation [**spoiler alert**: Yes, it can!].

Levering himself proves a biblically literate Catholic thinker. His biblical reflection on Mary goes far beyond proof texting, displaying an impressive grasp of biblical-theological themes that span the Testaments and unite redemptive history, including the theme of God-fearing mothers who wait upon the Lord for the gift of a child. Mary stands at the zenith of these mothers of God's covenant people. Levering sees Mary as the fulfillment of Israel, Isaiah's "daughter of Zion" from whom salvation comes (Isa 62:11). Moreover, as the paradigm of the faithful disciple, Mary is the embodiment of the church as well as Israel. As the mother of Jesus and therefore the bringer of salvation, Mary's story is the hinge between the old and new covenants and stands at the center of redemptive history. In Levering's words, "No role in salvation history, other than that of Jesus, is more exalted or decisive" (p. 63).

No one disputes the significance of Mary's role in the story of

---

37. See Matthew Levering, *Mary's Bodily Assumption* (Notre Dame, IN: University of Notre Dame Press, 2015).

38. Tradition with a capital "T" here refers to the Roman Catholic teaching that Tradition and Scripture are two distinct, equally authoritative modes of communicating the one Word of God: "Sacred Tradition and Sacred Scripture make up a single sacred deposit of the Word of God" (*Dei Verbum*, 10, as cited in *Catechism of the Catholic Church*, 97).

39. Levering, *Mary's Bodily Assumption*, 7.

Jesus. If Protestants have been reluctant to celebrate Mary, that is largely out of a concern to respect the literal sense of Scripture that is the sole basis for doctrine, and for fear of encouraging an exaggerated Marian devotion. Several recent Protestant documents affirm Mary as a model of faithful discipleship.[40] So far, so biblical. The question is how Catholics employ a mode of biblical reasoning to arrive at the aforementioned dogmas.

After the account of Jesus's birth, there are relatively few explicit biblical statements about Mary the mother of Jesus. Tellingly, however, Levering suggests that typology is "in" the literal sense, and he gets considerable theological mileage from an analysis of the term "woman." For example, from Jesus's words from the cross to Mary and the beloved disciple in John 19:26–27 ("Woman, behold your son!"; "Behold, your mother!"), he concludes that Mary is the "mother" of all disciples, and the church. Yet none of the Synoptic Gospels reports this episode, nor is it self-evident that Jesus meant anything more than that he was committing his mother to the disciple's care. The disciple certainly understood Jesus's words in that way because "from that hour the disciple took her to his own home" (John 19:27). It does not logically follow that *all* disciples "should imitate the beloved disciple by recognizing Mary as their mother" (p. 66), as Levering claims.

Levering also observes that Mary "literally follows Jesus to the cross" (p. 66). Yes, others were also present, but according to Levering her presence was required as part of her unique vocation as Jesus's mother. Further, he says that Mary's love "was powerful enough to suffer with Jesus." Yet the plain sense of the text says no more of her suffering than would be appropriate of any mother who had to witness the capital punishment of her child, which is what I think Simeon is prophesying (Luke 2:34–35).

---

40. See, *inter alia*, Scot McKnight, *The Real Mary: Why Evangelical Christians Can Embrace the Mother of Jesus* (Brewster, MA: Paraclete, 2007); Tim Perry, *Mary for Evangelicals: Toward an Understanding of the Mother of Our Lord* (Downers Grove, IL: InterVarsity, 2006); Perry, "An Evangelical Word to Catholics" in Timothy George and Thomas G. Guarino, eds., *Evangelicals and Catholics Together at Twenty* (Grand Rapids, MI: Brazos, 2015), 119–29).

Levering's most elaborate textual weaving pertains to Jesus calling Mary "woman" in John 2:4 and 19:26, at Cana and the cross, each an occasion for the purification of the people, because the water Jesus changed into wine at Cana would normally have been used for Jewish rites of purification (John 2:6), and the blood shed on the cross was shed for the remission of sin. Levering then links Jesus's use of "woman" to Genesis 3:2, where Eve is simply called "the woman." Whereas death came from the first "woman," life comes from Mary, the new Eve. Mary is thus the mother of the new covenant who participates in the work of redemption accomplished on the cross. Mary is also the "woman" of Revelation 12:1 who is beset by a dragon just as she is on the verge of childbirth (the child is Christ, and perhaps Christians). Levering never says that Mary's suffering was salvific, but he does insist that just as she participated in Jesus's incarnation, "her suffering at the foot of the cross was uniquely united with her Son's suffering" (p. 71).

A final typological connection allows Levering to make a connection between the Bible and the doctrine of Mary's bodily assumption, namely, the idea that she is in heaven with Jesus with a glorified body. Revelation 12:1 depicts the "woman" in heaven, with a crown of twelve stars. It doesn't really matter whether the twelve stars represent the tribes of Israel or Jesus's apostles, for by this time Mary is everywoman: the old Israel; the new Eve; the Mother of God, Jesus, and the church. For our purposes, however, what is interesting is Levering's suggestion that the woman in heaven (Mary) is with her Son not simply as a disembodied soul, but rather as an embodied participant in the new resurrection order. The Catholic doctrine of Mary's bodily assumption is not unbiblical, says Levering, for it is the conclusion of a chain of typological connections.[41]

---

41. To be more precise, Levering's concatenation of "woman" texts falls into the category of "homological" types, as opposed to "christological" or "tropological." Homological types are less defined than the other two categories, which makes them "difficult to grab hold of, but it also makes them flexible" (Benjamin J. Ribbens, "Typology of Types: Typology in Dialogue," *Journal of Theological Interpretation of Scripture* 5 [2011]: 93).

A chain is only as strong as its weakest link.[42] Perhaps this is why, in his book on Mary's bodily assumption, Levering acknowledges that typological exegesis cannot stand on its own, for it is prone to fanciful exaggerations. Legitimate typology must attest God's saving power in Christ (no problem here) "and must have its truth confirmed liturgically and theologically by the community of believers (the Church) guided by the Holy Spirit."[43] Once again, the assumption appears to be that it is the Roman community that has been so guided. But why should we assume that?

Why Catholics Never Sing Sola for Their Fathers

As we have seen, Levering argues that the Marian doctrines like bodily assumption are not unbiblical because they are the result of the Catholic Church's typological mode of biblical reasoning. How should Protestants evaluate Levering's Protestant strategy to establish Catholic doctrine?[44] Let me make three summary points in response.

First, the real issue when Protestants and Catholics come to differing biblical interpretations is the locus of authority. I find Levering's case for Mary as the new Eve to be creative and worthy of a deeper examination than I can offer here, but prima facie I think his argument enjoys only a fairly low canonical plausibility. The intertextual connections are weak, far too weak in my opinion to serve as the basis for official Catholic dogma (or to deem those who deny it heretical), and the emphasis that Mary participates in the saving work of Christ cuts against the grain of the biblical text. For Catholics, however, the true meaning of Scripture is a joint product of the biblical text and the church's developing tradition of reading it. The typological connections that suggest Mary is the new Eve, or the mother of the church, or queen of heaven, are true

---

42. In my view, the weakest link in Levering's typological chain is his attempt to connect the "woman" in heaven (Rev 12:1) with the "ark" within God's heavenly temple (Rev 11:19). If the ark of the covenant that contained the Word of God on two tablets of stone is a type of Mary's womb, one might have expected twins!

43. Levering, *Mary's Bodily Assumption*, 110.

44. For a point-by-point evangelical evaluation, see Allison, *Roman Catholic Theology and Practice*, 135–43, 202–5.

because the church has said they are, not because they are clear biblical teachings. So, when Levering suggests that Marian dogma is biblical, "biblical" here means "how Catholics have come to read the Bible in the tradition of the church." Catholic doctrine is not unbiblical in the sense of "not being directly contrary to Scripture," yet at crucial points it does appear *suprabiblical,* in the sense of supplementing what the Bible directly teaches (or what is directly implied) with ideas derived from somewhere else.[45] For Protestants, the church's say-so does not make it so. What is *not* biblical, therefore, is requiring Christians to affirm doctrine that simply *may* (or may not!) be biblical. The bodily assumption of Mary is thus an example of premature dogmafication.

Second, *sola scriptura*—the principle that Scripture alone is the only infallible authority and proper ground for establishing doctrine—gives rise to a distinct mode of biblical reasoning. This is not the place to set forth a complete theological method and hermeneutic, but I do want to argue that *sola scriptura* (a) should not be identified with naive biblicism and (b) involves more than being "not unbiblical."[46] *Sola scriptura* names not simply a principle but a pattern of theological authority.[47] The church has a place in this pattern, as does church tradition, but it is ministerial rather than magisterial, fallible rather than infallible. In a nutshell, *sola scriptura* means that the Bible alone authorizes doctrine, yet the Bible that authorizes is not alone, for the Spirit who speaks in and through Scripture does not do so independently of the church's tradition and teaching ministry. Everything depends on how these things are placed in the pattern of authority, a point to which I shall return in the conclusion.

---

45. I would argue that the doctrine of the Trinity, in contrast to the Marian dogmas, is "directly implied" by what Scripture explicitly says, even if it took the church three hundred years to articulate it. See further Fred Sanders, *The Triune God* (Grand Rapids, MI: Zondervan, 2016), esp. chaps. 6–8.

46. For a critique of naive biblicism, see Christian Smith, *The Bible Made Impossible: Why Biblicism Is Not a Truly Evangelical Reading of Scripture* (Grand Rapids, MI: Brazos, 2011). While Smith's critical aim is often on target, he fails adequately to distinguish what he calls biblicism and the Reformers' pattern and practice of appealing to biblical authority (i.e., *sola scriptura*).

47. For a fuller exposition of this pattern, see my *Biblical Authority after Babel,* 123–46.

Third, while *sola scriptura* is often thought to be a distinctly *Protestant* mode of biblical reasoning, church fathers like Irenaeus held to something very much like *sola scriptura* too. According to John Behr, an Eastern Orthodox theologian (and thus an impartial judge of Roman Catholic/Protestant disputes), when Irenaeus appealed to tradition as the "canon of truth," he was appealing to the faithful distillation of Scripture's content, which is ultimately Christ: "For Irenaeus, the canon of truth is the embodiment or crystallization of the coherence of Scripture, read as speaking of the Christ who is revealed in the Gospel."[48] Irenaeus insists that Scripture, not the church, is the "pillar and bulwark" of the truth (cf. 1 Tim 3:15), because Scripture is how the apostles handed down their proclamation.[49] What is more, Irenaeus says that it is his gnostic opponents that allege "the truth was not delivered by means of written documents, but through a *viva voce.*"[50] Behr explains that Irenaeus's opponents deny the Scripture's authority and clarity, insisting that they "need to be interpreted in the light of a tradition which is not handed down in writing but orally."[51] Levering is no gnostic, nor does his mode of biblical reasoning rely on tradition conceived as a second source of revelation in addition to Scripture. A case could nevertheless be made that Protestants rather than Catholics are the true heirs of Irenaeus's approach to Scripture and tradition.

Finally, let me make brief mention of John Webster's theological project, and his essay "Biblical Reasoning," as a way of making a Protestant parry of Levering's Catholic thrust. The main strength of Webster's "theological theology" is that it accords pride of place to the triune God's communicative presence and activity. This leads Webster to view Scripture, interpretation, the church, and tradition alike as creaturely elements in a divine economy in which the Son and

---

48. John Behr, *The Formation of Christian Theology*, vol. 1, *The Way to Nicaea* (Crestwood, NY: St. Vladimir's Seminary Press, 2001), 36.

49. Irenaeus, *Adv. Haer.* 3.11.8.

50. Irenaeus, *Adv. Haer.* 3.2.1. English translation from *The Ante-Nicene Fathers*, ed. Alexander Roberts and James Donaldson (New York: Charles Scribner's Sons, 1903), 1:415.

51. Behr, *The Way to Nicaea*, 40.

the Spirit are the primary agents. In this vision, theology's main task is to assist the church to remain faithful to the gospel as Scripture articulates it. The reference point and norm for all the church believes, says, and does is the Word of God written. Hence theology is biblical reasoning: figuring out what the text says (exegetical reasoning) and representing in intelligible concepts what one has heard and understood (dogmatic reasoning).[52]

In a number of seminal essays, Webster eloquently expresses his concern about the tendency of both Roman Catholicism and post-liberal Protestantism to elevate ecclesiology and the practices of the church at the expense of the divine economy and the work of Son and Spirit. In particular, the Roman Catholic *totus Christus*—the idea that Christ (the head) and the church (his body) together make up the "whole Christ"—is especially noteworthy.[53] Webster rightly sees that the church's magisterium—the authority of its teaching office when it comes to interpreting Scripture—is not simply a power play or a concession to social constructivist theories of meaning but rather a dogmatic claim, having to do with the pattern of theological authority. If the church is part of the whole Christ, then it participates in Christ's offices of prophet, priest, and king.

By way of contrast, Webster insists, with most Protestants, on the asymmetry of divine and human action: "God's work and the work of the church are fundamentally distinguished."[54] Jesus Christ himself is prophet, priest, and king. Calvin insists that the church "has Christ as its sole Head."[55] *Totus Christus* blurs the distinction between the head and his body, between the Lord and the church as the domain of his

52. See John Webster, "Biblical Reasoning," in *The Domain of the Word: Scripture and Theological Reason* (London and New York: T&T Clark International, 2012), 115–32.

53. *Catechism of the Catholic Church*, para. 795. See further Kimberly Baker, "Augustine's Doctrine of the *Totus Christus*: Reflecting on the Church as Sacrament of Unity," *Horizons* 37 (2010): 7–35.

54. John Webster, *Word and Church: Essays in Christian Dogmatics* (Edinburgh and New York: T&T Clark, 2001), 196.

55. John Calvin, *Institutes of the Christian Religion*, ed. John T. McNeill, trans. Ford Lewis Battles (Louisville: Westminster John Knox, 1960), IV.6.9.

Word. The salient point is that Levering's mode of biblical reasoning relies on *totus Christus* (i.e., the church participating in Christ's prophetic ministry via the magisterium) whereas Webster's mode of biblical reasoning tries to do justice to *solus Christus*. In Webster's words, "Roman Catholic rejection of *sola scriptura* in favor of Scripture *and* tradition is thus a corollary of a rejection of the ecclesiological implications of *solus Christus*."[56] Beneath the surface skirmishes over scriptural interpretation lies the deeper disagreement over the lordship of Christ and the place of the church in the pattern of interpretive authority.

WHERE THE CONFLICT REALLY LIES: LEVERING'S ROMAN SUBSTANCE

To this point, I have examined only two of Levering's nine chapters. My main purpose in doing so was to set out his key assumptions pertaining to his use of Scripture to establish doctrine. Indeed, I am purposely not taking the bait, for doing so would be to lay out well-worn Protestant arguments about each of these nine doctrines. However, as I mentioned earlier, I don't want these trees to distract me from the forest, by which I mean the overarching framework Levering is here assuming about what it means to be biblical. This framework is the pattern of theological authority in which the church looms large—too large, in my opinion. It is therefore somewhat ironic that, though he has written several chapters pertaining to the church (e.g., the Eucharist, the seven sacraments, monasticism, saints, and papacy), he has not written a chapter on the church per se (i.e., ecclesiology). For this is where the conflict really lies.[57]

Alvin Plantinga's book *Where the Conflict Really Lies: Science, Religion, and Naturalism*[58] works something of a plot twist in the story

---

56. Webster, *Word and Church*, 25.

57. Noll and Nystrom agree: "The central difference that continues to separate evangelicals and Catholics [is] . . . the nature of the church" (*Is the Reformation Over?*, 237).

58. Plantinga, *Where the Conflict Really Lies: Science, Religion, and Naturalism* (Oxford: Oxford University Press, 2011).

of religion and science. The real conflict is not between biblical faith and scientific fact but between scientific explanation and a materialist worldview (metaphysical naturalism). In similar fashion, I want to suggest that the real conflict between Protestants and Roman Catholics is not between Scripture and tradition but between catholicism and one particular tradition (Romanism). What disagreements I still may have with Levering have less to do with his drawing on catholic tradition, much less biblical theology, than they do with the way his underlying Romanism—by which I mean the pattern of theological authority that gives pride of interpretive place to the Roman magisterium— exaggerates the nature and function of the institutional church. There is a parallel between a scientism that reduces readings of the Book of Nature to what accords with materialism, and Romanism that reduces the range of legitimate readings of Scripture to what accords with the magisterium.

Calvin's treatise "On the Necessity of Reforming the Church" (1543) calls attention to two broad areas where Protestants disagree with Rome. Both areas pertain to ecclesiology. The "soul" of the doctrinal matter has to do with the role of the church in salvation: "All our controversies concerning doctrine relate either to the legitimate worship of God, or to the ground of salvation."[59] What Calvin calls the "body" of the disagreement has to do with church government and sacraments. To these two I wish to add a third: the "heart" of the disagreement pertains to interpretive authority and the magisterium. In the Catholic framework of biblical reasoning, all roads—soteriological, ecclesiological, and interpretive—lead *through* Rome.

What the Church Is and Does

Let me begin with some brief comments on the nature and function of the Roman Church. These will help set the context for our engagement with Levering's biblical reflections. Recall, first, that

---

59. John Calvin, "On the Necessity of Reforming the Church," in *Calvin: Theological Treatises*, ed. J. K. S. Reid (Philadelphia: Westminster, 1954), 187.

though Levering does not treat it as a discrete doctrinal item, the church hovers over every chapter insofar as his biblical reflections, and Catholic biblical reasoning generally, arise from the liturgically inflected communal process of the church-thinking-with-Scripture.

Again, while I welcome Levering's exercises in biblical reasoning, especially those that attend to the history of redemption, I have to question some of the conclusions he draws regarding the place of the church in this redemptive history. For example, in the Eucharist the church participates in the union and communion with Christ that his broken body and shed blood on the cross make possible, but when Levering says, "the Eucharist saves us from the punishment of death" (p. 89), I have respectfully to demur. Nor is it the baptismal water alone that unites us with Christ's saving death, but the Holy Spirit through faith in the Word (cf. Gal 2:20). Scripture presents baptism and the Lord's Supper as signs and seals—not the effective (or even instrumental) causes—of salvation. That epithet is reserved for Christ's death and resurrection alone. What is at stake in saying this, of course, is the gospel. What exactly is the good news? That the church makes salvation possible, or that Christ saves? Admittedly, this is a blunt dichotomy, but at least it puts the issue on the table.

Say what you like about Friedrich Schleiermacher, the father of modern liberal theology, but his treatment of the "antithesis" between Protestantism and Roman Catholicism remains insightful: "[Protestantism] makes the individual's relation to the Church dependent on his relation to Christ, while [Roman Catholicism] contrariwise makes the individual's relation to Christ dependent on his relation to the Church."[60] Karl Barth makes a similar point about Roman Catholicism tying the possibility of dogmatics too closely to church tradition, and the agency of Jesus Christ to the agency of the Catholic

---

60. Friedrich Schleiermacher, *The Christian Faith*, ed. H. R. Mackintosh and J. S. Stweart (New York: T&T Clark, 2008), §24, 103. Richard John Neuhaus says something similar: "For the Catholic, faith in Christ and faith in the Church are one act of faith" ("The Catholic Difference," in *Evangelicals and Catholics Together: Toward a Common Mission*, ed. Charles Colson and Richard John Neuhaus [Nashville: Thomas Nelson, 1995], 216).

Church: "Their presupposition is that the being of the Church, Jesus Christ, is no longer the free Lord of its existence, but that He is incorporated into the existence of the Church, and is thus ultimately restricted and conditioned by certain concrete forms of the human understanding of His revelation and of the faith which grasps it."[61]

Leonardo De Chirico (see above) makes what is perhaps the most recent penetrating evangelical criticism of the Catholic concept of the church as a continuation of Christ's incarnation and thus an instrument in mediating grace to fallen nature through the sacraments. He builds on John Stott's brilliant suggestion that "the essentials of evangelicalism may be encapsulated in the combination of the two adverbs *hapax* and *mallon*."[62] To say *hapax* ("once and for all") is to express the finality of God's revelation (word) and redemption (work) in Christ. For example, Jude urges his readers "to contend for the faith that was once for all [*hapax*] delivered to the saints" (Jude 3). Similarly, Paul says that Christ "died to sin, once for all [*ephapax*]" (Rom 6:10; cf. 1 Pet 3:18; Heb 7:27). The Spirit's coming was also *hapax* because the day of Pentecost is unrepeatable, yet the work of the Spirit is not "once for all" but ongoing, "more and more" (*mallon*) as he progressively transforms saints in the image of Christ. For example, Paul commends the church at Thessalonica for their brotherly love, yet urges them to show this love "more and more [*mallon*]" (1 Thess 4:9–10).

De Chirico's contention is that the Roman Catholic theological framework is guilty of a "blurring" of time, namely, the distinction between "once for all" and "more and more": "Roman Catholic ecclesiology rests on the idea of the continuation of the incarnation of the Son of God in his mystical body, that is, the Church."[63] In other words, Roman Catholics view the incarnation in ongoing *mallon* rather than definitive *hapax* terms: "The unique mediation of Christ yields to the

---

61. Karl Barth, *Church Dogmatics* I/1, 2nd ed. (Edinburgh: T&T Clark, 1975), 40.

62. John Stott, *Evangelical Truth: A Personal Plea for Unity, Integrity, and Faithfulness*, rev. ed. (Downers Grove, IL: InterVarsity, 2003), 33.

63. De Chirico, "The Blurring of Time Distinctions in Roman Catholicism," *Themelios* 29/2 (2004): 41.

mediation of the Church."[64] Even the choice of the twelve apostles is no longer "once for all" but "more and more" (i.e., an apostolic succession): "In short, the *hapax* of the time of Christ continues in the *mallon* of the time of the Church."[65] To be precise, the church's time participates in the time of Christ sacramentally. In the words of the *Catechism of the Catholic Church*, "The Church's mission is not an addition to that of Christ and the Holy Spirit, but its sacrament."[66] De Chirico worries that the church participates not only in the incarnation but also in the redemption that was accomplished on the cross: "The *hapax* of Calvary is dissolved in the *mallon* of the Mass."[67] The *Catechism* appears to bear this out: "The sacrifice of Christ and the sacrifice of the Eucharist are *one single sacrifice*."[68] We see, then, that what might seem innocuous at first, this blurring of the time, results in the *totus Christus* whereby Christ and the church make up the "whole Christ's" person and work. It is this whole picture—call it the *totus Vaticanus*—that Protestants think lacks biblical support.

Do Levering's biblical reflections provide any evidence to corroborate this concern, shared by Schleiermacher, Barth, and De Chirico alike, that the Roman Church errs in claiming for herself the mantle that belongs to Christ alone?[69] This is the forest obscured by the trees, the Roman elephant in the room, that we need to bring into sharper focus.

The Church as Sacrament vs. the Material Principle of the Reformation

We can get a better handle on the Catholic Church's sacramental self-conception—its view of its role of mediating grace to sinners and thereby helping them to get right with God—by examining the

---

64. Ibid., 42.
65. Ibid., 43.
66. *Catechism of the Catholic Church*, para. 738.
67. De Chirico, "Blurring of Time," 44.
68. *Catechism of the Catholic Church*, para. 1367 (emphasis original).
69. For an analysis of the claim that the Roman Catholic Church continues the three offices of Christ, see Mark Saucy, "Evangelicals, Catholics, and Orthodox Together? Is the Church the Extension of the Incarnation?" *Journal of the Evangelical Theological Society* 43 (2002): 193–212.

Protestant doctrine of justification vis-à-vis the three Roman *p*'s: pardon, penance, and purgatory.

PARDON AND/OR PERFECTION?

Probably no doctrine is more significant in the history of Protestant/Catholic relations than justification by faith, which Luther called "the principal article of all Christian doctrine."[70] Justification by faith is, in the words of more recent Anglican evangelicals, "the heart and hub, the paradigm and essence, of the whole economy of God's saving grace."[71] De Chirico worries that here, too, the Catholic blurring of time turns the *hapax* of justification—*declared* righteous—into the *mallon* of gradually *becoming* righteous.[72]

Levering has clearly taken the time to listen carefully to Protestant concerns as expressed, rigorously and vigorously, by Luther, including Luther's belief that the church has erred by claiming for itself "what belongs only to Christ" (p. 129). Levering understands the exclusionary force behind *sola fide*: faith alone justifies, not charity or works. And, when he reflects on Paul's account of union with Christ and the gift of forgiveness that accompanies Abraham's simple trust in the promises of God, my Protestant heart is strangely warmed. But then my heart skips a beat when he channels the Council of Trent and asks, "Does the movement of justification change our hearts so that . . . we are *made* truly just and not merely *imputed* to be just?" (p. 133, emphasis mine).[73]

I sympathize with anyone trying to parse the *ordo salutis*. Yet, it is the special gift of the Reformation to the one, holy, apostolic, and catholic church to insist that justification is a *hapax*, a once-for-all declaration by God that "there is therefore now no condemnation for those who are in Christ Jesus" (Rom 8:1). To be sure, Levering has

---

70. Martin Luther, *Commentary on the Epistle to the Galatians* (Cambridge: Hames Clarke, 1953), 143.

71. R. T. Beckwith, G. E. Duffield, and J. I. Packer, *Across the Divide* (Abingdon, UK: Marcham Manor, 1977), 58.

72. De Chirico, "Blurring of Time," 44.

73. Levering does not offer a biblical reflection on the Catholic position that justification is "conferred in Baptism, the sacrament of faith" (*Catechism of the Catholic Church*, para. 1992).

an important point: the *ongoing* transformation of the heart is linked to God's *once-for-all* justifying gift. Evangelicals who think they can have Jesus as Savior but not as Lord could learn a thing or two at this point from Roman Catholics—or from the Reformers themselves. At the same time, I think it is important not to confuse the once-for-all of justification with the process of sanctification. Both have their ground in Christ and our union with Christ by faith through the Spirit, but we should not blur their distinction. The transformation of the heart is the fruit of justification, not its condition: "For we are his workmanship, created in Christ Jesus for good works" (Eph 2:8–10).[74] Justification is the moment of our creation in Christ, by God's declarative fiat; sanctification is the process by which we increasingly become obedient like Christ and produce good works.[75] Hence, we are justified by faith alone, yet the faith that justifies is not alone: "Justification is not *by* works, but neither is it *without works*."[76]

PENANCE AND PURGATORY

According to Roman Catholics, justification is conferred at baptism. The heart is transformed, and is now able to do works of charity and thus improve upon the initial gift of grace. What should we do about sins committed after baptism? Here, I confess, I wish Levering had tried to show why the sacrament of penance, another "liturgical practice,"[77] is not unbiblical. He does briefly mention indulgences granted by the pope "as a participation in the church's treasury of merits, to which

---

74. For a fuller exposition of this point, see Calvin's "Antidote Against the Council of Trent," and A. N. S. Lane, *Justification by Faith in Catholic-Protestant Dialogue: An Evangelical Assessment* (London and New York: T&T Clark Continuum, 2003).

75. Stott makes the same point: "Justification is instantaneous . . . Sanctification, however, is gradual" (*Evangelical Truth*, 79).

76. Tony Lane, *Exploring Christian Doctrine* (London: SPCK, 2013), 196. See further Calvin's response to Cardinal Sadolet on precisely this point: "We deny that good works have any share in justification, but we claim full authority for them in the lives of the righteous. For, if he who has obtained justification possesses Christ, and at the same time Christ never is where his Spirit is not, it is obvious that gratuitous righteousness is necessarily connected with regeneration" (Calvin, "Reply to Sadolet," in *Calvin: Theological Treatises*, 236).

77. *Catechism of the Catholic Church*, para. 1480.

the pope has the 'keys'" (p. 142), and this is a kind of penance.[78] The mention of indulgences occurs in his chapter on purgatory, which is a kind of penance writ large, or rather, postmortem. The point at issue is whether the Bible teaches that sinners have to undergo further punishment despite Christ's finished (i.e., *hapax*) work on the cross. The real issue, to put it starkly, is whether Christ's work is sufficient.[79]

Levering helpfully reminds us that, for Luther, the treasure of the church is not the accumulated merit of Christ and the saints but "the Holy Gospel of the glory and the grace of God."[80] Luther also thought that the true church was where "Christ and His Word" are; everything else is smoke and mirrors, smells and bells. Levering begins his defense of purgatory with a biblical reflection on the state of the soul in the intermediate state after death but before the end-time resurrection, when it is "away from the body" but "at home with the Lord." Levering is more confident than I am about the extent to which Scripture enables us to know much about the intermediate state and what the saints are doing in it. I am particularly unsure about the biblical grounding of the notion that the rewards of saints who have passed on can be shared with both the living and the dead.

Levering wisely refrains from appealing to 2 Maccabees to support the doctrine of purgatory, as Protestants do not acknowledge it as canonical. He instead appeals to 1 Corinthians 3:10–14 and the idea that those whose work falls short will be saved "but only as through fire." Here is his key premise: "Christ has paid the penalty of sin and has perfectly forgiven us, but we nonetheless must go through the penitential experience of suffering and death so as to be fully configured to him in love" (p. 154). This makes sense, I submit, only if one assumes that justification includes actually becoming holy (i.e., inner transformation). Protestants read 1 Corinthians 3 as referring not to

---

78. See the *Catechism of the Catholic Church*, para. 1478.
79. See further Stephen Wellum, *Christ Alone: The Uniqueness of Jesus as Savior* (Grand Rapids, MI: Zondervan, 2017), ch. 10, "The Sufficiency of Christ: The Reformation's Disagreement with Rome."
80. Luther, "The Ninety-five Theses," in *Martin Luther: Selections*, thesis 62 (p. 496).

making people righteous so that they merit the reward *of* heaven, but of evaluating their earthly works for the sake of determining their rewards *in* heaven. Furthermore, to say that the merits of the saints are necessary is tacitly to deny the infinity of Christ's merits and the sufficiency of his work. In contrast, the Reformation doctrine of justification, whereby God declares there is no condemnation for those in Christ because his infinite merits are imputed to them, "renders purgatory useless."[81]

The Church as Interpretive Authority vs. the Formal Principle of the Reformation

We come now to the heart of the matter, namely, the Reformers' concern to put the church in its correct place in the pattern of theological authority. *Sola scriptura* is partly exclusionary, insisting that there can be no other locus of magisterial authority (i.e., Scripture, not the church), yet it is also exclamatory, testifying to the authority of the Spirit speaking in the Scriptures to the whole church. Here, too, we need to call attention to temporal drift, namely, the tendency of the Roman Church to say that its living tradition "participates" in the dynamic time of revelation. To quote De Chirico once more, "The *hapax* sense of biblical revelation is opened up to being integrated with tradition that is mediated by the Magisterium."[82] It is worth noting that the Latin term *pontifex,* from which we get the English term *pope,* means "bridge builder."

Levering appropriately concludes his book by considering the papacy, probably the single most visible and concentrated point of Protestant/Catholic dispute. He is aware but apparently undeterred by the checkered history of the papacy, though it is not entirely clear how, given this history, he can then claim that the papacy is "one of the ways in which the church's ability to make unified doctrinal judgments is assured" (p. 172). Luther objected precisely to the pope's appropriating rightful say-so about the meaning of Scripture to the

---

81. Allison, *Roman Catholic Theology and Practice,* 219.
82. De Chirico, "The Blurring of Time," 45.

hierarchical institution of the church at Rome. What better way to rebut Luther than to establish the papal primacy by Scripture alone—if such a thing can be done? Levering boldly makes the effort, giving it the old college (of cardinals) try . . .

The focus of Levering's biblical reasoning is the apostle Peter in his capacity "as an instrument of unity in the church" (p. 172).[83] Peter's confession and Jesus's response to it—"You are Peter, and on this rock I will build my church" (Matt 16:18)—obviously loom large in Levering's account.[84] It is a text that has long been tugged in the interpretive war between Protestants and Catholics over the papacy. Interestingly, Levering adds "Rock" after Peter (p. 178), thereby making transparent the connection between Peter and the "rock" on which Jesus will build his church. The problem is that the two words are not identical. Peter's name in Greek (*Petros*) could be translated "a loose stone" or "piece of rock," whereas *petra* means "a (mass of) rock." The Gospel of Matthew has used this latter term before, when Jesus says, "Everyone then who hears these words of mine and does them will be like a wise man who built his house on the rock [*petran*]" (Matt 7:24). The suggestion, then, is that the rock is not Peter himself but the truth of Jesus's teaching that he is the Christ that Peter confesses. One does not build a church upon a loose stone, much less a loose cannon (remember Peter's denial), but one can build a church on Jesus's preaching and teaching and on the prophets and apostles that attest it (Eph 2:20).

We need to look elsewhere in the New Testament to round out the biblical view of Peter.[85] Jesus tells Peter, "I have prayed for you that your faith may not fail. And when you have turned again, strengthen your

---

83. Ironically, my college mentor, Robert Gundry, recently published a monograph arguing from a close reading that Matthew's Gospel consistently portrays Peter as a *false* disciple! See Gundry, *Peter: False Disciple and Apostate according to Saint Matthew* (Grand Rapids, MI: Eerdmans, 2015).

84. For a survey of interpretations of this passage, see Oscar Cullmann, *Peter: Disciples, Apostle, Martyr. A Historical and Theological Study* (Philadelphia: Westminster, 1962).

85. See further Larry R. Helyer, *The Life and Witness of Peter* (Downers Grove, IL: IVP Academic, 2012); and Markus Bockmuehl, *Simon Peter in Scripture and Memory: The New Testament Apostle in the Early Church* (Grand Rapids, MI: Baker Academic, 2012).

brothers" (Luke 22:31–32). The context is Peter's imminent betrayal of his Lord, and Jesus wants Peter to know that not only will he forgive Peter but he is counting on Peter to minister to the other apostles. If Luke's intent was to "authorize" Peter as first among equals, it is odd that in volume 2 (Acts) Peter gives way to the apostle Paul. Even more telling is the episode in Galatians 2 where Paul recalls his having to stage an intervention because of Peter's failure to preserve the gospel in the face of the circumcision party. Though Peter had been eating with Gentile believers in Antioch, certain emissaries from Jerusalem appear to have intimidated him, because afterwards he separated himself from them. Paul says that when he came to Antioch, "I opposed him [Peter] to his face, because he stood condemned" (Gal 2:11). Peter was the leader, all right, but not in a good sense: "And the rest of the Jews acted hypocritically along with him" (Gal 2:13).[86] Levering acknowledges that popes may betray Jesus, as Peter did, yet "they are preserved from corrupting the gospel" (p. 186). Yet Paul's judgment is unequivocal. Peter's conduct "was not in step with the truth of the gospel" (Gal 2:14).

We must remember Peter's depiction in Matthew and Luke when we turn to his portrayal in the Fourth Gospel. When Jesus commands Peter to "Tend my sheep" (John 21:16), it is likely that he is speaking to Peter as a representative of all fallible church leaders. Again, in Acts 13 Paul supersedes Peter, becoming the focus of the rest of the book.[87] Moreover, though Matthew 16:19 seems to indicate Peter as the recipient of the "keys of the kingdom of heaven," in John 20:23 Jesus gives the ability to forgive sins (which is what the keys allow one to do) to the disciples collectively.[88] Indeed, later in the book of Acts Paul tells

---

86. Levering briefly treats this passage, acknowledges Paul's authority, but says that Peter's primary mission remains of preaching "the gospel to the circumcised" (Gal 2:7). If this is so, then one wonders why Paul, rather than Peter, is not the vicar of Christ, particularly in light of his mission to preach the gospel to the Gentiles.

87. Note, too, that Paul explicitly says he received the gospel, and his apostolic authority, "not . . . from any man . . . but . . . through a revelation of Jesus Christ" (Gal 1:12), and that Jesus appointed Paul, not Peter, as apostle to the Gentiles (Rom 11:13; 1 Tim 2:7).

88. For a fuller exposition and evaluation of the differences between Roman Catholic and Protestant views of the keys of the kingdom, see my *Biblical Authority after Babel*, 168–74.

the elders of the church in Ephesus that the Holy Spirit has made them guardians "to feed the church" (Acts 20:28 KJV). There is no explicit biblical evidence that Jesus singled out Peter to be the steward in the eschatological household of the Lord or charged him with preserving its visible unity. As previously noted, Peter failed miserably in this very charge at Antioch and had to be corrected by Paul.

From another angle, there is biblical evidence that unity does not always require someone to personify it. Israel was a united twelve-tribe confederacy under Yahweh. Their request for a king—a single individual who would visibly represent and embody their unity—was prompted by a desire to be "like all the nations" (1 Sam 8:5), yet it displeased Samuel and the Lord (1 Sam 8:6–9). Like Israel's kings, the popes are symbols and guarantors of the visible unity of the Catholic Church. The church is "catholic" (universal) yet one, centered on Rome and the papacy. The big Catholic picture—the forest that embraces the doctrinal trees—is that the one true church of Jesus Christ "subsists in" the Church of Rome.[89] Divine authority "subsists in" Rome as well, to the extent that the dogma of papal infallibility underwrites the Magisterium (teaching authority) of the church: "The task of giving an authentic interpretation of the Word of God . . . has been entrusted to the living teaching office of the Church alone."[90] Or, as Protestants might paraphrase this statement of the Roman pattern of authority, "outside the Church there is no authorization."[91]

In his conclusion, Levering appeals to the sufficiency of Scripture to argue for its insufficiency, that is, for the necessity of preserving "a continuity in the transmission (*traditio*) of scriptural truth" (p. 189–90). In an important sense, I agree. Even "Scripture interprets Scripture" is not an isolated principle of authority but shorthand for a broader

---

89. For an informed evangelical analysis and evaluation, see further Leonardo De Chirico, *A Christian's Pocket Guide to the Papacy: Its Origin and Role in the 21st Century* (Fearn, Ross-shire, Scotland: Christian Focus, 2015), esp. ch. 2 and 6.

90. *Dei Verbum*, 10 § 2.

91. I am adapting the well-known Latin saying *extra Ecclesiam nulla salus* ("outside the Church there is no salvation").

pattern of authority, a pattern that, significantly enough, includes the church (see my conclusion below). Catholic doctrine is not unbiblical in the relatively unimportant sense that it makes appeal to Scripture, as both orthodox and heretical theologians do. However, I have argued that Catholic doctrine falls short of being biblical in the way that most mattered to the Reformers, namely, by according supreme authority to the Spirit speaking in the Scriptures even in matters of interpretation. Here I stand, reluctantly obliged to judge the Roman mode of biblical reasoning an example of not *sola* but *sorta scriptura*.

CONCLUSION:
REFORMATION AS COMIC POSSIBILITY
OR, WHY PROTESTANT DOCTRINE
IS NOT UNCATHOLIC

There was nothing funny about a gaping wound in the body of Christ in ancient Corinth, nor is the contemporary dismemberment of the church a laughing matter. On the contrary, these bodily lesions occasioned a heartfelt plea from the apostle Paul: "I appeal to you, brothers, by the name of our Lord Jesus Christ, that all of you agree, and that there be no divisions among you, but that you be united in the same mind and the same judgment" (1 Cor 1:10). How, then, do I make so bold as to speak of the "comic possibility" rather than the tragic actuality of the Reformation?

Comedy is first cousin to catholicity inasmuch as both involve a certain kind of felicitous unifying dynamic. As a literary genre, comedy is the story of protagonists overcoming obstacles to achieve a successful conclusion or happy ending. As a mark of the church, catholicity is the quality of achieving a differentiated unity, a fulsome wholeness. The Reformation was a comic possibility because the Reformers proposed a wholeness centered not on an imperial structure (Rome) but an imperial Word (the Bible as Word of the living God and the gospel of the Lord Jesus Christ).

We have examined Levering's claim that Catholic doctrine is not unbiblical. Let me now give some reasons why Protestant doctrine is not uncatholic. In the first place, the Reformation was less about starting a new church than retrieving the one ancient and true church. Carl Braaten writes, "The Reformers made their protest against Rome on behalf of the whole church, out of love and loyalty to the truly catholic church. After the split came, they continued to work for the reform of the church. . . . The Reformation was a movement of protest for the sake of the one church."[92] While it may seem counterintuitive, it is nevertheless true that the Reformers' main objection to Roman Catholicism was not its *catholicity* but its narrow focus on *Rome*. Calvin says as much in his 1539 letter to Cardinal Sadolet: "Our agreement with antiquity is far closer than yours . . . all we have attempted has been to renew the ancient form of the Church."[93]

Both Luther and Calvin have a high regard for catholic tradition as long as such catholicity is not defined by Rome rather than Romans (i.e., the gospel). The Reformers acknowledged that the church and her tradition have a part to play in the pattern of authority, namely, to hearken to and abide in the apostolic teaching through time in all places.[94]

Calvin does not violate the principle of *sola scriptura* when he encourages individuals to submit their biblical interpretations "to the judgment of the Church" as Scripture portrays the church, namely, as the sum total of those local congregations where God's Word is rightly preached and the sacraments rightly administered.[95] Nor does Luther violate *sola scriptura* in acknowledging the usefulness (but not infallibility) of

92. Carl A. Braaten, *Mother Church: Ecclesiology and Ecumenism* (Minneapolis: Fortress, 1998), 12.

93. Calvin, "Reply to Sadolet," 231. On Calvin's concern to remain catholic, see Randall C. Zachman, ed., *John Calvin and Roman Catholicism: Critique and Engagement, Then and Now* (Grand Rapids, MI: Baker Academic, 2008).

94. I am expanding on Michael Allen's and Scott Swain's description of the Reformers' understanding of tradition as "the church's stance of abiding in and with apostolic teaching through time" (*Reformed Catholicity: The Promise of Retrieval for Theology and Biblical Interpretation* [Grand Rapids, MI: Baker Academic, 2015], 34).

95. Calvin, *Canons and Decrees of the Council of Trent, with the Antidote* (1547), in *Selected Works of John Calvin: Tracts and Letters*, vol. 3 *Tracts, Part 3* (Grand Rapids, MI: Baker, 1983), 77.

church councils, provided that they are truly catholic (and not narrowly Catholic). Jaroslav Pelikan summarizes Luther's position as follows: "As a Protestant, he subjected the authority of church councils to the authority of the word of God; as a Catholic, he interpreted the word of God in conformity with the dogmas of the councils. . . . Catholic substance and Protestant principle belong together."[96]

"Catholic" and "Protestant" belong together. What a thought! Yet this is also what Philip Schaff dreamed of over a hundred years ago when he envisioned a future church that would combine the Petrine/Catholic emphasis on authority with the Pauline/Protestant emphasis on freedom "in a grand Johannean [*sic*] reconciliation."[97] What kind of child would such a union of Protestant and Catholic beget? Peter Leithart has christened it "Reformational Catholic,"[98] but I prefer "catholic evangelical" or "Reforming catholic," and the latter in this context because it better signals that the quest to be fully catholic is ongoing, and that the process requires curative, regular correction by the Word. Children of the Reformation, Protestants call the Church of Rome to further reformation, as we call our own churches, on the basis of God's Word.

Catholics and Protestants together. This is the comic possibility of the Reformation: a reforming catholic church. What Schaff conceived too dialectically, I am describing comically: the marriage of two estranged parties. Comedies often end with a marriage. The marriage I envision would have to be a divine comedy, however, for only the Holy Spirit can bring about on earth the communion the saints have with Christ in heaven.

"Let me not to the marriage of true minds / Admit impediments."[99] There are few if any impediments from the Protestant side. Roman

96. Jaroslav Pelikan, *Obedient Rebels: Catholic Substance and Protestant Principle in Luther's Reformation* (London: SCM, 1964), 76.

97. Philip Schaff, *History of the Christian Church*, 3rd ed., vol. 1 (New York: Charles Scribner's Sons, 1910), 358.

98. This is the vision of unity Leithart pursues in his *The End of Protestantism: Pursuing Unity in a Fragmented Church* (Grand Rapids: Brazos, 2016).

99. Shakespeare, *Sonnet 116.*

Catholics who believe the gospel are welcome at Lutheran, Presbyterian, and other Protestant Lord's Tables.[100] The only real impediments I see are those pertaining to the Roman institution.[101] Yet some in the Roman Catholic Church are reaching out. Matthew is already reading the Bible somewhat like an evangelical. This suggests to me a variation on the Catholics Come Home campaign that urged lapsed Catholics to return to Rome. I like the idea, but want to propose a variation. Rome is not home. Instead of Rome-home think rom-com: a romantic comedy featuring an evangelical catholicity bounded by the gospel, not by Rome. Let's head home, Matthew—home to the church in the heavenly Jerusalem (Heb 12:22) and to the comic possibility of uniting Protestants and Romans by reforming catholicity so that it is as deep and wide as the gospel itself.[102]

---

100. There are some exceptions to this Protestant rule, but these too may need to be corrected (reformed!) of their overly narrow catholicity.

101. Peter Leithart lists several such impediments, including papal infallibility and, in connection to the practice of restricting Communion to Roman citizens (so to speak), "sectarian exclusiveness" (Leithart, "What I Want from Catholics: Become More Protestant," *Ethika Politika* [October 28, 2015], accessed February 12, 2017, https://ethikapolitika.org/2015/10/28/what-i-want-from-catholics-become-protestant/).

102. I am grateful to Ryan Fields, Derek Rishmawy, and Dan Treier for their comments and suggestions on an earlier draft.

SUBJECT INDEX

SCRIPTURE INDEX